Is God a Delusion?

Is God a Delusion?

A Reply to Religion's Cultured Despisers

Eric Reitan

WILEY-BLACKWELL

A John Wiley & Sons, Ltd., Publication

This edition first published 2009
© 2009 Eric Reitan

Blackwell Publishing was acquired by John Wiley & Sons in February 2007. Blackwell's publishing program has been merged with Wiley's global Scientific, Technical, and Medical business to form Wiley-Blackwell.

Registered Office
John Wiley & Sons Ltd, The Atrium, Southern Gate, Chichester, West Sussex, PO19 8SQ, United Kingdom

Editorial Offices
350 Main Street, Malden, MA 02148-5020, USA
9600 Garsington Road, Oxford, OX4 2DQ, UK
The Atrium, Southern Gate, Chichester, West Sussex, PO19 8SQ, UK

For details of our global editorial offices, for customer services, and for information about how to apply for permission to reuse the copyright material in this book please see our website at www.wiley.com/wiley-blackwell.

The right of Eric Reitan to be identified as the author of this work has been asserted in accordance with the Copyright, Designs and Patents Act 1988.

Wiley also publishes its books in a variety of electronic formats. Some content that appears in print may not be available in electronic books.

Designations used by companies to distinguish their products are often claimed as trademarks. All brand names and product names used in this book are trade names, service marks, trademarks or registered trademarks of their respective owners. The publisher is not associated with any product or vendor mentioned in this book. This publication is designed to provide accurate and authoritative information in regard to the subject matter covered. It is sold on the understanding that the publisher is not engaged in rendering professional services. If professional advice or other expert assistance is required, the services of a competent professional should be sought.

Library of Congress Cataloging-in-Publication Data

Reitan, Eric.
  Is God a delusion? : a reply to religion's cultured despisers / Eric Reitan.
     p. cm.
  Includes bibliographical references (p.   ) and index.
  ISBN 978-1-4051-8362-8 (hardcover : alk. paper) – ISBN 978-1-4051-8361-1 (pbk. : alk. paper)   1. Apologetics.   2. Theism.   I. Title.
  BT1212.R45 2009
  261.2′1—dc22

                                                                                    2008017217

A catalogue record for this book is available from the British Library.

Set in Minion 10.5/13 by Graphicraft Limited, Hong Kong
Printed and bound in Singapore
By Fabulous Printers Pte Ltd

01   2009

To Russell Bennett and Baron Garcia, who demonstrated in their lives, each in his own way, what it means to live in a spirit of hope.

Contents

Introduction

At one point in his recent book, *The God Delusion*, Richard Dawkins expresses astonishment that "any circles worthy of the name sophisticated remain within the Church." He calls it "a mystery at least as deep as those that theologians enjoy" (2006, p. 60). His astonishment is occasioned by the Roman Catholic procedure for investigating candidates for sainthood, a procedure that he thinks can only be an embarrassment to more sophisticated Catholics. But his views here express a broader perplexity – a perplexity shared by other atheists – over why any morally sensitive and intellectually responsible adults would believe in God.

Dawkins' perplexity seems to be widely shared these days. The last few years have seen a flurry of books, both popular and academic, attacking religion in general and theistic religion in particular. In fact, a recent *Time Magazine* article declared that "Dawkins is riding the crest of an atheist literary wave" (Van Biema 2006, p. 50).

Examples aren't hard to find. Sam Harris, in his 2004 book *The End of Faith*, lists religious faith alongside ignorance, hatred, and greed as the demons "that lurk inside every human mind." Of these demons, he thinks faith "is surely the devil's masterpiece" (p. 226). In his *Letter to a Christian Nation* (2006), Harris continues the assault, arguing that religious faith "is on the wrong side of an escalating war of ideas" (p. 80) and that the very survival of the world depends on the victory of those on the *right* side of this war: the side opposing religious faith.

Others who belong to the side Harris favors include the philosopher Daniel Dennett, who seeks to demystify religion in his 2006 book, *Breaking the Spell: Religion as a Natural Phenomenon*. While Dennett displays a philosopher's caution about expressing his conclusions too boldly, it is clear where his sympathies lie: religion, for him, is a potent and potentially dangerous force that needs to be studied scientifically so that it can be controlled. The possibility that religion might be directed towards a reality inaccessible to science, that belief in a transcendent God of love might be *true*, is not a matter Dennett finds worthy of serious attention. He thinks that the arguments for God's existence are weak, dispensing with them in "a scant six pages" (as he declares with apparent pride in a defense of Dawkins published in the March 2007 issue of *The New York Review of Books*).[1] And since he thinks the existence of religious belief can be readily explained without invoking the idea that there is some kind of *supernatural force* making itself felt on the human psyche, Dennett is happy to view religion as delusional. He finds little reason to think the delusion useful, and so the only interesting question is just how pernicious it is.

More recently, the physicist and amateur philosopher Victor Stenger has cranked out a little book entitled *God: The Failed Hypothesis* (2007), in which he purports to show that recent advances in science pretty decisively establish that God does not exist. He then mirrors (more concisely, but with less rhetorical flair than Dawkins, and less eloquence than Harris) the charge that not only don't we need religion to have moral and meaningful lives but religion is an important source of evil in the world.

And for the most angry and rhetorically charged attack, we have Christopher Hitchens' recent screed, *god is not Great: How Religion Poisons Everything* (2007). This pugilistic manifesto digs through the annals of religious history and doctrine to uncover the very worst that religion has to offer – and then holds up these disturbing phenomena as representative of the very essence of religion (while doing some furious rhetorical hand-waving to conclude that heroic figures such as Dietrich Bonhoeffer and Martin Luther King, Jr., were not really religious at all). As Hitchens puts the point, "religion has caused innumerable people not just to conduct themselves no better than others, but to award themselves permission to behave in ways that would make a brothel-keeper or an ethnic cleanser raise an eyebrow" (p. 6). While he admits that "nonreligious organizations have committed similar crimes," Hitchens maintains that religion lacks any redeeming features that might counterbalance its evils. It is steeped in misrepresentation, and it "is ultimately grounded on wish-thinking" (p. 5).

Of course, the range of works attacking religion is hardly exhausted by this list. Other recent books that should probably be included are biologist Lewis Wolpert's *Six Impossible Things Before Breakfast* (2007), Carl Sagan's posthumous essays, *The Varieties of Scientific Experience* (2006), and David Mills's recently revised and updated *Atheist Universe* (2006). Attacks on particular religious doctrines (such as the doctrine of biblical inerrancy or the doctrine of hell), or particular versions of religious life (especially fundamentalism), are legion (and I am to blame for at least a few of those attacks[2]). And every few years, a scholar in my discipline of philosophy comes out with a new philosophical attack on the rationality of theistic belief in general or Christianity in particular. Some of the best include J. L. Mackie's classic *The Miracle of Theism: Arguments For and Against the Existence of God* (1982), Michael Martin's *Atheism: A Philosophical Justification* (1990) and his follow-up, *The Case Against Christianity* (1991). In its modern incarnation, this sort of philosophical attack on religion (especially Christianity) has been going on at least since Bertrand Russell's 1927 essay, "Why I am Not a Christian" (Russell 1961b).

But it is one thing when academic philosophers address the question of God's existence, with a primary target audience of fellow scholars or undergraduate students taking a philosophy of religion class. In terms of philosophical acumen, Dawkins' *The God Delusion* is dwarfed by the works of Mackie and Martin (and is, in my judgment, rendered puerile in comparison with the writings of the most thoughtful and meticulous of the atheist philosophers, William Rowe). But Dawkins has what Mackie and Martin and Rowe can only dream of: a major bestseller and a growing crowd of followers who seem to hang on his every word. The recent books by Harris, Dennett, Stenger, and Hitchens have also become bestsellers.

What we have today is a surge of scientists and other intellectuals who have been coming out of the closet to voice, not just skepticism, but overt *hostility* towards theistic religion, even in its most seemingly benign forms. These "new atheists," as I will call them, are distinguished by their outrage. Belief in God, they tell us, is not just irrational but dangerous – even evil. And the public, apparently hungry for such frank expressions of animosity, have been gobbling it up, turning one book after another into a bestseller.

The reasons are probably varied. The September 11 attacks, orchestrated and perpetrated by religious fanatics, have doubtless had their effect. Sam Harris makes fruitful use of our dread of religious extremism to play up what he takes to be the inherent dangers of religion itself. I do not doubt that many have looked in horror at what, apparently, religion can do – and then seen the seeds of similar horrors in their own backyards, their own churches and religious upbringings. There is also the evident power, in America, of the religious right's unified voting bloc – a power that has unsettled not only political liberals but also many moderates (and even a fair number of secular conservatives). And then there are the recent assaults on public science education, perpetrated by religious conservatives in the guise of "Intelligent Design Theory."

But I will leave the historical and sociological explanations to others more schooled in these disciplines. The fact is that religion is being challenged in a way that, while not entirely unprecedented in history, is surely notable. This is not to say that religion has become unpopular, or that belief in God is waning. Rather, it is to say that those who oppose religion – especially theistic religion – are becoming noisier and more vocally angry, and they are pulling out the stops. And leading the cavalry charge (I almost wrote Calvary charge!) is Richard Dawkins, who seems to style himself a kind of C. S. Lewis of atheism.

Dawkins' *The God Delusion* offers up, in one place, the most important attacks that are currently being pressed against religion and theistic belief. These attacks can be summarized as follows:

- *all* the traditional arguments for God's existence are very bad ones;
- despite claims to the contrary, science *can* investigate the existence of God; and when such a scientific investigation is pursued, we see that God's existence is highly improbable at best;
- the existence of religious belief can be satisfactorily explained without making any reference to a supernatural reality;
- we do not need religion to provide us with a basis for morality, or to give meaning to our lives;
- religion is dangerous, even in its moderate forms, because it encourages blind faith that is immune both to rational criticism and to the urgings of conscience;
- religion is a source of division and enmity among people, needlessly magnifying the violence in the world.

These charges are not trivial, and Dawkins clearly believes each one. And so he thinks religion is not only irrational, but one of the roots of evil in the world.[3] Given these convictions, it's no wonder that Dawkins cannot understand why any intelligent, morally sensitive people would believe in God.

This book is a sustained effort to clear up Dawkins' perplexity. It is, in other words, a systematic rebuttal of the main arguments found in *The God Delusion* and, more broadly, in the "atheist literary wave" that Dawkins surfs.

This book is not, however, an attempt to convince atheists and agnostics that they ought to become theists. My aim is very different from the project that Sandra Menssen and Thomas Sullivan, for example, set for themselves in their remarkable recent book, *The Agnostic Inquirer* (2007). In that book, the authors ask whether an agnostic might have good reasons to become convinced that there is a God who has revealed Himself in the world – that is, whether a case can be made that the probability of such a God's existence exceeds 0.5, so that belief in God becomes the most reasonable judgment. This question dominates much of religious apologetics, both historical and contemporary, and Menssen and Sullivan offer an important new contribution to that tradition – by arguing that the content of putative revelatory claims might count as evidence for the existence of a good God who has revealed Himself.

By contrast, my aim is not to convince atheists and agnostics that they should believe in God but rather to show that those who do believe in God are not thereby irrational or morally defective. Contrary to the angry arguments of the new atheists, I will argue that allegiance to theistic religion is entirely consistent with being a decent, reasonable person. But I think that, in our ambiguous and mysterious world, equally rational people can believe different things. On my view of rationality, the fact that a reasonable person could be a theist does not preclude that a reasonable person might also be an atheist. Agnostics should *not* expect to find arguments here that aim to compel them to accept God's existence. But I do hope they will be convinced that the decision to embrace theistic religion can be both rational and benign.

The Spirit of Schleiermacher

A little over two hundred years ago, a young theologian named Friedrich Schleiermacher published a little book that responded to a similar flurry of disdain for religion. The book was entitled *On Religion: Speeches to its Cultured Despisers*. In that book, Schleiermacher faced head-on the contempt for religion that was rampant among the intellectual elite in Europe at the turn of the nineteenth century – a contempt born out of the Enlightenment, the budding scientific revolution, and the growing clashes between organized religion and the advocates of rationality and progress.

As the title of this book suggests, the spirit of Schleiermacher is a powerful inspiration for the ideas and arguments that make up my reply to the new atheists. Schleiermacher has justifiably been called the father of modern theology, but at the time that he published his *Speeches* he was a little-known hospital chaplain. What turned this book by an unknown into the talk of the intellectual world was the daring way in which he steered a course between the polarized forces of traditional religion and the intellectual world of the Enlightenment. His aim was not to preserve a calcified past or the dogmas that were the target of so much scorn among religion's "cultured despisers." Rather, his aim was to show these cultured despisers that they had *missed the point* of religion.

In the very same stroke, of course, he showed that many of the most ardent defenders of traditional religion were missing the point as well. Schleiermacher wasn't defending in all its details what organized religion had become at the dawn of the modern age, and he certainly wasn't trying to beat back the forces of modernity. Rather, he was trying to show that the essence of religion was both immune to the accusations leveled by its cultured despisers and fully compatible with the growing insights of the modern age. According to Schleiermacher's understanding, "religion itself" is something that only a minority in history has really grasped and appreciated, "while millions, in various ways, have been satisfied to juggle with its trappings" (1958, p. 1).

It may well be that the target of religion's cultured despisers, in Schleiermacher's day as well as our own, is not religion itself but, rather, its trappings. And, of course, Schleiermacher's own religion was not only theistic but Christian. The points he was making about religion in general extended to theistic religion and to Christianity itself.

In my view, it is one of the great tragedies of history that the trend in theology launched by Schleiermacher at the turn of the nineteenth century was beaten back by reactionary forces less than a century later, and has been thoroughly eclipsed – especially in the popular picture of religion today – by the rise of fundamentalism.[4] On Schleiermacher's analysis as well as my own, religious fundamentalism, at least insofar as it embraces fundamentalism, does not have the right to call itself *religion* at all. The "God" of fundamentalism has no legitimate claim on the title.

Thus, while this book defends the rationality of theistic religion against the charges leveled by the angry new atheists, readers shouldn't expect me to defend the versions of theism they most directly attack. I teach and work in Oklahoma, which is at least one "buckle" of the American Bible Belt. And I learned soon after coming here that when I describe my faith to my students, calling myself "Christian" strikes many as akin to describing an eighteen-legged purple animal with an elephantine nose, and then calling it a horse.

I will not be defending the doctrine of biblical inerrancy because I think it is both mistaken and dangerous. I will not be defending the doctrine of hell because I think that it is mistaken and (at least in its most traditional formulations) dangerous. I will not be defending the divine command theory of ethics (that is, the theory that morality is the product of God's decrees) because I think it is both mistaken and dangerous. I will not be defending the legitimacy of "faith" understood as stubborn belief without regard for evidence because faith in *that* sense is a dangerous and inappropriate basis for forming one's convictions. I will not be defending a strong doctrine of religious exclusivism because I think it is both mistaken and – that's right – dangerous. I will not be defending the patriarchal subordination of women or the heterosexist marginalization of gays and lesbians because I think that these things are objective moral evils. I will not be defending "Young Earth Creationism" because I think it is mistaken, dangerous, and, well, silly.

There is much that comes under the guns of Dawkins and his allies that I *will* defend (for example, the merits of the cosmological argument for God's existence, the evidentiary value of religious experience, and the value of "faith" when that term is properly understood). But a principal task in this book will be to "stake out" the proper territory for theistic religion – to identify the kind of theistic religion that morally sensitive and intellectually responsible people can embrace without it being a "mystery"; a kind of theistic religion that, I will argue, is immune to the challenges raised by Dawkins and the other new atheists. What should become clear is that many actual religions tread shamelessly outside this territory, into the domain of superstition and ideology; and when they do so, they render themselves appropriate fodder for Dawkins' attacks. Dawkins' mistake is not that he attacks these runaway religions. His mistake is to blithely assume that theistic religion itself falls prey to these attacks. It does not.

And so my argument here, while occasioned by the recent "atheist literary wave," should be understood to be as much a critique of some dominant contemporary manifestations of religion as it is a critique of religion's cultured despisers. In fact, I'd started writing a book with a very different title when I read *The God Delusion*. Reading Dawkins' book inspired a shift of focus. The book I'd been writing bore the working title, *How the Religious Right Gets Religion Wrong*. A geology colleague recently suggested I should title this book *A Pox on Both Your Houses*. My hope, however, is to be at least a bit less pugnacious than that.

In that spirit, let me say that much of what Dawkins and the other new atheists have to say is important. Their concerns about the harms done in the name of religion need to be taken seriously, and the underlying reasons for so much religious violence need to be explored. In fact, insofar as *The God Delusion* nicely summarizes the main objections of contemporary atheists to religious faith, it seems to me it should be required reading for all who have yet to seriously confront a forceful statement of these objections. I share Dawkins' disdain for those expressions of faith that seek to "immunize" believers against all critical arguments by, among other things, warning them "to avoid even opening a book like [*The God Delusion*], which is surely a work of Satan" (Dawkins 2006, pp. 5–6).

I think all religious believers should take to heart the words that Simone Weil, the early twentieth-century mystic and philosopher, wrote in her correspondence with a Catholic priest friend: "For it seemed to me certain, and I still think so today, that one can never wrestle enough with God if one does so out of pure regard for the truth. Christ likes us to prefer truth to him because, before being Christ, he is truth" (1951, p. 69). If more Christians (and Jews and Muslims, etc.) lived out their faith journeys with Weil's idea close to their hearts, I cannot but believe that much of the violence done in religion's name would be avoided. And, at the very least, I believe that Dawkins' *The God Delusion*, if approached seriously, will inspire *some* wrestling with God.

Put another way, I share with the new atheists their disdain for those who stubbornly cling to religious beliefs for no reason at all, without regard for arguments or evidence, with no thought to the implications of their beliefs or the objections that might be leveled against them. This kind of stubborn attachment to religious beliefs is what Dawkins and Harris call "faith." And while Alister McGrath, in *Dawkins' God* (2005), rightly criticizes the adequacy of this understanding of faith, it would be a mistake to think that no religious believers conceive of faith in precisely these terms.[5]

Many, in fact, live out their religious lives in the grip of a "faith" that is just as Dawkins and Harris describe it: they cleave to their beliefs out of mere willful stubbornness, without regard for truth, and they proudly call it a virtue. While there are (as I will argue) understandings of faith according to which it may be the virtue that religious believers claim it to be, this understanding is not one of them.

The reasons for condemning "faith" in this sense are well articulated by the new atheists. But there is a distinctively religious reason that most atheists ignore: faith in this sense is idolatrous. It involves devotion to one's own concept of God rather than to the truth about God. In this respect, Dawkins may be closer to an authentic religious faith than most fundamentalists: he is devoted to atheism because he is devoted to *the truth*, because he sincerely wants to believe the truth about God.

It is my conviction that theism and other forms of supernatural religion are born out of a combination of rational insight, profound experiences of a distinctive kind, and morally laudable hope. But, along with Schleiermacher, I believe that the germ of religion born from these sources needs to be refined and shaped by careful and humble reflection in open-minded discourse with others. The religious vision that can arise out of such discourse is not the pernicious delusion that Dawkins takes to be the hallmark of all supernatural religion.

But it is an unfortunate fact of history that the germ of this religious vision has consistently been co-opted for political and economic gain, corrupted by our more mean-spirited impulses, obscured by our blinkered and parochial thinking, and – perhaps – distorted by the kinds of impulses that Dawkins and Dennett take to be the evolutionary basis for religion itself.[6] The results have been religious traditions that – while preserving the germ of what I might presumptuously call "true religion," and while offering fleeting glimpses of what that germ might evolve into – are also laden with crud.

And in some of the more pernicious modes of religious expression, the germ has been thrown away altogether and the crud has been lifted up. Human beings have been encouraged, indoctrinated, even coerced into the worship of rubbish.

Ideology and Hope

Perhaps, given religion's sordid history, it is not surprising that the cultured despisers of religion would find it a mystery why any intelligent and morally sensitive persons would embrace theistic belief. I do not begrudge them their befuddlement. Rather, I question what they do in the face of it.

Dawkins, for example, thinks that this mystery cannot be solved so long as we assume that theists are being reasonable and morally sensitive in their theism. Instead, the mystery can only be solved by invoking selective stupidity.[7] On Dawkins' view, if people who are otherwise intelligent and morally sensitive also believe in God, it must be because their intelligence and moral sensitivity have, at this point, failed them. Sam Harris's *The End of Faith* makes a similar claim, albeit with greater subtlety and eloquence.

But in his own discipline, Dawkins becomes incensed whenever a mystery of evolution – some complex biological system that hasn't been explained yet in Darwinian terms – is treated as a refutation of Darwin's theory. When intelligent design theorist Michael Behe, author of *Darwin's Black Box* (1996), invokes such mysteries as reasons to conclude that evolutionary theory can't explain the organized complexity we find in living organisms, Dawkins treats this as an intellectual cheat.

To throw up one's arms and declare a Darwinian explanation impossible is simply a way to shut down intellectual inquiry. Can the complexity of our immune system be explained on the assumption that all complex systems evolved gradually from simpler ones through natural selection? To assume that the answer is *no* – and to declare, "It must be divine intervention!" – just because it hasn't been done yet is intellectually irresponsible. "*Hasn't* been done!" should not be equated with "*Can't* be done!"

But here is the parallel question: Can the fact that there are theists who seem to be intelligent and morally sensitive be explained on the assumption that these theists are *exercising their intelligence and moral sensitivity* in the formation of their theistic beliefs? For Dawkins to assume that the answer is no – and for him to declare, "It must be selective stupidity!" – just because *he* hasn't been able to figure out how the exercise of intelligence and moral sensitivity can generate religious belief . . . well, why isn't *that* intellectually irresponsible?

Let's be honest: Dawkins is no more qualified to pursue a good faith effort to find rational foundations for theism than a creationist is qualified to pursue a good faith effort to find Darwinian explanations for complex biological phenomena. Of course, the typical creationist lacks the biological training necessary to pursue the effort with any competence. But there are exceptions: Michael Behe is an accomplished professor of biochemistry. If Dawkins is right about Behe's failings, this only goes to show a general point of no small importance: even accomplished scholars can go wrong in their thinking when they have an ideological axe to grind. Put simply, creationists would be too delighted by the failure to find Darwinian explanations to keep doggedly going until success is achieved.

In order to keep doggedly looking for a certain kind of explanation, even in the face of initial failures to find one, we need some confidence that such an explanation is out there to be found. It is this confidence that keeps scientists going despite all the false starts and failed experiments. They have faith in the power of science to explain events – not in the naive sense of "faith" that Dawkins and Harris foist upon religious believers, but in a very real sense of the word. For scientists, their faith is a kind of methodological presumption that a naturalistic explanation is available, if only we keep at it long enough. It is, in a sense, a species of hope. In a later chapter, I will argue that there is a kind of religious faith very similar to this faith of the scientists. But for now I want to make a different point.

Some of the people I have most admired have not only been devoutly religious but their religion has been theistic. They have shaped their lives according to a love of God that buoys them through difficult challenges and seems to radiate back through them as a love and compassion for the world and everything and everyone in it. They are thoughtful and open to critical discussion of their convictions. They are slow to anger, slow to condemn, and even quicker to forgive.

These people are, admittedly, no more typical of theistic believers than they are of the general population. And they have no connection at all to the fundamentalism that is the primary target of today's cultured despisers of religion. But they do believe in God. And they do align themselves with religious traditions (the ones I've known best have been Christians, Sikhs, Hindus, and Jews, but there are many examples within Islam and other faith communities as well).

The new atheists would have us believe that the religiosity of these rare individuals is an anomaly in their character, something they possess in spite of their intelligence and moral sensitivity. Their belief in God, their religious faith, their allegiance to a historic religious tradition – all these things exemplify where their intelligence and moral sensitivity have failed them.

For the sake of Friedrich Schleiermacher and Simone Weil and Martin Luther King, Jr., as well as too many personal friends and inspirations to name, I hope that Dawkins and the other cultured despisers of religion are wrong. I hope, in other words, that theistic religion can be, and often is, a vital constituent of a life lived with compassion and intellectual integrity.

To say that the religious faith of these rare individuals springs from their intelligence and moral sensitivity is not to say they all have carefully worked out philosophical arguments demonstrating the reasonableness of theistic faith. Their intellects and compassion may operate on a more intuitive level. It's the job of philosophers to trace out carefully the rational pathways that intuitive insight often surges through too quickly for plodding intellects to follow.

My hope is that such pathways can be found. The new atheists, whose life experiences and personal heroes are almost certainly very different from my own, do not have this hope. And therefore, just like the creationists who will give up the search for Darwinian explanations at the first sign of intellectual difficulty, the new atheists lack the tenacity to keep looking for rational pathways to theistic faith.

Overview

The search for these pathways requires hope, but it also requires philosophical diligence. And such diligence requires a serious effort to think through many of the most important ideas and arguments developed in the philosophy of religion. As such, my reply to the cultured despisers of religion may serve as a kind of introduction to that field.

In Chapters 1 through 3, I focus on the two key concepts that form the basis of the philosophy of religion: the concepts of "religion" and "God." I argue that the new atheists are continually in danger of either misconstruing these concepts or considering only one meaning among many. Most significantly, they fail to see the difference between theistic religion that is principally characterized by *fear* of a supernatural tyrant, and theistic religion that is chiefly characterized by *trust* in a transcendent good. These things are so fundamentally distinct that to conflate them is like confusing medieval alchemy and contemporary chemistry.

In Chapter 4, I take up the question of how science and religion are related. In the course of doing so, I explore the distinction between religion and superstition, and I consider the worry that when religion makes claims that fall outside the scope of scientific inquiry it renders religious assertions meaningless. In Chapters 5 and 6, I explore the traditional arguments for the existence of God. I argue that, while the best of these arguments do not *prove* God's existence, they do something else of no small importance: they show that it is reasonable to believe in the existence of a necessary being that explains the existence of the empirical world. Such a being would constitute a reality fundamentally distinct from the world we encounter with our senses. It would amount to a supernatural reality that explains the existence of the world.

In Chapters 7 and 8, I appeal to two ideas that the new atheists dismiss rather quickly – religious experience and faith – to build on the foundation for theistic religion that philosophical reasoning lays down. I argue that the phenomenon of religious experience supports the rationality of believing in a transcendent good. Faith, understood as a species of hope and a decision to live as if a hoped-for reality is true, can take us the rest of the way towards belief in something like the Judeo-Christian God: an infinite personal spirit whose essence is love. The hope that underlies such belief I call the "ethico-religious hope," and I argue that living in this hope is fundamentally at odds with engaging in the pernicious practices that the new atheists attribute to faith. There is, in effect, a "logic of faith" that precludes intolerance, fear-driven violence, and persecution.

In Chapter 9, I turn to the problem of evil – that is, the problem of reconciling belief in a transcendent God of love with the existence of the evils in this world. I argue that these evils are insufficient to dash the ethico-religious hope. To the contrary, the scope and magnitude of evil in the world entails that for many of us, our lives will have positive meaning only if we live in that hope – only if we have faith in something like a God of love.

Finally, in Chapter 10, I focus on what I take to be the source of the violence, oppression, and cruelty that have so often gone on in the name of religion. It is not religion *qua* religion that is responsible. Rather, these things are caused by ideologies of exclusion that are only contingently linked to theistic religion. While such ideologies are often overlaid upon religious doctrines and practices, they needn't be. And such ideologies often operate independently of religion. Religion, in short, is only a convenient vessel through which these ideologies sometimes operate. But at least in the sense of "religion" defended here, the essence of religion stands opposed to these dangerous ideologies. To attack religion is therefore to attack what may be one of our most important resources for fighting the very evils that so inflame the new atheists' outrage.

Our task must be to nurture authentic religion, to pursue the compassionate and thoughtful discourse that can purge it of the forces that corrupt it. We must find ways, not to stamp out religion, but to let *true* religion loose upon the world.

Contrary to what the new atheists might say, that can only be a thing of beauty.

1

On Religion and Equivocation

In "Why I Am Not a Christian," Bertrand Russell prefigures by about 80 years many of Richard Dawkins' complaints about religion and theistic belief. After dispensing with (or so he thinks) the arguments for God's existence, Russell launches into an attack on the character of Christ, focusing on Christ's purported endorsement of the doctrine of hell. As Russell sees it, the doctrine "that hellfire is a punishment for sin . . . is a doctrine that put cruelty into the world and gave the world generations of cruel torture; and the Christ of the Gospels, if you can take him as his chroniclers represent Him, would certainly have to be considered partly responsible for that" (Russell 1961b, p. 594).

After impugning Christ's character, he turns to the Christian religion which he claims "has been and still is the principal enemy of moral progress in the world" (p. 595). Then he brings religion *as such* under fire. "Religion," he says, "is based primarily and mainly upon fear . . . fear of the mysterious, fear of defeat, fear of death. Fear is the parent of cruelty, and therefore it is no wonder if cruelty and religion have gone hand in hand" (p. 596). Finally, he turns his sights on God, saying that the concept of God "is a conception derived from the ancient Oriental despotisms. It is a conception quite unworthy of free men" (p. 597).

But what does Russell mean by "religion" here? What does he mean by "God"? Is religion in *every* sense "based on fear"? Is *every* conception of God "derived from the ancient Oriental despotisms"? For Russell, the concept of God is that of a terrible tyrant in the sky, dispensing arbitrary rules and ruthlessly punishing those who question his authority. The cowering masses, terrified of the world and its dangers, project their fears into the heavens, imagining this cosmic tyrant who, while deadly and capricious, can be appeased. Out of their efforts at appeasement, *religion* is born.

And when appeasement does no good (as it surely won't, since its object is a fiction), there is the inevitable effort to place blame: *we* haven't been good enough, or *you* haven't been good enough. Those wicked Sodomites have brought God's wrath upon us. It's the fault of the infidels or the heretics. To appease God, we must defeat His enemies.

Gradually, perhaps, this attitude takes on an otherworldly dimension: The rewards for our efforts at appeasement will come in *another* life. And if we fail to defeat God's enemies in this life, have no fear: they will roast in the next.

It's no wonder, if this is Russell's only image of religion, that he thinks of it as evil.[1] It's no wonder that, eighty years later, Russell's spiritual protégé, Richard Dawkins, is on a righteous crusade to stamp out religion from the world.

But perhaps what Russell is describing is not *the* phenomenon of religion and *the* concept of God. After all, our language is messier than that. One word often refers, not just to one concept, but to a cluster of related ones. The philosopher Wittgenstein (1953) once suggested that many terms – such as the term "game" – extend over a range of phenomena that are related only by what he called "family resemblances" (p. 32, remark no. 67). My cousin looks nothing like my daughter. But my daughter looks like me, I look like my mother, my mother looks like her brother, and he looks like my cousin. We call both professional football and peek-a-boo "games"– even though it is hard to find *anything* they have in common – because they are connected by such "family resemblances."

So it may be with both "religion" and "God."[2]

The Meanings of "Religion"

When we use the term "religion," we might mean a system of doctrines. Then again, we might mean a body of explanatory myths, or a social institution organized around shared beliefs and ritual practices, or the personal convictions of an individual, or a person's sense of relatedness to the divine. Sometimes we treat it as synonymous with "comprehensive worldview" and other times as synonymous with "spirituality."

Pretty much everyone would agree that the beliefs shared by most Southern Baptists, insofar as they are Southern Baptists, comprise a religion; and most would agree that the beliefs shared by biochemists, in their role as biochemists, do not. But while some people would be inclined to call secular humanism a religion, others would staunchly resist doing so.

The fact is, we use the term "religion" in a variety of ways. And this fact makes it difficult to talk precisely about religion, let alone attack it with valid objections. Whenever usage is so varied, there is a real danger that one will fall prey to what philosophers call *equivocation* – that is, the fallacy of using the same term in different senses in the course of a single argument or discussion, without noticing the shift.

This is the treacherous conceptual quagmire into which Bertrand Russell waded eighty years ago, and into which the new atheists slog cavalierly today. To his credit, Dawkins *tries* to define his terms. But he fails to do so with a philosopher's care, and he is too swept up in his own rhetoric, the joyous excesses that make his attacks on religion so entertaining (at least to those who aren't deeply offended by them). Sam Harris and Christopher Hitchens, by contrast, never define their terms, leaving it up to their readers to figure out what they are so fervently attacking when they attack "religion."

To see more fully the conceptual challenges faced by anyone who wants to attack religion, consider some contrasting definitions. Paul Griffiths (1999), in his book *Religious Reading*, takes religion to be an account of things distinguished from other kinds of accounts by virtue of being *comprehensive, unsurpassable,* and *central.* For an account to be comprehensive, "it must seem to those who offer it that it takes into account everything, that nothing is left unaccounted for by it" (p. 7). An account is unsurpassable if it cannot be "replaced by or subsumed in a better account of what it accounts for" (p. 9). And to be central, an account "must seem to be directly relevant to what you take to be the central questions of your life, the questions around which your life is oriented" (p. 10).

Contrast this definition with the one offered by William James in *The Varieties of Religious Experience* (1914). James defines religion as "the feelings, acts, and experiences of individual men in their solitude so far as they apprehend themselves to stand in relation to whatever they may consider the divine" (p. 31). And he takes "the divine" to mean "only such a primal reality as the individual feels impelled to respond to solemnly and gravely, and neither by a curse nor a jest" (p. 38).

Again by way of contrast, consider the view of sociologist Emile Durkheim, who takes religion to be essentially a social phenomenon. For Durkheim, religion is a product of the "inter-social sentiments," which are those that bond the individual to society by representing the individual as a member of a greater whole to whom he or she has binding obligations.[3] Durkheim sees religion as "a form of custom, like law and morality," that distinguishes itself from other customs in that "it asserts itself not only over conduct but also over *conscience*."[4] For Durkheim, the metaphysical speculations so typical of religious doctrine are merely instrumental and incidental: they function solely to achieve the effect of socializing the individual members of society, creating a conscientious allegiance to societal rules.

Or consider the theologian John Hick (1989a), who sees religious traditions, with their dogmas and practices, as attempts to orient religious practitioners towards an ultimate reality, a "noumenal Real" that transcends the grasp of human language and cognitive faculties. He takes it that human beings are alienated from "the Real" and from one another, at least in part because the Real is just too vast for us to grasp. All we can do is tell mythological stories, formulate metaphors, and devise ritual practices that connect us to it experientially. These stories, metaphors, and practices are supposed to move us away from our self-centered starting points, towards other-centeredness, and finally towards Reality-centeredness. The measure of a religion's "truth," for Hick, is not the literal truth of its teachings, since these are "about that which transcends the literal scope of human language" (p. 352). The measure of religious truth is, instead, its capacity to jar us out of our self-absorption and into a way of life shaped by a living connection with a Reality we cannot put into words.

So, which is it? Is religion a comprehensive and unsurpassable account of everything that matters to a person? If so, the naturalism of secular humanists would qualify as their religion. Or is religion a private matter of how the individual relates subjectively to what is taken to be the fundamental reality? If so, the physicist's awe and wonder at the vast beauty of the cosmos would be a religion. Or is religion a social construct, its metaphysical pronouncements (if any) an incidental by-product of its goal of creating loyalty, obedience, and cohesion among society's members? If so, Marxist ideology would have been the religion of the former Soviet Union.[5] Or is religion an attempt, through metaphors and ritual practices, to bring our lives into alignment with an inexpressible transcendent reality? If so, then most world religions would paradoxically *be* religions even as they reject the accuracy of Hick's account (since they don't typically take themselves to be engaged in merely metaphorical discourse).

The point, of course, is that "religion" is used in all these ways and more. Each account has justification in ordinary usage. And there is probably even greater diversity with respect to the cognate term, "religious." Consider all the things we call "religious": beliefs, stories, practices, ways of life, experiences, communities, persons, etc. When we call these things "religious," do we always mean the same thing?

Of course not.

Einsteinian Religion and the Feeling of Piety

What this means is that if the new atheists want to say religion is evil, they need to tell us what sense of "religion" they have in mind. Likewise for "God."

Do they?

Christopher Hitchens (2007) never even tries. But when we look at the details of his attack, we see an interesting trend. He claims, for example, that the faith of Dietrich Bonhoeffer, a Lutheran pastor who was executed for resisting the Nazis, was no real "religion" at all but "an admirable but nebulous humanism" (p. 7). When he refers to Bonhoeffer again, it is to point out that he risked and sacrificed "in accordance only with the dictates of conscience" rather than "on orders from any priesthood" (p. 241), implying that one is being *religiously* motivated only if one acts out of obedience to authorities of an organized religious hierarchy. That Bonhoeffer was part of a priesthood seems to miss his attention. The possibility that Bonhoeffer's conscience might have been informed by his faith never enters Hitchens' radar screen.

Concerning Martin Luther King, Jr., Hitchens claims that King was not a Christian in any "real" sense because he preached forgiveness of enemies and universal compassion rather than a rabid retributivism culminating in a doctrine of hell. The lynchpin of his case against the view that King was a real Christian is summarized in the following observation: "At no point did Dr. King . . . ever hint that those who injured and reviled him were to be threatened with any revenge or punishment, in this world or the next, save the consequences of their own brute selfishness and stupidity" (p. 176).

So, in Hitchens' view, an ethic of love and forgiveness is less central to Christianity than the doctrine of hell. Someone who believes that "God is love" and claims to have experienced that love as a source of spiritual support can turn out, on Hitchens' account, not to be a Christian in anything but a "nominal" sense. But while King was no true Christian, Hitchens treats Father Wenceslas Munyeshyaka, the Catholic priest in

Rwanda who was charged with aiding the death squads and raping refugee Tutsi women, as channeling the true spirit of the Christian faith (pp. 191–2). I would, of course, reverse these assessments. Anyone who, like Father Wenceslas Munyeshyaka, could call his mother a "cockroach" because she is Tutsi, strikes me as utterly divorced from religion even if he wears its trappings. I would argue, with Schleiermacher, that a deep connection to the essence of religion is rare compared to those who "juggle with its trappings," and that this rare connection is most clearly represented in the lives of such people as Bonhoeffer and King.

But to say these things requires an account of what I mean by "religion." Instead of offering his own account, Hitchens' strategy seems to be this: if it is good, noble, or tends to inspire compassion, then it isn't "religion." It is "humanism" or something of the sort. With no clear definition to guide him, Hitchens is free to locate only what is cruel, callous, insipid, or banal in the camp of religion, while excluding anything that could reliably motivate the heroic moral action exemplified by Bonhoeffer and King. When "religion" is never defined, but in practice is treated so that only what is poisonous qualifies, it becomes trivially easy to conclude that "religion poisons everything."

Do the other cultured despisers of religion do any better?

Consider Dawkins. In the first chapter of *The God Delusion*, Dawkins tries to distinguish "Einsteinian religion from supernatural religion" (p. 13). He stresses that it is only religion in the "supernatural" sense that he intends to attack. But his main purpose seems to be to deflate the pretensions of theists who want to quote Einstein as their ally.[6] Perhaps because of this polemical aim, his account of the kind of religion he wants to attack is fatally underdeveloped.

Dawkins rightly points out that, when Einstein professed to be religious, he wasn't referring to belief in a personal God but to the humility and "unbounded admiration" that thoughtful people feel when they contemplate the "magnificent structure" of the universe. At one point, Einstein expresses his understanding of religion this way:

> The most beautiful and most profound experience is the sensation of the mystical. It is the sower of all true art and science. He to whom this emotion is a stranger, who can no longer wonder and stand rapt in awe, is as good as dead. To know that what is impenetrable to us really exists, manifesting itself as the highest wisdom and the most radiant beauty which our dull faculties can comprehend only in their primitive forms – this knowledge, this feeling is at the center of true religiousness. (Frank 1947, p. 284)[7]

This awe in the face of an extraordinary and mysterious reality which puts all our self-conceits into their proper place – this is what Einstein meant by "religion." For him, religion was essentially a *feeling*, not belief in a personal God.

But in this respect, Einstein was hardly original. When he understands religion as a feeling, he is following in the footsteps of Friedrich Schleiermacher. Schleiermacher's first published work, *On Religion: Speeches to its Cultured Despisers*, was written while he hobnobbed with Schlegel and other intellectual romantics in turn-of-the-nineteenth-century Berlin. In many ways, his *Speeches* could have been written to today's "cultured despisers" of religion. What Schleiermacher did in the *Speeches* was argue that these cultured despisers didn't really understand *religion* at all. For Schleiermacher, religion is not essentially about beliefs or doctrines or knowledge, nor is it about practices or ethical norms. Religion is neither a "knowing" nor a "doing." It is, instead, a distinctive *feeling*.

By "feeling," Schleiermacher didn't mean some rush of emotion, but rather a kind of primal experience – or, perhaps better, a *way* of experiencing. He called it the feeling of *piety*, and in the *Speeches* he tried to describe it as the awareness of "the Infinite in the finite."[8] Later, in his magnum opus, the *Glaubenslehre* (usually translated as *The Christian Faith*), he described it as "the feeling of absolute dependence." Sometimes, instead of "feeling," he used the term "self-consciousness," although it is clear that what we are conscious *of* in our experience of piety is not our isolated ego but the self *in relation* to something beyond us.

These brief sketches do not, without elaboration, give us an adequate sense of what piety is like (we will consider it more carefully in later chapters). But it doesn't take much reflection on Einstein's humble wonder in the face of a mysterious reality to conclude that what Einstein was feeling was piety in Schleiermacher's sense.

There is a crucial difference, for Schleiermacher, between the feeling of piety and any attempt to explain it. He identifies religion with the feeling. As soon as you begin to explain it in conceptual terms you are doing *theology*, and you've left religion itself behind.[9]

Schleiermacher did acknowledge the reality of religious *communities*, or religions. He thought these came into existence because, as social creatures, we couldn't keep so profound an experience to ourselves. It's natural that religion should *express* itself communally. But religion, in its essence, remains a personal feeling.

In some ways, this point is really very obvious. One commentator on Schleiermacher puts it this way: "Is it not evident to all that when a person is most deeply immersed in religious reality – when he is *being* most religious – he is least conscious of the ideas commonly thought to be its substance, for instance, God, freedom, and immortality?" (Christian 1979, p. 52).

Being religious is about being swept up in a unique feeling. In this respect, at least, *all* religion is Einsteinian.

Of course, Schleiermacher did not share Einstein's *naturalism* – that is, his tendency to explain this feeling in purely natural terms, without invoking a transcendent cause. In the *Glaubenslehre*, Schleiermacher takes the feeling of piety to be our first inkling of a connection to something beyond the world of the senses, something that is the absolute ground of our being. In Schleiermacher's mature theology, the religious feeling turns out to be our first direct experiential link to a God of love.

But given Schleiermacher's view of religion, his differences with Einstein are not on the level of religion in its primary sense. They both experience the feeling that is religion's essence. Where they differ is in their theology – that is, in how they *explain* the feeling to themselves and others. While Schleiermacher would certainly have disagreed with Einstein's theology, he would have had no grievance at all with Einstein's *religion*.

And so, Dawkins' division between "Einsteinian religion" and "supernatural religion" proves to be a crass oversimplification. In important ways, Schleiermacher's religion was *both* "Einsteinian" *and* supernatural.

But I can already imagine Dawkins' reply: *I mean to say, simply, that the term "religion" is either understood in a way that includes belief in a supernatural God, or in a way that does not. That is a mutually exhaustive dualism, and my target is everything in the former category. And I wish physicists would stop using the terms "religion" and "God" in the Einsteinian way, since it misleads the masses.*

I am prepared to grant that when Dawkins heaps accusations on the doorstep of *religion*, he means what I will call "theistic religion" – that is, any use of "religion" that includes belief in a supernatural God. But my point is that even this use of the term is rich in variations. It can refer to someone's account of the world in terms of God's activities (*à la* Griffin), or to a solemn personal experience interpreted as an encounter with God (*à la* James), or to a feeling of absolute dependence that gives rise to theistic belief (*à la* Schleiermacher), or to a social institution that invokes the idea of God to bring about adherence to societal norms (*à la* Durkheim), or to communal metaphors and rituals aimed at aligning individuals with a God who defies direct description (*à la* Hick). It might or might not include belief in the power of intercessory prayer, or in miracles that defy natural laws, or in the inerrancy of some holy book.

With so many possible meanings, anyone who launches a critical discussion of theistic religion in general needs to be cautious. For example, if someone wants to distinguish between "Einsteinian religion" and "theistic religion," it would be risky, in a moment of rhetorical flourish, to say what Dawkins says in the following passage: "The metaphorical or pantheistic God of the physicists is light years away from the interventionist, miracle-wreaking, thought-reading, sin-punishing, prayer-answering God of the Bible, of priests, mullahs and rabbis, and of ordinary language. Deliberately to confuse the two is, in my opinion, an act of intellectual high treason" (p. 19).

Here, Dawkins poses a sharp dichotomy between the metaphorical God of Einstein and a very *particular* understanding of a supernatural God,[10] which he dubs the one of "ordinary language" (as if, in ordinary usage, "God" means just one thing).

In any event, Dawkins claims that the target of his arguments is *not* some particular brand of theism. "I am not attacking any particular version of God or gods," he says. "I am attacking God, all gods, anything and everything supernatural, wherever and whenever they have been or will be invented" (p. 36). And yet, swept up in rhetorical excess, he lavishes enormous attention on the "misogynistic, homophobic, racist, infanticidal, genocidal, filiacidal, pestilential, megalomaniacal, sadomasochistic, capriciously malevolent bully" whom he takes to be the God of the Old Testament (p. 31). (I left out "jealous and proud of it" as well as "a petty, unjust, unforgiving control-freak" and "a vindictive, bloodthirsty ethnic cleanser.")

Imagine an author who sets out to prove that music glorifies violence but who spends most of the book fixated on gangsta rap and then attributes the vices of the latter to music in general. As already noted, this kind of mistake is called *equivocation*. Dawkins' rhetorical excesses and inattention to nuanced differences do not just make him susceptible to this fallacy. When he tries to make the case that religion is pernicious, Dawkins moves willy-nilly from an attack on *particular* religious doctrines and communities to conclusions about religion and belief in God *generally*. And this, of course, is entirely typical of religion's cultured despisers.

The Art of Equivocation

Perhaps Dawkins would have less trouble with theistic religion were it as personal as Einstein's religion was. Schleiermacher was well aware of this inclination among religion's cultured despisers. In one tongue-in-cheek passage from his *Speeches*, he expresses the views of his hostile audience as follows:

> Those of you who are accustomed to regard religion simply as a malady of the soul, usually cherish the idea that if the evil is not to be quite subdued, it is at least more endurable, so long as it only infects individuals here and there. On the other hand, the common danger is increased and everything put in jeopardy by too close association among the patients. (Schleiermacher 1958, p. 147)

Schleiermacher delights in the metaphor, imagining how his audience sees religion's dangers "heightened by the proximity of the infected," increasing the risk that this "feverish delirium" will spread through the whole society, until "whole generations and people would be irrecoverably ruined" (p. 147).

In response, Schleiermacher argues that while religion in its basic sense is a private feeling, it cannot *stay* comfortably private. In Schleiermacher's view, "If there is religion at all, it must be social, for that is the nature of man" (p. 148). In fact, the impulse to association is especially strong in the case of religion, in part because of the sheer power of the religious experience. More significantly, the *content* of religious feeling is an impulse to communalism. "How," he asks, "should he wish to reserve what most strongly drives him out of himself and makes him conscious that he cannot know himself from himself alone?" (p. 149)

The content of the religious feeling includes an awareness of "man's utter incapacity ever to exhaust it for himself alone" (p. 149). Hungry for what others can bring to our understanding of the feeling, we are drawn into association with others.

But ordinary human language isn't up to the task of expressing what we so urgently long to express. And the content of religious feeling is not something "to be tossed from one to another in such small morsels as the materials of a light conversation" (p. 150). And so religious communities inevitably adopt a more intimate form, akin to that of close friendship and love, "where glance and action are clearer than words, and where a solemn silence also is understood" (p. 150).

For Schleiermacher, these genuine religious communities, born from the religious feeling and the desire to share it, are antithetical to any "endeavoring to make others like ourselves" (p. 149). In such communities, each member is "full of native force seeking liberty of utterance and full at the same time of holy desire to apprehend and appropriate what others offer" (p. 151). And so there is no room for hostility towards divergent understandings. Schleiermacher disparages the "wild mania for converting to single definite forms of religion" (p. 155).

If hostility and rivalry are part of a community that calls itself religious, they originate in something other than the primal source of religion. They are, in a real sense, corruptions. The primal religious feeling teaches that "everything is holy . . . whether it is embraced in his system of thought, or lies outside, whether it agrees with his peculiar mode of acting or disagrees" (p. 56). To the extent that organized religion loses sight of this feeling, it is a failure.

Organized religion ceases to be *true* religion if it becomes about dividing human communities into in-groups and out-groups. While Schleiermacher believed that alternative theological speculations inevitably follow from the religious feeling, he also believed that, because the essence of religion is an awareness of something far greater than ourselves, anyone who truly has this awareness "must be conscious that his religion is only part of the whole; that about the same circumstances there may be views and sentiments quite different from his, yet just as pious" (p. 54). Schleiermacher therefore believed that anyone with true religion, no matter how they understood their religious experience (no matter what their theology), would be characterized by a "beautiful modesty" and a "friendly, attractive forbearance" (p. 54).

He thus reprimanded his generation's cultured despisers of religion with words that still resonate today: "How unjustly," he said, "do you reproach religion with loving persecution, with being malignant, with overturning society, and making blood flow like water" (pp. 54–5). For Schleiermacher, religious feeling is "the natural and sworn foe of all narrowmindedness, and all onesidedness" (p. 56). Any organized "religion" that cultivates narrowmindedness or in-group/out-group divisions has lost its connection with the feeling of piety. A community that uses the concept of heresy to attack enemies of the faith has nothing to do with religion in Schleiermacher's sense – even if, in keeping with Schleiermacher's own theology, it includes belief in God.

But when Dawkins makes his case in *The God Delusion* that religion is pernicious, he focuses on the role that religion plays in dividing humanity into opposing groups. He maintains that religion is a "divisive force." He calls it "a *label* of in-group/out-group enmity, not necessarily worse than other labels such as skin color, language, or preferred football team, but often available when other labels are not" (p. 259). He insists that, with respect to enduring conflicts such as the one in Northern Ireland, "without religion there would be no labels by which to decide whom to oppress and whom to avenge" (p. 259). It is socialization into one religious community or another, starting in childhood, that creates the division. Dawkins claims that if we "look carefully at any region of the world where you find intractable enmity and violence between rival groups," it is a "very good bet" that religion serves as the basis for the division (p. 260).

But it is religion *as a social phenomenon* that can set human communities against one another or socialize children into rival "religious" identities. And, if Schleiermacher is right, religion as a social phenomenon can serve this divisive role only when it has lost touch with the *substance* of the original religious feeling, thereby ceasing to be authentic religion at all.

Seen from Schleiermacher's perspective, Dawkins' argument amounts to this: "There exists this social phenomenon that was originally born out of religion (understood as a feeling of piety), but which has become alienated from this source. And this social phenomenon, which has nothing to do with true religion, is a cause of violence and misery. Therefore, religion is a cause of violence and misery."

It doesn't take a logician to see that this argument is bad, even if we take "religion" in Dawkins' argument to include only its "supernatural" forms. After all, Schleiermacher believed in God but what Dawkins is attacking is entirely divorced from the theistic religion of Schleiermacher and his many spiritual children.

The fact is that Dawkins attacks "supernatural religion" in *one* sense and applies his conclusions to "supernatural religion" in *any* meaningful sense. If one were looking for examples of equivocation to include in a critical thinking textbook, one couldn't do much better than Dawkins' arguments against religion.

Examples abound. Dawkins explains at length why he is hostile to "fundamentalist religion," by which he means organized religion that affirms the literal inerrancy of a holy book (such as the Bible). He also explains at length why he is hostile to moral absolutism – which he never defines but which seems to mean something like "unquestioned belief in the truth of certain moral principles, taken to hold without exception, and believed without acknowledging the possibility of error." He concludes – rightly, in my view – that both of these phenomena are dangerous (pp. 282–301).

But how are they related to religion in general? Fundamentalism is only one form of religion. Moral absolutism is at best associated with the religion of some (but not others). One can be a moral absolutist without being especially religious and one can be religious without being a moral absolutist.

So how does Dawkins move from condemning fundamentalism and absolutism to condemning religion as such? Following in the footsteps of Sam Harris, he appeals to the concept of faith. He maintains that religion – even "moderate" religion – asserts that "unquestioning faith" is a virtue. "Faith," he says, "is an evil precisely because it requires no justification and brooks no argument" (p. 308). And the more that "faith" is encouraged, the more likely people are to cling to dangerous beliefs "on faith" and thus become dangerous fanatics. The more that someone's beliefs are shielded from critical scrutiny by virtue of being part of their "religious faith," the harder it becomes to criticize religious doctrines *before* they lead to violence and tragedy.

Again, I agree with Dawkins – *if* "faith" means "stubborn belief that is indifferent to evidence and immune to rational criticism." But for Dawkins' argument to work, this sort of "faith" must be essential to religion in *any* meaningful sense.

Is it? Not for Schleiermacher. Not for Simone Weil, who believed, as we saw, that "one can never wrestle enough with God if one does so out of a pure regard for truth." Not for me. Not for Russell Bennett, former pastor of Fellowship Congregational Church in Tulsa, whose funeral was packed with people of every religious faith and none at all, who was described by a Jewish rabbi as one of "the Thirty-Six" (referring to the Jewish fable that, in every generation, there are thirty-six truly good souls who preserve the world through their gentle but persistent commitment to a life of love, and who are so humble they would never admit to being one of this number). Not for Paul Ashby, current pastor of this same church, who has long meditated on the question of why Tibetan Buddhism, despite terrible oppression under the Chinese occupation, has never given rise to a suicide bomber. Not for most of the congregation at this church.

I mention this church, not because it is unique (it's not) but because it is the church I know best. It is the church where my children are learning not merely about Christianity but how to critically reflect on all religious doctrines in a spirit of curiosity and devotion to a truth that transcends human understanding.

Is there *faith* in such a church? Absolutely, but not in Dawkins' sense. For the sense of faith that is present at churches like it, we need to look elsewhere (I will offer my own proposal in Chapter 8). Is this community *religious*? Absolutely – but not if "faith" in Dawkins' sense is taken to be the essence of religion.

Religion, even organized religion, needn't be any of the things Dawkins accuses it of being. Often, of course, religious communities look just as Dawkins describes. But when this happens, it may be because the community has lost touch with the essence of religion in Schleiermacher's sense – perhaps because the evolutionary forces that Dawkins and Dan Dennett describe as the *source* of religion have swept through and disconnected the community from the primal religious feeling, making the community *about* something else (such as social control in Durkheim's sense). Contrary to what Dawkins and Dennett think, the evolutionary forces they discuss do not explain religion. Rather, they explain why authentic religion is so rare.

The Eloquent Equivocations of Sam Harris

In *The End of Faith* (2004), Sam Harris raises equivocation on the meaning of "religion" to a high art, wraps the ambiguity in mellifluous prose, plays up our fear of religious extremists, launches stinging attacks on Christian fundamentalism, and then lets the force of rhetoric do the work of implicating all religion in the impending demise of human civilization. His message is simple: humanity is headed towards Armageddon, and the blame lies as much with your Aunt Ruth, who faithfully drives to her United Methodist Church every Sunday to sing hymns and pray and listen raptly to Pastor Jim, as it does with Al Qaeda fanatics.

This is a rather scathing portrait of a book that won the 2005 PEN/ Martha Albrand Award (which until 2006 was awarded annually to a new American author of nonfiction). In terms of the criteria used to determine the award recipient, namely "literary and stylistic excellence," Harris's book is exceptional. But while such excellence deserves recognition, one of the risks of stylistic brilliance is that it can blind readers (and authors!) to weak argumentation. And one of the problems most easily obscured is equivocation.

Is Harris guilty of the charge? Like Dawkins, he accuses religion in general of endorsing "faith" construed as blinkered allegiance to irrational beliefs. But Harris has other arguments as well. I want to consider two of them – both targeting religious moderates. The first implicates these moderates in the supposed threat to human civilization as we know it; the second accuses them of a deep intellectual dishonesty, according to which they betray both reason *and* faith.

Harris is astute enough to recognize a difference between religious extremists and religious moderates. The former blow themselves up on crowded buses, demand the deaths of infidels or abortion doctors, and celebrate at the funerals of gays with signs announcing "God Hates Fags"; the latter pray over their meals, recite traditional creeds, think everyone should try to live in peace, and look forward to listening to the cantor on Friday evening, or belting out a good hymn on Sunday morning, etc. The extremists are prepared "to burn the earth to cinders if it would put an end to heresy," while the moderates "draw solace and inspiration from a specific spiritual tradition, and yet remain fully committed to tolerance and diversity" (2004, p. 14).

What could be wrong with the latter? The problem, according to Harris, is that they perpetuate "a terrible dogma" – namely, that "the path to peace will be paved once each of us has learned to respect the unjustified beliefs of others." He thinks these moderates endorse "the notion that every human being should be free to believe whatever he wants about God." And, on his view, this notion "is one of the principal forces driving us toward the abyss" (pp. 14–15).

The *abyss*, no less! Perhaps so, but is it fair to saddle *all* "religious moderates" with this "terrible dogma"? Schleiermacher may well be the spiritual grandparent of so-called "moderate" Christians today. If you don't read him carefully, you might come away thinking he endorses the naive respect for religious diversity that Sam Harris foists onto all religious moderates. After all, he claims that the religious person will "listen to every note that he can recognize as religious" (Schleiermacher 1958, p. 149), regardless of sect or denomination, recognizing that "there may be views and sentiments quite different from his, yet just as pious" (p. 54). There is, in Schleiermacher, a strong basis for a pluralism that looks for what is valuable in every religion, setting aside charges of heresy in favor of "this beautiful modesty, this friendly, attractive forbearance" (p. 54).

And Schleiermacher says all of this while devoting his life to the Christian faith. Surely then, here is one of Harris's "religious moderates" who "draw(s) solace and inspiration from a specific spiritual tradition" while remaining "fully committed to tolerance and diversity."

But it would be an appalling mistake to accuse Schleiermacher of teaching Harris's "terrible dogma." Schleiermacher, in these passages praising tolerance of religious diversity, is describing the *nature* of the religious mind and thereby offering a measuring stick by which to decide whether a so-called faith community is truly *being* religious.

Respect for religion in all its forms does not equal respect for all those who *call* themselves religious, even those who behave in ways utterly at odds with what anyone moved by religious piety would do. Harris's "religious extremists" would be singled out by Schleiermacher as lacking authentic religiosity. From Schleiermacher's perspective, there is no religion there to respect. He would condemn it as a perversion, all the more horrific because of the essential beauty of what has been perverted.

Schleiermacher, in a manner typical of the religious moderates I know, combines a sharp critical stance towards extremist and fundamentalist religion with an interest in culling from every religious tradition some insight into the transcendent. My experience is admittedly anecdotal but my point isn't about statistical frequency. It's about whether Harris's sharp dichotomy – between religious extremists who would raze the earth to expunge heresy and doe-eyed moderates who think everyone should just be allowed to believe whatever they wish – is fair. Schleiermacher, once again, stakes out a perspective from which *both* of Harris's alternatives would have to be condemned.

Like Schleiermacher and Harris, I condemn both alternatives. Unlike Harris, I do not plunge headlong towards the wholly unwarranted conclusion that there are no other alternative accounts of religion but these.

In a follow-up argument, Harris betrays an even more astonishing caricature of religion. He begins this argument as follows:

> The only reason why anyone is "moderate" in matters of faith these days is that he has assimilated some of the fruits of the last two thousand years of human thought. . . . The doors leading out of scriptural literalism do not open from the *inside*. The moderation we see among nonfundamentalists is not some sign that faith itself has evolved; it is, rather, the product of the many hammer blows of modernity that have exposed certain tenets of faith to doubt. (Harris 2004, pp. 18–19)

Harris then notes that "from the perspective of those seeking to live by the letter of the texts, the religious moderate is nothing more than a failed fundamentalist." He reiterates his misguided charge that religious moderation "does not permit anything very critical to be said about religious literalism," since fundamentalists are "merely practicing their freedom of belief", and so concludes that, "by failing to live by the letter of the texts, while tolerating the irrationality of those who do, religious moderates betray faith and reason equally" (pp. 20–1).

But why, exactly, are religious moderates supposed to have betrayed religious faith? On Harris's view, it is because they do not "live by the letter of the *texts*." And why is it that religious moderation cannot, on his view, be seen as representing the evolution of religion to a more advanced form? Because he thinks that "the doors leading out of *scriptural literalism* do not open from the *inside*."[11]

Religion, for him, is about scriptural literalism. The *fundamentalist* view of religion, as blind allegiance to a *text*, is also Harris's definition! Since *that* is what he takes the essence of religion to be, and since we cannot escape literalism from "the inside," he concludes that there is nothing within religion itself that enables this escape. Since Harris relegates religious feeling to the margins, the fact that this feeling is sharply at odds with fundamentalism cannot, for Harris, count as an internal impelling cause of religion's evolution. Religious moderates are therefore represented as people without the integrity of their convictions, people who are simultaneously unwilling to accept where literalism leads (because of the influence of modern insight and rationality) and unwilling to accept where modernity and rationality lead (because of a nostalgic attachment to the text).

We aren't led to this conclusion unless we accept the equation that Harris makes between *fundamentalism* and religion. Harris never considers the possibility that fundamentalism may be the perversion, that fundamentalism may be the betrayal of authentic religion. He blithely equates religion with fundamentalism, and the rest is easy: fundamentalism is irrational; it has no resources for transcending itself. If religious moderation is born out of fundamentalism, it can only be because these moderates can't stomach fundamentalism but are unwilling to follow reason to its conclusion.

Had Harris offered, at the start of the book, a narrow stipulative definition of "religion," and said that he was only attacking religion in that very narrow sense, I would have praised the book for identifying a dangerous phenomenon and explicating precisely what made it so dangerous. But instead, Harris allows his attacks to sweep indiscriminately across anything that calls itself religious – except when "religion" is used as a label for a specific phenomenon he wants to call "spiritual practice" (his treatment of which we will consider in Chapter 7). Harris is careful to rescue what he loves from his promiscuous assault.[12] What he fails to explore is whether there are other things, to which he is personally indifferent, that are equally undeserving of his attack.

The Truth amidst the Mudslinging

And yet, amidst all their equivocation, Dawkins and Harris get something right: organized "religions" have not typically been what Schleiermacher and other religious progressives have lifted up. Schleiermacher himself admits that every real religion is corrupt in one or many ways. After all, religious communities are human ones, subject to all the failings to which humanity is susceptible. And there may be things about these communities that make them distinctively vulnerable to certain kinds of corruption.

This is something I could hardly deny. My family and I drive an hour to church every week. On the way there, I don't pay much attention to the sights but on the way home I see all the churches that we are passing: Amazing Grace Holiness Church on the right, followed a few miles further on by First Pentecostal Holiness Church (all this holiness along one small stretch of highway!). Once we get into the countryside with nothing but cows for company, we pass Ventures of Faith Ministries whose sign proclaims it to be the "World Outreach Center." I can never resist the comment, which inevitably makes my wife groan: "Strategically situated for world outreach!"

Once we take off the freeway and follow the single-lane highway home, we pass a Baptist church whose name I can't recall but which posts a variety of messages on its sign. For a time last summer, the message read, "Prayer conditioned inside!" (I didn't get it until my wife pronounced it with an Oklahoma accent). Later, when Oklahoma was in the grip of an extended heat wave, the sign said, "Think it's hot *here*?"

Once we get closer to home, we pass through a small town whose most prominent landmark is a red-and-blue-painted auto repair shop (with lightning bolts!) calling itself "God's Garage." On the property is a sign pointing the way to an affiliated church. I can't recall its name but I think of it as the church where everyone has a well-tuned car.

Of course, we could shorten our Sunday drive if we were willing to worship at any of these churches. We could avoid it altogether were we to worship at one of several dozen that exist in our town. So why don't we?

Our reasons have much in common with those that Dawkins and Harris voice for disdaining religion. Of course, there are churches in our town that don't fall prey to their criticisms. If other considerations were not in play, we could spare ourselves the drive. But the reality is that any real-world religious community – what Schleiermacher called a "positive religion" – will have flaws.

As social animals, most of us must therefore choose between a *flawed* religious community and no real *living* religion at all. If we want religion in our lives, we must decide which flaws we can live with, given our idiosyncrasies and life histories. It is like choosing a spouse: no spouse is perfect, so you need to find one whose flaws you can live with and who can live with your flaws.

But sometimes (perhaps often) these flaws are so monumental that Schleiermacher can only agree with the cultured despisers of religion when they accuse positive religions of displaying characteristics entirely at odds with "true religion." Choosing these positive religions is not choosing religion at all and may even lead to the death of religious feeling. Again, the analogy to an intimate relationship is apt: if we are to find a loving life partner, we must choose among imperfect mates. But some flaws are so great they render a loving relationship impossible.

When corruption of religious communities is pervasive, the situation may be akin to finding a mate amidst a crowd of abusive alcoholics. While some of those close at hand might not be abusive drunks, one may need to travel far to find a *compatible* mate.

The religious world we live in may well be like a world dominated by abusive drunks. The reality is that organized religions have historically served a dangerously divisive role. The concept of heresy has shaped virtually every actual religious tradition in history. And this concept has clearly played a role in fomenting violent conflict. Sam Harris may well be right that we have the moderating power of *secular* culture to thank for the fact that there aren't more American churches at each other's throats.

But Dawkins himself observes that religion is not the only thing that has served as a "label of division." Beneath this use of religion is an *underlying drive to divide* that will seize just about anything to do its work: religion, skin color, national identity, kinship groups, language differences, even (as Dawkins notes) sports team allegiances (2006, p. 259).

No one can deny Harris's charge that the history of religion is fraught with the willingness to sacrifice critical reflection at the altar of fundamentalism. But under the surface, other drives may be at work. Human beings crave power and privilege. And this drive is so strong that it can even take hold of a philosophy of radical *egalitarianism* such as Marxism and use it as a basis for imposing the very class divisions that Marx abhorred, vesting party members with privilege while the majority languish, too afraid of the KGB (the heresy police!) to voice dissent.

And then, of course, there is the human desire for certainty, for relief from doubt. Sometimes that certainty is sought in a radical relativism:

"Whatever I believe is right for me, just because I believe it." Sometimes it's sought in a fanaticism that won't admit the possibility of error or a naive trust in someone else to do your thinking for you.

These drives have taken hold of religious communities repeatedly through history. In Schleiermacher's day, the cultured despisers of religion saw all this corruption and (in Schleiermacher's words) it made positive religion "the object of a quite pre-eminent hate" (1958, p. 214). We see that hate today in the spewing vitriol of Dawkins, the righteous outrage of Harris, the cold intellectual disdain of Dennett (like a researcher studying cancer under a microscope).

In response to this hatred, Schleiermacher does not deny the pervasiveness of corruption but asks the cultured despisers of religion to "forget for once this one-sided view and follow me to another." He goes on:

> Consider how much of this corruption is due to those who have dragged forth religion from the depths of the heart into the civil world. Acknowledge that much of it is unavoidable as soon as the Infinite, by descending into the sphere of time and submitting to the general influence of finite things, takes to itself a narrow shell. (Schleiermacher 1958, p. 216)

In short, consider the possibility that these positive religions were born out of the inner life of religious feeling and the urgent need to share it in community with others. If that is true, we need to ask what forces took hold of these communities, ultimately wringing from them every trace of the religion that gave them birth.

These are questions I will return to in the final chapter, once I have more adequately characterized the kind of "religion" I want to defend. For now, I simply want to note that Dawkins and Harris, in a manner characteristic of the angry new atheists, ignore the possibility that, when religion becomes a tool of division or a venue in which critical reflection is shut down, religion *has lost its way.*

Under some important definitions of "religion," that's precisely what's happened.

Definitions therefore matter a great deal. We need to be careful to use our terms precisely and to acknowledge different meanings of a word. The new atheists display an all-too-common failure in this respect. The evils of "religion" in one sense are treated as the evils of "supernatural religion" in general – even though supernatural religion in Schleiermacher's sense is essentially *opposed* to the very things Dawkins and Harris and Hitchens blame it for. This is true even though Schleiermacher's religion was neither the atheistic religion of some Buddhists nor the impersonal deism of the Enlightenment. It was theistic, with a loving and redeeming God at its heart. It was communal, finding its fullest expression in communities of faith. But it had no room for divisiveness or blind allegiance to pronouncements from on high.

Religion of this sort may be hard to find in the buckle of the Bible belt, but it can be found even there.

And it's worth the drive.

2

"The God Hypothesis" and
the Concept of God

Although Dawkins flails mightily against religion, his book isn't called *The Religion Delusion*. It's called *The God Delusion*. In Schleiermacher's terms, Dawkins' main concern may not really be with religion at all, but with a particular *theology* that has become wedded to religion: specifically, a theology that affirms the existence of God.

And so, even if I'm right that Dawkins' attacks on *religion* are mired in equivocation, that doesn't mean his book fails to achieve a different objective, perhaps his main one: to refute what he calls "the God Hypothesis" (2006, p. 31). Since my purpose in this book is to defend *theistic* religion – that is, religion in which the feeling of piety is directed towards *God* – a successful refutation of the so-called God Hypothesis would be a telling blow against my aim, regardless of how innocuous the feeling of piety may be as a feeling.

When Dawkins introduces God as a *hypothesis*, he is using the language of science. A hypothesis is a proposition we test in the light of observation. Put in overly simple terms, scientists make a prediction based on the hypothesis. They ask, "What should we expect to observe *if* this hypothesis is true?" If the prediction "comes true," the hypothesis lives to be tested another day. If it doesn't, the hypothesis has been falsified.

Sometimes, things really are this simple. Suppose there's a glass of liquid on my kitchen counter. I hypothesize that it's water and make a prediction: "If I swig this, it will quench my thirst without harming me." I swig, and my mouth is promptly roasted by a strong exothermic reaction.

My hypothesis has been falsified. Were I still able to talk, I might say, "Dang! What's sulfuric acid doing in my kitchen? I'm a philosopher, not a mad chemist!"

But things are not always this simple. Suppose a friend tells you there's a wild boar in the woods. Although boars haven't been seen in your neck of the woods for generations, you decide to check it out. You formulate your hypothesis: "There's a wild boar in these woods." And you make your prediction: "If I wait quietly in a tree, I'll eventually see a boar." And then you keep lookout in your tree until your provisions run out. You head home, never having seen the boar.

Has your prediction been falsified? Suppose the woods are enormous. In that case, failing to see a boar *might* mean there isn't one . . . or it might just mean bad luck. As with other hypotheses about the existence of a particular thing, seeing a boar will confirm your hypothesis, but failing to see one won't falsify it.

Of course, if you sit in your tree for weeks and never see a boar, you might start to doubt your friend's reliability. If you look for other boar signs (prints, etc.) and find none, you might say to yourself, "These woods look *just* the way I'd expect a boar-less forest to look." And you might conclude that it isn't reasonable to believe the "boar hypothesis." We might say that the hypothesis has been *weakly* falsified.

Victor Stenger, in *God: The Failed Hypothesis* (2007), tries to show that the God Hypothesis is weakly falsified by science in just this way. As he puts it, "The observed universe and the laws and parameters of physics look just as they can be expected to look if there is no God" (p. 164). Stenger's case appeals to physics but Dawkins invokes evolutionary biology to make a similar point in *River Out of Eden*. According to Dawkins,

> In a universe of electrons and selfish genes, blind physical forces and genetic replication, some people are going to get hurt, other people are going to get lucky, and you won't find any rhyme or reason in it, nor any justice. The universe that we observe has precisely the properties we should expect if there is, at bottom, no design, no purpose, no evil, no good, nothing but pitiless indifference. (Dawkins 1995, p. 133)

Christopher Hitchens (2007, pp. 66–7) gestures towards a similar argument when he tells the anecdote about Laplace, the scientist who was asked by Napoleon Bonaparte why his astronomical theories didn't mention God. Laplace replied that he *didn't need that hypothesis*. Since Laplace didn't think he needed the God Hypothesis, and since his reply to Bonaparte was both daring and clever, Hitchens is convinced: there is no God. (Yes, Hitchens' reasoning is *exactly* that horrific.)

This line of thinking, which invokes science to refute God's existence, will be challenged with care in Chapter 4. For now, I want to make three points. First, if you've been wandering in an enormous forest for days and seen no boar signs, all you can reasonably say is that "things look like we'd expect in the absence of a boar . . . so far." Those looking to weakly falsify the God Hypothesis should remember that the universe is a mighty big forest.

Second, moving from "Things look just as we'd expect in the absence of a God" to "The God Hypothesis is likely false" assumes that how the universe would look were the God Hypothesis true is different from how it would look otherwise. Were I to look at pine branches in the woods and conclude that "they look just as we'd expect were there no boar hereabouts," we wouldn't treat that as even *weak* falsification of the boar hypothesis, since a boar's presence would have no effect on how pine branches look.

Of course, Stenger and Dawkins assume that the observable universe would look different to scientific eyes were the God Hypothesis true.[1] My third point is that whether they are right about this depends enormously on what the God Hypothesis actually *says*. The same can be said for their claim that belief in God is pernicious. Whether this is true depends on what "God" means.

So how *do* the new atheists define "God"?

New Atheist Definitions of God

In *God: The Failed Hypothesis*, Stenger offers a "scientific God model," according to which God is defined by the following attributes:

1 God is the creator and preserver of the universe.
2 God is the architect of the structure of the universe and the author of the laws of nature.
3 God steps in whenever he wishes to change the course of events, which may include violating his own laws as, for example, in response to human entreaties.
4 God is the creator and preserver of life and humanity, where human beings are special in relation to other life-forms.
5 God has endowed humans with immaterial, eternal souls that exist independent of their bodies and carry the essence of a person's character and selfhood.
6 God is the source of morality and other human values such as freedom, justice, and democracy.

7 God has revealed truths in scriptures and by communicating directly to select individuals throughout history.

8 God does not deliberately hide from any human being who is open to finding evidence for his presence. (2007, pp. 41–2)

This is clearly a list of things many theists believe; but if Stenger's aim is to define God for the sake of investigating whether God exists, this list is seriously problematic. It includes things that aren't attributes of *God* at all. Since criterion 1 designates God as creator and preserver of the universe (and, by implication, of "life and humanity"), what criterion 4 adds is that humans are special among living things. But that's a claim about *humans*. Likewise, criterion 5 is about humans (we have immortal souls) and, at best, about what God has *done* (He's "endowed" us with these souls, or, better, created beings – us – who possess them). But would God not have *been* God had He refrained from creating creatures like us? Criteria 3 and 7 are also about what God supposedly *does*, while criterion 8 is about what God *doesn't* do (He doesn't hide from those who seek Him). But there are presumably many things God doesn't do. Why treat this one as a defining characteristic?

Suppose there is no scientific evidence to suggest that a supernatural being "steps in whenever he wishes to change the course of events," by (for example) violating natural laws in response to human prayers (Stenger's criterion 3). Have we shown that there is no God? Only if such intervention is part of the very definition of God. But is it possible to believe in God's existence and yet deny that God ever violates natural laws? Absolutely. That's what Schleiermacher believed. Does that make him an atheist?

Or consider the great twentieth-century theologian, John Hick, who argues that in order to create a world in which we can develop as autonomous beings with a sense of our own independent identity, God must place Himself at an "epistemic distance" from us – that is, He must *hide* from us (2001, p. 42). And so, in a sense, Hick rejects Stenger's criterion 8. Does he thereby reject the existence of God?

If criteria 3 and 8 are part of the very definition of God, then many devout theologians turn out not to believe in God as defined. But what that tells us, of course, is that Stenger's definition is faulty. Theologians can and do disagree about these and other matters even if they share belief in God's existence.

It's hard to avoid the judgment that Stenger is tailoring his definition to suit his conclusion. He knows full well that his case against God amounts at best to weak falsification: Nothing we've seen in the woods supports belief in a wild boar . . . so far. But if the woods are enormous, and our ability to observe it and understand what we see profoundly limited, why should we expect to make observations that clearly support the presence of a boar? The case for weak falsification is strong only if two things are true: first, the boar *would be noticed* if it weren't hiding; second, *it isn't hiding*. And so Stenger needs criterion 8 to be part of his definition of God in order to make his case, and thus blithely includes it even though doing so makes little theological sense.

In fact, I personally accept criterion 8, at least under a certain description (although I'd never define God in terms of it). History is replete with examples of people who report ineffable experiential encounters with the divine. For reasons that will become clear in later chapters, I think an extraordinary experience of this sort (a religious rather than an empirical one) is the only way to encounter God, and we should not expect, even if God exists, to find unambiguous empirical evidence of that fact.

What follows – at least if we assume that God isn't hiding from those who earnestly seek evidence of Him – is that persons who seek God *through an openness to extraordinary modes of experience* will frequently have such experiences, ones that support theistic belief. Something along these lines is surely what most theists mean when they say God doesn't hide from those who seek Him: those who earnestly seek God will experience His presence in their lives, not with their eyes or ears, but at the level of feeling (in something like Schleiermacher's sense).

Do they? Absolutely. It happens across cultures and eras and religious differences. On this evidence, criterion 8 seems true: God does not deliberately hide from those who seek Him. But Stenger is characteristically unwilling to attach the slightest evidentiary value to religious experiences. He insists that the evidence must come from science. And his understanding of God is tailored to that view. He takes criterion 8 to mean that God would leave clear signs of His existence in the empirical world studied by science.

Put simply, Stenger defines "God" by trolling through things theists typically believe and including in his definition anything that can help make the God Hypothesis susceptible to weak scientific falsification. But is this the best way to arrive at a definition? Surely not. But then, how should we arrive at one?

In *The God Delusion*, Dawkins defines "the God Hypothesis" as the hypothesis that "*there exists a superhuman, supernatural intelligence who deliberately designed and created the universe and everything in it, including us*"

(2006, p. 31). For Dawkins, then, "God" refers to a being characterized by a list of attributes that includes being superhuman, being supernatural, being "an intelligence," and being the creator and designer of everything.

Unlike Stenger, Dawkins doesn't smuggle into his definition claims that are mainly about humans. You get the sense that he's trying to extract from particular conceptions of God a common thread of meaning. He is, I think, trying to fairly express common usage.

We can ask at least two questions about his efforts. First, how close does he get to common usage? But the deeper question is this: When it comes to a term like "God," one that religious believers generally agree names a being *who transcends human understanding*, how legitimate is it to define God in terms of common usage? After all, common usage reflects the very human understanding that God supposedly transcends.

The Supremely Good God of Traditional Theism

Our first question is this: How well has Dawkins captured the dominant account of God? In the Christian tradition (to which I can best speak), theologians have pursued a two-thousand-year-long critical dialogue about God's properties and, while disputes continue, there is also a dominant consensus – one that surely trickles down to the laity through their seminary-trained pastors.

And what is that picture? Any good introductory philosophy of religion text will tell you, but I am particularly fond of the summary offered by atheist philosopher William Rowe (2007). He describes the "God of the theologians" as follows: "The dominant idea of God in western civilization, then, is the idea of a supremely good being, creator of but separate from and independent of the world, all-powerful (omnipotent), all-knowing (omniscient), eternal, and self-existent" (p. 6). Of the properties listed here, most are fairly self-explanatory for a rough-and-ready understanding of God. The exceptions are the last two. By "eternal," theologians mean one of two things: *everlasting* (existing for all time), or *atemporal* (existing outside of time). Most theologians have preferred the latter (although I suspect the former is the more popular understanding). By "self-existent," theologians have meant that God *explains His own existence*, rather than being explained by something else (an idea we will return to in Chapter 6).

So, how close does Dawkins get to this theological understanding? An all-powerful and all-knowing being could readily be described as "super-human," and that may be what Dawkins has in mind. And "supernatural" is sometimes taken to mean existing outside the natural world and its laws. A God who is independent of the world and outside of time would fit the bill. So, "supernatural" might well cover these attributes.

Dawkins' definition doesn't include self-existence – an oversight I will return to later. But for now, I want to focus on Dawkins' most glaring oversight: he makes no mention of God's goodness.

For Dawkins, this is no accidental omission. In *The God Delusion*, he barely mentions the so-called "problem of evil" – long viewed as the most important challenge to God's existence – because he thinks it is no real problem at all. Put simply, the problem is this: Why is there evil in the world, if there exists a morally perfect and all-powerful God, one who could eliminate evil and presumably would want to?

Dawkins says this problem is "childishly easy to overcome," because it is "an argument only against the existence of a good God. Goodness is no part of the *definition* of the God Hypothesis, merely a desirable add-on" (p. 108). And so he excludes goodness from his definition, almost as a favor: Remove that pesky goodness and spare those poor theists the embarrass-ing problem of evil. But is Dawkins right to think that goodness is "merely a desirable add-on"?

The New Testament offers only one account of God that has the form of a definition, in 1 John 4, verses 8 and 16: "God is love." Christian theologians have routinely insisted that love – a moral property – is what makes God truly *God*, rather than, say, just a powerful tyrant in the sky.

Some may be understandably cynical about this insistence that God is love, given how many Christians seem to have gone to Herculean lengths to reconcile brutality and cruelty with their faith in such a God. But there are many Christians for whom the doctrine that God is love has proved far more than an empty mantra.

An obvious example is Martin Luther King, Jr. Both Dawkins and Hitchens want to distance King – a Baptist preacher – from the theism they attack, perhaps because they admire him. We've already encountered Hitchens' rather stunning claim that King can't be viewed as a proper Christian because he chose to love and forgive his enemies rather than publicly announce they'd roast in hell. In defiance of every reputable theologian, Hitchens thinks hell is more central to Christianity than the love and mercy of God.

Dawkins is less outrageous, if no less muddled. He claims that, "Although Martin Luther King was a Christian, he derived his philosophy of non-violent civil disobedience directly from Gandhi, who was not" (2006, p. 271). While this is partly true, it is terribly misleading (even setting aside Christian influences on Gandhi).

Consider King's autobiographical sermon, "Pilgrimage to Nonviolence." Here, King shares his personal struggles with the Christian love ethic. He claims that at one point he'd "almost despaired of the power of love to solve social problems." It was, he says, Gandhi that changed his mind. As King puts it, "As I delved deeper into the philosophy of Gandhi, my skepticism concerning the power of love gradually diminished, and I came to see for the first time that the Christian doctrine of love, operating through the Gandhian method of nonviolence, is one of the most potent weapons available to an oppressed people in their struggle for freedom" (1986, p. 38). King concludes that the civil rights movement was one in which "Christ furnished the spirit and motivation and Gandhi furnished the method" (p. 38).

To say that King's Christianity had no part in his commitment to nonviolence is therefore a gross mischaracterization. And his Christian faith did more than just provide him with an ethic. Again, his words in "Pilgrimage to Nonviolence" are telling:

> God has been profoundly real to me in recent years. In the midst of outer dangers I have felt an inner calm. In the midst of lonely days and dreary nights I have heard an inner voice saying, "Lo, I will be with you." When the chains of fear and the manacles of frustration have all but stymied my efforts, I have felt the power of God transforming the fatigue of despair into the buoyancy of hope. I am convinced that the universe is under the control of a loving purpose, and that in the struggle for righteousness man has cosmic companionship. Behind the harsh appearances of the world there is a benign power. (King 1986, p. 40)

These are the words of a deeply religious man, whose faith in a loving God not only provided the "spirit and motivation" for his commitment to nonviolence, but whose inner experience of a "loving purpose" at work beneath the surface of a seemingly hostile world gave him the will to persevere in that commitment despite dangers and failures.

This wasn't faith in a God for whom goodness was just "a desirable add-on." As his own words make clear, King's pilgrimage to nonviolence was fueled by faith in a God whose very essence is love.

But King's example hardly settles the matter. For every Martin Luther King there is a Fred Phelps (pastor of Westboro Baptist Church who, with a congregation made up of his extended family, has been on a homophobic campaign that's included picketing Matthew Shepherd's funeral with signs displaying such slogans as "God Hates Fags"). And for every Fred Phelps, there are a dozen Jerry Falwells and Pat Robertsons, whose platitudes about love are combined with teachings that subordinate women, condemn to hellfire those with different beliefs, and drive gay Christians to suicide.

It's hard not to notice Bertrand Russell's vitriolic reaction to Christianity, a vitriol mirrored in Dawkins' and Hitchens' lavishly disparaging rhetoric. For those poisoned against Christianity, it may be hard to take seriously the idea that Martin Luther King represents "real" Christianity, while Robertson and Falwell represent a distortion.

And so it's not surprising that the new atheists wouldn't pay attention to the Christian idea that a God without goodness is no God at all. But as unsurprising as this is, it's a *serious* mistake – one that may be rooted in the way they go about trying to define "God."

Non-Substantive Definitions of "God"

Both Dawkins and Stenger define God in terms of a list of attributes. A definition of this kind – what I'll call a "substantive definition" – is what I typically get when I ask students to define "God." Some say God is "a perfectly loving and all-powerful spirit," others that He is "the creator and preserver of the universe." Some define God as "the ultimate tyrant, who lays down arbitrary laws and then roasts anyone who doesn't obey them." Still others (who've done the reading) define God as "an omnipotent, omniscient, perfectly good, eternal, unchanging, and self-existent spiritual being."

Occasionally, however, I get definitions that do not fit this model. Two stand out. The first runs as follows: "God is whatever it is that I feel connected to when I'm in the grip of worship." The other is this: "God is the best possible being."

Those who have studied philosophy will recognize the latter as a variant on St Anselm's famous definition of God as "something than which nothing greater can be thought" (Anselm 1998, p. 87). Those with more esoteric reading interests may recognize the former as similar to

Schleiermacher's definition from the early sections of the *Glaubenslehre*. There, Schleiermacher calls the basic religious experience "the feeling of absolute dependence," by which he means a kind of immediate consciousness of ourselves as utterly dependent on something that grounds our very existence and makes possible everything we experience and everything we do – in Schleiermacher's language, "our receptive and active existence" (1928, p. 16).

For Schleiermacher, "God," in that term's "original signification," is just the name for this *something*. God is whatever it is that we depend on absolutely, "the Whence of our receptive and active existence" (p. 16). The concept of God emerges for us the moment we not only have this feeling of absolute dependence (which, for reasons we will consider in Chapter 4, cannot be *about* anything in the empirical world), but treat the experience as veridical, that is, as an experience of something real.

For Schleiermacher, theology's task is to reflect on religious experience with the care necessary to develop an understanding of God. This is the task Schleiermacher sets for himself (what philosophers today might call a phenomenological study of religious experience, aimed at describing its "intentional object"). Any list of God's attributes would be the result of such a study, and the definition of God therefore *precedes* any attempt to develop such a list.

Schleiermacher's definition is *ostensive* – that is, a definition achieved by pointing (literally or figuratively) at the object named by a term. Imagine you are at a party and a friend asks, "Who is Leroy Jones?" Assuming you know Leroy and he's there, you might answer by pointing him out. Your friend may still know next to nothing *about* Leroy but at least he now knows where to look to find out. Likewise, once Schleiermacher has defined "God," we still know next to nothing *about* God. For that, we must do the hard work of theology.

For the moment, let us leave Schleiermacher's definition and turn to Anselm's account of God as "something than which nothing greater can be thought." Actually, I like my student's version better: God is the best possible being.

When I ask my students what makes something the best possible being, they typically mention being all-powerful, all-knowing, and perfectly good. But when I ask whether it is better to be immutable or mutable, their eyes glaze over. When pressed, they'll sometimes say that God is *whichever is better, but they're not sure which that is.*

But this answer is interesting, especially in terms of what it tells us about the Anselmian definition: this definition doesn't say what God's attributes *are*. Instead, it gives us a standard for deciding whether an attribute would belong to God. A disposition to suspend natural laws, for example, would be a property of God if and only if it is better to meddle in this way than not.

Is it? Theologians have disagreed. Schleiermacher argues that a God who meddled in the course of natural events would be less great than one who didn't. He says that "the capacity to make a change in what has been ordained is only a merit in the ordainer, if a change is necessary, which again can only be the result of some imperfection in him or his work" (1928, p. 179). In other words, it would be good for God to meddle only if He didn't design nature right in the first place. But a "greatest possible being" would get things right the first time, and so would never meddle.

Of course, many theologians disagree with Schleiermacher. But my point is that the Anselmian definition of God leaves room for such disagreement. Rather than offering a fixed set of attributes, Anselm's definition offers guidelines for pursuing a kind of theological research program. His definition is not ostensive like Schleiermacher's (I'd be inclined to call it formal) but shares with Schleiermacher's definition the fact that it provides a starting point for understanding God, not a comprehensive list of attributes.

And if, as most theists would agree, God transcends our finite understanding, wouldn't it be better to define "God" in a way that makes our understanding of the divine susceptible to development in the light of critical reflection? What we need is a definition that points us to something without presuming to describe every key detail; a definition that gets all of us "looking in the same direction" so that we can have a debate about the properties of what we're looking at.

Of course, any definition of this sort will make it difficult to test the God Hypothesis scientifically, even if it were theoretically possible to do so. And so the new atheists may view such a definition as a deliberate evasion of their efforts at falsification (I can almost hear their indignation).

My initial response to such views is simply this: *Get over it*. Since the God Hypothesis concerns a reality that transcends the world investigated by science, it can't be investigated scientifically anyway (a point I will defend in Chapter 4), and such indignation is irrelevant. Theologians and philosophers of religion should not be forced, out of deference to those scientists who want to subject everything to *their* methodology, to adopt a definition of God unsuitable to its subject matter.

At the same time, we need to heed the warning implicit in a parenthetical remark by Daniel Dennett in *Breaking the Spell*: "How to turn an atheist into a theist by just fooling around with words – if 'God' were just the name of *whatever it is* that produced all creatures great and small, then God might turn out to *be* the process of evolution by natural selection" (2006, p. 215).

Dennett's concern here is important but he carries it too far. Struck by the radical evolution of the concept of God through history, he thinks it's a mystery why people today "insist on calling the Higher Power they believe in 'God' " (p. 208). He wonders why it is that, since contemporary concepts of God preserve so little of what the ancients would have recognized, we don't just "let go of the traditional terms along with the discarded conceptions" (p. 208).

The answer that Dennett leaps to is *brand loyalty*. If the Coca-Cola company were to change the formula of its flagship beverage (as it did some years ago), and take the original formula off the market (as it did briefly before thinking better of it), they'd still want to call the new drink Coke. If they called it "Goober Ale," they wouldn't be able to take advantage of existing brand loyalty. Dennett thinks something like this is going on when liberal theologians still call the object of their worship "God."

Dennett's perspective here makes sense if ancient anthropomorphic conceptions of God have nothing important in common with those abstract modern ones that, in Dennett's words, refer to "a Higher Power . . . whose characteristics are beyond comprehension – aside from the fact that they are, in some incomprehensible way, good, not evil" (p. 206). But I think there is something they have in common – and Dennett has, I think, unwittingly hit upon what it is with his rather derisive observation that even the most abstract and mystery-laden conceptions of God insist that, "in some incomprehensible way," God is good.

The Ethico-Religious Hope

The philosopher John Bishop (1998) points out that underlying the Anselmian definition of God as something "than which a greater cannot even be conceived" is the idea that the concept of God "has to be the concept of that which is worthy of worship." And, as Bishop notes, worship "requires a uniquely excellently worthy object" (p. 176).

Bishop follows up this insight with a line of thought that strikes me as even more important. He supports what he calls a "functionalist" understanding of God: he thinks that belief in the existence of God serves an important function in the "psychological economy" of devout theists (p. 176). Put simply, belief in God does an important job – namely, to provide a warrant for a certain kind of hope.

Bishop notes that although we may sincerely believe that a virtuous life is valuable in itself, it remains true that, given the world in which we live, we may have "thoughts of hopelessness, alienation or despair that tempt us to think that, though living life lovingly may indeed be the highest value, suffering, finitude and death – especially as they affect virtuous and vicious alike – make a mockery of commitment to such a life, robbing it of its meaningfulness and point" (p. 183).

Put another way, no matter how much we may endorse the intrinsic value of a benevolent life, we may still look around and see a universe that is utterly indifferent to such a life, a fundamental reality that cares nothing about happiness, fairness, loving relationships, or even life itself. We look at the world and see what Dawkins claims to see: a universe of "pitiless indifference," in which all our projects, our cherished memories, our efforts to be better people, are ultimately swallowed up by death.

But we can hope for something better. When Bishop tries to articulate the content of this hope, he characterizes it as the hope "that lives lived lovingly . . . are not deprived of meaningfulness and point by suffering, finitude, and death" (p. 183). But this strikes me as too negative to even really be a hope. The hope is better expressed by King who held not only that benevolent lives aren't stripped of meaning by the grim facts of life but that this is true *because of the nature of the universe*: "Behind the harsh appearances of the world there is a benign power."

But the negative statement of the hope may help us to flesh out King's more positive formulation. Stated negatively, the hope is that the universe is not what Dawkins says it is, and what it appears to be if reality is nothing more than what scientific investigation can discern: a universe of "pitiless indifference." To understand what this means, we need to consider what the material universe seems to be pitilessly indifferent to. In brief, it seems indifferent to *the good*.

But what does that mean?

When we think about what is good, what come to mind first are the things we value in a nontrivial way: loving relationships; a gesture of kindness unasked for; a moment of tenderness at the end of the day, when an exhausted mother strokes her sleeping child's hair; a dog's enthusiastic greeting; a pleasant meal among friends; a life lived with integrity. All the things, in short, that it breaks our hearts to imagine as nothing but the fleeting by-products of matter and energy grinding away according to mechanistic laws – laws that will soon grind them out of existence again.

To offer any deeper philosophical analysis of the good, beyond this rough understanding, is to wade into the thick of centuries' worth of philosophical controversy. But I think I should offer something in the way of analysis here, even if it will inevitably be sketchy and controversial.

When we say that something is good, I think we mean more than just that we happen to value it. We mean that there is something about it which calls out for a valuing response in us. And when it comes to the most important goods, I think we mean that there is something fundamentally wrong with those who don't value it. Those who don't value human life and welfare, for example, are sociopaths.

Some of the things we value are things we want to have. When we say we value them, what we really mean is that we value having them or experiencing them: an aromatic cup of coffee, a healthy body, an electrifying first kiss. But there are other things whose existence we value even if we can't have or experience them – for example, our children. We may value our experience of them, but we also value their continued existence apart from such experience. And we don't just happen to value it. We think we should value it. Anyone who didn't would be defective.

There is a saying attributed to St Augustine that captures the central idea here: "I'd rather *have* a diamond, but I'd rather *be* a mouse." In other words, there are some things that it is good to *be*, things whose existence as such has value, even if no one as a matter of fact values them. While the diamond has value to me as a possession, the mouse's existence has value in itself, apart from whether anyone values it as a possession. Sometimes such things are said to be inherently valuable or objectively good.

Among those things we tend to regard as objective goods, the most significant are almost certainly persons. We ought to value persons, not merely as something to have or possess but as beings whose existence has merit for its own sake. And when we value persons for their own sakes, we express that by actively caring about their welfare, that is, about what is good for them: their needs (what they must have to exist at all, like food and water), and their interests (those things which help them to flourish, such as education and intimacy). At a minimum, this entails not capriciously interfering with their ability to pursue their good. But it will also mean, when appropriate, helping to promote their welfare.

The essence of morality seems to lie in this: caring about what is good for those whose existence has objective value – especially persons, but also animals and perhaps plants. Those who do this we call good in the moral sense. And it seems that we should value the moral goodness in persons, regardless of what that goodness does for us. And so it is not only persons who are objectively good. So is their moral goodness. And some things that spring from moral goodness – such as loving relationships – are also good objectively. Even if we don't have loving relationships, we should value their existence.

But if the fundamental reality is nothing but what Dawkins takes it to be – "electrons and selfish genes, blind physical forces and genetic replication" – then the fundamental reality cares nothing for any of this. With a sociopath's indifference, the physical universe kills persons as readily as it shatters inanimate things.

Everything we care about – and, more significantly, everything we *should* care about – is something that the universe of "blind physical forces" just *doesn't* care about. A materialist view of reality turns morality and goodness into the idiosyncratic concerns of a single species that might never have existed (and if we hadn't, the universe wouldn't have cared a whit). When we are gone (as we will be), the universe will once again just be a world of meaningless facts and events. The world of things *without* life, *without* personality, *without* a capacity to care – this, according to the scientific picture endorsed by Dawkins and Stenger and others, is the ultimate reality.

Juxtaposed against this picture, there is the hope that the essence of the universe is characterized by something else – what Martin Luther King called "a loving purpose." It is the hope that there is something fundamental that eludes empirical investigation and which is essentially on the side of goodness. In such a universe, the moral agent who cares about the good is in tune with the fundamental truth about the universe in a way that the sociopath is not.

William James characterized the essence of religion as the conviction that "the visible world is part of a more spiritual universe from which it draws its significance" and that "union or harmonious relation with that higher universe is our true end" (1914, p. 485). But what is the point of believing in such a higher and more fundamental reality? The point is to open a space in which we can hope that, despite what the universe looks like through an empirical lens, the universe is fundamentally on the side of goodness.

I will call this the *ethico-religious hope.*

For some, my thinking here will recall Immanuel Kant's moral argument for God's existence. Kant maintains that the highest good we can hope for consists in happiness being possessed by those who are morally virtuous. He also thinks that the empirical world offers no real hope that the virtuous will be happy. But a commitment to morality requires us to believe in the fulfillment of this hope – and only a transcendent moral being, or God, can fulfill it. Since reason requires a commitment to morality, it thereby demands that we believe in God.[2]

It is not my purpose to defend Kant's argument. I am not arguing here, as Kant does, that reason requires us to believe in the best picture of things that we can hope for. My aim at this point is to offer an account of what "God" means, not to argue that we should believe in the existence of a being fitting this account (my arguments that it is reasonable to believe in such a being will come later). Furthermore, Kant's hope is that the most virtuous life will also be the happiest. The hope I want to call attention to is broader and vaguer than this. It is the hope that the universe is fundamentally *on the side of* goodness.

This hope might express itself as the hope that those who care about the good will be rewarded by God. But I prefer to express it as the hope that when we live a moral life we are more in harmony with the essence of the universe, more true to reality, than those who choose the path of moral indifference or brutality. When we are virtuous, we come into alignment with the fundamental reality, and thus into relationship with it. And this connection offers more intrinsic fulfillment than any terrestrial prosperity ever could.

God: The Ethico-Religious Hope Fulfilled

With the ethico-religious hope characterized in this way, we can return to the task of defining God. Put simply, "God" in the most general sense has to be understood as a being whose existence would fulfill our ethico-religious hope. When we ask whether God exists, we are therefore asking whether there actually exists a reality that fulfills this hope – an ultimate reality that makes it true that the universe is fundamentally on the side goodness even though the physical laws of nature are pitilessly indifferent to it. If the answer is yes, then "God" in the most significant sense of that word exists – even if there does not exist a being who meddles with the laws of nature in response to petitionary prayer, or who possesses omnipotent powers, or who dictated the text of some particular holy book. And if the answer is *no*, then the world might for all we care be full of super-human entities (such as the almighty "Q continuum" from the *Star Trek* universe), but there would be no God.

This account unites abstract liberal conceptions of God with more traditional ones, highlighting a common thread of meaning that Dennett ignores: "God" names that which, in our intuitions and numinous visions, suggests that our ethico-religious hope is not in vain.

But if this is right, then in order to flesh out a complete theological picture of God, we will need to ask about the conditions under which the universe, on the most fundamental level, would not be indifferent to the good.

The most obvious answer is this: the fundamental reality in the universe (that which ultimately explains the existence and significance of everything else) would actually have to care about the good. But this answer assumes that the fundamental reality has the capacity to care. It assumes that at the foundation of the universe is something personal – not in the anthropo-morphic sense, certainly nothing remotely human, but rather in the sense that at the core of reality is something that is capable of valuing goodness, of caring for what is objectively good. Caring and valuing are activities of an agent, some*one* who does these things. Our ethico-religious hope is most clearly and obviously fulfilled, then, if the universe is the creation of some-one who cares about the good.

But couldn't our ethico-religious hope be fulfilled by something less personal – perhaps a spiritual reality as impersonal as the physical one but whose laws, unlike physical laws, operate to preserve and perpetuate the good?

Such a universe would clearly be more satisfying to our moral natures than the universe of pitiless indifference attested to by Dawkins. But with-out some agency to explain why the laws of the universe support the good, the universe isn't really saying "yes" to goodness. It's just doing its blind mechanistic thing and it so happens, by happy accident, that these mech-anisms line up with the good. In such a universe, we are the only ones who are capable of being moral – that is, of valuing what we should and act-ing accordingly. For the universe to care, it seems there must be at its root a purposive mind that endorses goodness.

If "God" refers to a reality that fully satisfies our ethico-religious hope, God must therefore be construed as personal. And I don't believe that the liberal theologians who, in Dennett's words (2006, p. 206), have cast a "fog of mystery . . . over all the anthropomorphic features that have not been abandoned outright," are denying this. They're just not committing themselves to God as a person in any ordinary sense. What they are committed to is the existence of that which fulfills our ethico-religious hope. Whatever that something is, it needs to be morally good, and so it will need to closely resemble a personal God even if our usual ideas of what a person is like don't apply. And so, as they gesture towards an inexplicable reality, they have every right to call it God –and not just out of brand loyalty.

What else would a God who fully satisfied our ethico-religious hope need to be like? Such a God, it seems, would have to preserve every good thing we could ever rightly care about from the meaningless destruction offered by a universe of pitiless indifference. Conceived in this way, God cares about and sustains all real objective goods – that is, everything whose *existence* ought to be valued. And so God commands a degree of devotion that no single one of those goods could by itself properly claim. Everything that it is fitting for us to love is sustained and preserved in the bosom of God. Hence, to believe in such a God is to believe in a being worthy of unprecedented love, trust, and gratitude. The act of expressing such devotion is what we call worship.

Hence, this account of God succeeds in capturing what those who are *devoted* to God, who regard God as worthy of worship, have in common. Those who have no such devotion may well define God in ways that pay no heed to God's role in satisfying our ethico-religious hope. Those who see God as an enemy or a fanciful delusion may have no qualms about leaving goodness out of their account. But devoted theists cannot.

Because I think this is what all devout theistic understandings of God have in common, I have some worries about Schleiermacher's ostensive definition, according to which "God" names the source of our feeling of absolute dependence. What if this "Whence of our active and passive existence" proved cruel or indifferent to morality? Schleiermacher's definition would, it seems, still have to label it "God" – an implication that I think Schleiermacher himself would deplore.[3]

This implication can be avoided only if the experience of a being that fulfills our ethico-religious hope is already part of the feeling of absolute dependence. In fact, this seems to be Schleiermacher's view: Benevolence is implicit in the feeling of piety from the start. But if this is Schleiermacher's view, then his ostensive definition is really parasitic on a more basic understanding of God. The original religious sense is not just the sense of being absolutely dependent, but of being sustained by a perfect benevolence. Had it been otherwise, the source of that feeling wouldn't have a claim on being God. It's only because the feeling of piety is laden with optimism, with a sense of goodness, that it is a religious feeling at all.

Perhaps what Schleiermacher should have said is this: the primal religious experience, which he calls piety, is our first experiential encounter with a reality that can fulfill our ethico-religious hope. Were it not for this experience, we might not even know there was such a thing to hope for. But in the grip of this experience, we immediately experience ourselves as connected to a reality that makes our hopes come true.

I take Dennett's warning seriously: we cannot let "God" mean just anything. If the ultimate reality is indifferent to goodness, it isn't God – even if it is "a superhuman, supernatural intelligence who deliberately designed and created the universe and everything in it, including us." Were we able to prove the existence of such a being, but it turned out to be malign, we'd have proved the existence, not of God, but of the Devil.

Continuity from the Ancients: Plutarch and Zoroaster

In response to Dennett's claim that ancient and modern understandings of "God" are so divergent that brand loyalty offers the only rationale for using the same term, I've proposed a thread of meaning shared by all devoted theists: they all see God as a being whose existence would fulfill the hope that reality is, in its most fundamental aspect, unswervingly on the side of goodness. And what would do the most to fulfill this hope? A creator who cares about what is good and acts decisively to preserve it.

But Dennett may well point out that this understanding of God simply is not what the ancients had. Ancient peoples frequently believed in tyrannical deities who were cruel, vindictive, and petty. Goodness was simply not the hallmark of their gods. Rather, it was "superhuman and supernatural" power.

I do not deny this. In fact, belief in a tyrannical deity is hardly a relic of the past but manifests itself often enough today. But there is a difference between groveling before a tyrant, in the hopes of remaining in the tyrant's favor, and devoting oneself to God. The former isn't worship but appeasement – an outward show of loyalty accompanied by an inner spirit of enmity. We cannot be devoted to what we obey out of fear. Among those who are devoted to God, God must be construed as impeccably trustworthy. A cruel streak, a hint of capriciousness, and devotion would be impossible. As I understand it, the concept of God (with a capital "G") was born when the idea was born of a being we can trust absolutely, one worthy of worship.

This distinction is made powerfully by the ancient Greek thinker Plutarch, in his essay "Superstition" (1993). Here, Plutarch draws a sharp line between true religion, which worships a benevolent deity, and what he calls superstition, which involves the fearful efforts to curry favor with deities who are capricious tyrants. The superstitious believe in gods but "mistake their kindness for terror, their fatherliness for despotism, their care for us for cruelty, and their superiority to anger for savageness and brutality" (p. 6). In Plutarch's view, "The superstitious fear the gods, but take refuge with them. They flatter them, but abuse them. They pray to them, but blame them" (p. 6).

Plutarch holds that atheism is actually a reaction to the evils of superstition. Superstition is ruinous to those caught up in it because they cannot shrug anything off as just plain bad luck. Everything is "a blow from god or an assault of some daemonic power" (p. 7). Better to be an atheist:

> If an unbeliever is in deep distress, one can wipe his tears, cut his hair, or change his mourning-clothes: but what can you say to the superstitious man? How can you help him? He sits outside in a sackcloth or clad in filthy rags, he rolls naked in the mud and proclaims his sins and trespasses – he ate or drank something, or took some path that heaven forbade. (Plutarch 1993, p. 7)

In short, Plutarch understands the essence of superstition to be the belief that you are at the mercy of supernatural beings who are not merciful. They are enemies you can neither fight nor resist. All you can do is appease them.

Plutarch's superstitious man sounds very like the psychological picture of those in the grip of "battered wife syndrome" who see their spouse as inescapable and so embroil themselves in rituals of appeasement that do no good. Such efforts are hardly evidence of devotion. What motivates them isn't love, trust and gratitude, but helpless fear.

The idea that the God of religion must be construed as worthy of worship reaches farther back than Plutarch. Consider the ancient Persian prophet, Zoroaster, who may have lived as long ago as between 1700 and 1500 BC (Boyce 1979, p. 2). When Zoroaster was alive, the war god Indra – one of the so-called *daevas* – had become the dominant god in the Aryan pantheon (Zaehner 1961, p. 39). Zoroaster's career was defined by trenchant resistance to the worship of Indra and the other *daevas*. According to Zoroaster, because Indra was violent, arbitrary, and tyrannical, he was unqualified to be a god (Boyce 1979, pp. 21–2; Zaehner 1961, p. 37).

Zoroaster's dispute with his contemporaries was over what makes a being worthy of being called divine. In the language of Zoroaster's day, this was especially clear. The Iranian term for a divine being was "Yazata," which means a being "worthy of worship" (Boyce 1979, p. 21). For Zoroaster, the question was what made a being worthy of worship. His answer was *supreme goodness*.

What emerged from this insight was a theology characterized by the insistence that God's goodness is *the* fundamental divine-making property. The Zoroastrians would rather diminish God's power than his goodness. A less-than-omnipotent being could still be God if He remained perfectly good. But a superhuman, indestructible, and eternal spirit would *not* have "almost what it takes" to be God. If it were evil, then it would be the very antithesis of the divine.

In fact, belief in such an antithesis may be the most distinguishing feature of Zoroastrian theology. The Zoroastrian God, Ahura Mazda, exists from all eternity alongside an uncreated evil spirit of destruction and lies called Angra Mainyu. The world we know reflects the ongoing struggle between the creative efforts of God and the corrupting efforts of the Devil (Boyce 1979, pp. 19–21).

But this struggle is not interminable. The Zoroastrians believed that Ahura Mazda would prevail, that His very nature guaranteed victory. Goodness, by its nature, is generative. It establishes relationships and builds communities. Creation is an act of benevolence, a bestowal of the fundamental good: existence itself. As such, no essentially evil being could create anything. Angra Mainyu only destroys and corrupts what is already there, for that is the essence of evil.

In Zoroastrian thought, this means that evil by its very nature will eventually become self-destructive. The physical world, in addition to being a creation of divine goodness, is also a trap into which Angra Mainyu has been lured by his urge to destroy. As that trap closes in, Angra Mainyu and his demon hordes will find this urge turned inward and they will experience ultimate defeat. The creative power of goodness, by contrast, will endure, and a world free from evil will arise (Zaehner 1961, pp. 308–21).

For Zoroastrians, God's goodness involves compassion so boundless it extends even to Angra Mainyu. In one of the most compelling stories in

Zoroastrian mythology, Ahura Mazda reaches out the hand of love to Angra Mainyu. But the Devil mistakes compassion for weakness and so disdainfully rejects the gesture. It's the response God knew would come, but His loving nature wouldn't permit Him *not* to make the gesture (Zaehner 1961, p. 256).

Like Christianity, Zoroastrian beliefs included an afterlife, a heaven and hell. But mature Zoroastrian theology was universalist. Zoroastrian thinkers didn't deny that many would succumb to Angra Mainyu's corrupting influence, and so be damned. But human beings are creations of the only being with the power to create: the perfectly good God. This means that all humans – including the damned – have an essentially good nature. And once he's sucked them in, Angra Mainyu can't resist the urge to gloat over their gullibility and so reveal all his promises for lies. Like a malicious schoolboy who's succeeded in conning a credulous child, he can't help but stick out his tongue and go, "Nya, nya! Fooled you!" And so the damned are disavowed of their delusions – Angra Mainyu himself sows the seeds of their salvation. And Ahura Mazda's compassion does not exclude them. By the end of the age, they are freed from hell, and every human soul that has ever lived joins in loving communion with the creator (Zaehner 1961, pp. 306–8).

I devote so much attention to Zoroastrian thought in part because I find in it an antidote to some of the blinkered thinking that has gripped so much of Christian theology in relation to the doctrine of hell. But more importantly, we discover in Zoroastrianism a mythological defense of the idea that there is no true divinity unless it can satisfy our ethico-religious hope. Ahura Mazda's goodness is the reason for the very existence of the universe, and is thus the most important truth *in* the universe. In the end, every good thing is salvaged from Angra Mainyu's clutches. Evil may have its day but it cannot prevail, even in the souls of the damned, because the universe is on the side of goodness.

Concluding Remarks

Here then, summed up in the mythology of an ancient religion, we have the central point of this chapter: Other divine attributes may be debatable, but for anyone *devoted* to God, goodness is not. A proper definition of "God" will leave a great deal open for debate. But goodness – the very thing that Dawkins treats as merely a "desirable add-on" – cannot be excluded from our understanding of God without removing the object thus defined from the space God fills in the lives of devout theists. What Dawkins defines as "God" is therefore the god of superstition, the dangerous power that, if we believe in it, will inspire subservience rather than devotion.

What I am defending in this book is not the god of superstition, nor any so-called "religion" organized around the efforts to appease such a deity. When I defend theistic religion, I have in mind a religion born out of seminal religious feeling – the intuition of something grander and more wonderful in the universe than what we encounter with our senses – and elaborated in the most optimistic conceivable terms. This grander reality that I sense behind the surfaces of things is nothing less than the fulfillment of my deepest hopes: a God worthy of devotion.

The new atheists seem to have no idea that theistic religion in this sense even exists. When Dawkins claims that it is "childishly easy to overcome the problem of evil" because one can "(s)imply postulate a nasty god" or "a god with grander things to do than fuss about human distress," he betrays his profound failure to understand the role that belief in God serves for devout theists (Dawkins 2006, p. 108). This failure is characteristic: the cultured despisers of religion don't understand their subject. And so they treat real problems for religious belief (such as the problem of evil) as trivial, while devoting enormous attention to concerns that, in Plutarch's terms, are problems for superstition.

Borrowing Plutarch's words, today's despisers of religion have confused true religion with superstition, and "trying to escape superstition, they fall headlong into the harsh and obdurate ways of the atheists, leaping right over piety, which lies between" (Plutarch 1993, p. 12).

3

Divine Tyranny and the Goodness of God

On September 5, 2005, a faux news article from the satirical web magazine, *Dateline: Hollywood*, reported that televangelist Pat Robertson blamed Hurricane Katrina on the decision to have Ellen Degeneres, a lesbian, host the Emmy Awards. According to the article, the comments were made during a Sunday airing of the conservative Christian news show that Robertson hosts, *The 700 Club*: "'By choosing an avowed lesbian for this national event, these Hollywood elites have clearly invited God's wrath,' Robertson said on 'The 700 Club' on Sunday. 'Is it any surprise that the Almighty chose to strike at Miss Degeneres' hometown?'"[1]

The story is fake but it was retold as if it were authentic, quickly becoming a popular urban legend. The reason is clear enough: the story was believable. Although Robertson did not say what was attributed to him, he and other public voices of the American religious right have routinely made claims of the same general sort. What the *Dateline: Hollywood* satire did was what the best satire always does: highlight the truth through exaggeration.

Only days after the publication of the *Dateline: Hollywood* article, reality mimicked satire: In a rambling monologue during the September 12, 2005 broadcast of *The 700 Club*, Robertson suggestively linked Hurricane Katrina to American attitudes and policies on abortion.[2] A few years earlier, in a guest appearance on *The 700 Club* shortly after the 9/11 attacks, Jerry Falwell made international news by blaming the attacks on "the pagans, and the abortionists, and the feminists, and the gays and the lesbians who are actively trying to make that an alternative lifestyle, the ACLU, People For the American Way, all of them who have tried to secularize America".[3] Although Robertson distanced himself from the comments in the ensuing furor, at the time he professed to "totally concur."

These kinds of comments have predictably fueled current anti-religious rhetoric. Hitchens (2007) takes Falwell's claims about the 9/11 attacks to epitomize an ancient practice of using disasters "to overawe the gullible with the mightiness of god's disapproval" (p. 148). In Hitchens' view, religious leaders use "the suspicion that a calamity might also be a punishment" to further their own moralistic agendas:

> After New Orleans, which suffered from a lethal combination of being built below sea level and neglected by the Bush administration, I learned from a senior rabbi in Israel that it was revenge for the evacuation of Jewish settlers from the Gaza Strip, and from the mayor of New Orleans . . . that it was god's verdict on the invasion of Iraq. You can nominate your own favorite sin here, as did the "reverends" Pat Robertson and Jerry Falwell after the immolation of the World Trade Center. In that instance, the proximate cause was to be sought and found in America's surrender to homosexuality and abortion. (Hitchens 2007, p. 149)

I share Hitchens' disdain for this practice. My question is this: what has been done to the concept of God when we are fed this idea that hurricanes and earthquakes are the roarings of an angry deity?

Schleiermacher certainly found no place for this idea in *his* concept of God. In one sermon, he insists that "this idea of the wrath of God" can find no foundation in Christianity. "On the contrary," he declares, "the more we focus our own attention and that of others on this notion, the further we depart from the true spirit of Christianity" (1987, p. 153).

As a general comment on all forms of divine anger, I suspect Schleiermacher would have difficulty making his case. I have witnessed my wife's anger when our children are needlessly hurt or threatened by others – a protective rage that powerfully expresses her love. I haven't seen it culminate in violence (although, were our children's lives in danger, I suspect it might). Rather, what I have witnessed are words of indignation so impassioned that their targets can only feel ashamed of themselves. Such wrath can be beautiful. That my wife is capable of it is one reason I love her.

But there is a difference between a mother's wrath, born out of love, and a tyrant's wrath, born out of an overweening sense of entitlement. If we read Schleiermacher as arguing that the latter has no place in the Christian concept of God, he has a strong case.

In making that case, Schleiermacher offers a line of thought powerfully reminiscent of Plutarch. He asks us to imagine "what happens when the wrath of another is displayed against us." He thinks we respond in one of two ways:

We may arm ourselves against the other's anger in some way, if we can hope to win the battle. But how could we possibly win against God? Or else we are terrified if the other person has a superior power that we cannot escape. But how could we, as Christians, think of God in such a way that we would gladly have cause to flee him, or to be terrified of him? (Schleiermacher 1987, p. 158)

Clearly, Schleiermacher does not have in mind here the loving wrath of a mother who rushes to her wounded child's side. Often, such wrath carries no threat of harm. What power it has is moral power, the forceful show of care that calls attention to one's own failure to care enough. While such wrath might inspire violent resistance or quaking terror, its most significant property is its capacity to inspire remorse.

The tyrant's wrath, by contrast, is a deadly threat. The tyrant makes decrees and the huddled masses scurry to obey before his eyes fall upon them with displeasure. A tyrant rules by fear. He exercises his power capriciously and his laws are arbitrary. You do what the tyrant tells you to do . . . or else. It doesn't matter one whit what he tells you to do. His Word is Law, just because he says so. If you obey, it's not because of the merits of his decrees. You obey because, if you don't, he will smite you. The tyrant's wrath is nothing other than fury at being disobeyed. And this fury is often dangerously unpredictable, even indiscriminate.

Anyone who claims that Hurricane Katrina was a manifestation of God's wrath against sin does not have in mind a mother's loving anger. Mothers do not kill their beloved children in response to their beloved children being harmed. It is the tyrant's wrath that is being attributed to God.

In the face of the tyrant's wrath, you have the two choices that Schleiermacher presents: you can take up arms, or you can cower in terror. Real remorse happens only when you realize you've done something wrong, when you realize the gravity of the wrong and feel horror at what you've done. And so you'll never feel remorse in the face of a tyrant's wrath. Unlike the mother's loving anger, the tyrant's wrath isn't a reaction to some moral wrong but to *disobedience*. It's really nothing more than petulance at not getting his way. And so his wrath has no moral power to win you over. It can only make you into an enemy – one who fights, or one who fawns.

As we saw, Bertrand Russell (1961b) thought the concept of God "is a conception derived from the ancient Oriental despotisms" (p. 597).

Christopher Hitchens, in his derisive exegesis of the Ten Commandments, observes that the Pentateuch begins with "monarchical growlings about respect and fear, accompanied by a stern reminder of omnipotence and limitless revenge, of the sort with which a Babylonian or Assyrian emperor might have ordered the scribes to begin a proclamation" (2007, p. 99). Their picture of God is that of a tyrant.

But this picture cannot inspire devotion. We do not worship tyrants. We treat them as powerful enemies who we might, for self-interested reasons, need to appease. According to Plutarch's view of things, anyone who thinks of God as a tyrant is not religious but superstitious.

God conceived of as a tyrant is not the *God* of religion but the *god* of superstition. Such a god is fundamentally different from the God who fulfills our ethico-religious hope, as are the "religious" practices inspired by such a god (which will have the character of appeasement rather than worship). The "god" directly targeted by the cultured despisers of religion, the same one lifted up so often in fundamentalist teachings, *is not God* – at least not in any sense that can inspire devotion.

Nowhere in his book – not even in the title – does Christopher Hitchens capitalize "god." Perhaps we should treat this as an implicit recognition of the distinction I have been making (following Plutarch) between the *god* of superstition and the *God* of religion. But that would give Hitchens too much credit. He doesn't see the distinction. In general, the new atheists seem to think that those who are devoted to God are inexplicably loving and trusting the wrathful tyrant who could drown babies in New Orleans as a punishment for the so-called sins of a nation. But tyrants can only motivate the pretense of love and trust – outward displays of devotion, the often manic efforts to placate a capricious lord. A tyrant can inspire brutally precise obedience that cares nothing for who might get trampled in the effort to obey. But that is not the same as love.

The *god* Hypothesis may be pernicious. But it doesn't follow that the *God* Hypothesis is.

The Concept of Divine Goodness as a Tool of Criticism

My central point here can be approached in a different way. The fact that the concept of God *must* include perfect goodness is the very thing that makes it possible for progressive theists to say what we want to say about many of the teachings coming from contemporary "religious" authorities. What we want to say is what Zoroaster said to the worshipers of Indra: the being you claim to worship isn't God at all.

Consider James Dobson, who heads the right-wing Christian organization, *Focus on the Family*. Dobson believes that human flourishing depends on preserving the *right kind* of family – one that is, among other things, heterosexual. And he claims that the gravest threat to this kind of family is the so-called homosexual movement. According to Dobson, "For more than 40 years, the homosexual activist movement has sought to implement a master plan that has had as its centerpiece the utter destruction of the family."[4] In Dobson's view of things, "Traditional marriage between one man and one woman cannot co-exist with homosexual marriage. It will destroy the family."[5]

Dobson teaches that the greatest threat to our children isn't drugs or school violence or poor educational systems. It isn't neglect or abuse. So what is it? Here's Dobson's answer: "Moms and Dads, are you listening? This (homosexual) movement is *the* greatest threat to your children. It is a particular danger to your wide-eyed boys, who have no idea what demoralization is planned for them" (2001, p. 127). With these words, Dobson panders to the patently false prejudice that gays and lesbians are prone towards child molestation, thereby fueling hurtful homophobia.

There may be reasons for condemning homosexual relationships that are consistent with a picture of God as worthy of devotion – although I'm skeptical for reasons I've developed elsewhere (Reitan 2007a). But what Dobson offers here is nothing of the sort. It is, instead, the essence of what Jean-Paul Sartre (1948) took anti-Semitism to be: the effort to create a scapegoat for our failures so as to avoid responsibility for the hard work of building meaningful lives. If there are problems with our families, it's the homosexuals' fault, and the solution is to exclude them from full participation in social life. If we're struggling with the uncertainties of parenting, Dobson offers a mission: *keep the perverts out of our schools*. Do that and you can feel like a good parent even if you have no idea how to guide willful children to maturity.

Dobson's rhetoric encourages us to look outward for the source of our troubles, to blame and fear the one who is different. This kind of message has a long history of success among tyrants seeking to consolidate their power – and it is a message that Dobson attributes to the object of his allegiance. But it is a message unworthy of God. While there are dimensions of Dobson's ministry that reflect allegiance to a God of love, that image of God lives in unholy tension with the hate-mongering god of superstition.

I must acknowledge that my thinking here is colored by the impact of Dobson's ministry on people I love. Not long ago, close relatives of mine sought to deliver to Dobson a letter explaining the harmful impact that his anti-gay rhetoric has had on their lives. As they approached the Focus on the Family headquarters, they were arrested for their trouble.[6] But whatever my biases, my point is that the kind of argument I want to make against Dobson's teachings is possible *only because goodness is essential to my concept of God*. Take that away – as Dawkins and Stenger do in their definitions – and we lose a key tool for critically assessing religious teachings and practices.

Consider the doctrine of "plenary verbal inspiration," which holds that every word in the Bible is directly inspired by an infallible God. It isn't just the new atheists who find this doctrine abhorrent. So do many theists – at least those who are devoted to a *good* God. After all, would a good God have ordered the extermination of every child and non-virgin woman among the Midianites, as is reported in Numbers 31:9–18? Would a good God assign, as the penalty for raping an unpledged virgin, that the rapist marry his victim (Deuteronomy 22:28–9)? Would a good God call for the execution of children who curse their parents (Leviticus 20:9)?

I happen to think we can discover in the Bible a God worthy of worship – the God of radically universal love attested to by Martin Luther King, Jr. But we can't discover this God if we think of the Bible as a monolithic treatise written by God Himself. When the Bible is read in that way, we don't derive a picture of a God worthy of unfettered devotion. What we get is a picture of a capricious deity, sometimes merciful and loving, at other times jealous and tyrannical. If this way of reading the Bible is the only legitimate one, then the proper conclusion to draw – given God's essential goodness – is that the biblical god *is not God*.

But there are other ways to read the Bible. We can read it as a human testament to the encounter with God, one that evolves as human misconceptions crash up against a divine reality that transcends our understanding. In short, we can treat it as a rich historical archive unified by a common struggle: the struggle of flawed human beings to understand and respond to the divine, and to live as the people of God. We can see this struggle as ongoing, and the voices recorded in the Bible as participants in an enduring conversation that we ourselves have every right to participate in – rather than as a blunt authority intended to silence conversation.

Many Christians are not biblical literalists precisely because they take benevolence to be God's defining characteristic, and precisely because they cannot reconcile such a picture of God with a fundamentalist approach to the Bible.

By excluding goodness from his definition of God, what has Dawkins thereby done? He has erased the distinction Plutarch draws between the God of religion and the god of superstition. In the same stroke, he has excluded from his concept of God the very thing that can guard the concept from abuse – the very thing that can serve as a basis for criticizing dubious claims of divine inspiration; the very thing that, when it is part of theistic belief, helps theists resist co-optation by forces that would use religion to serve pernicious agendas.

And then Dawkins blames belief in God for these pernicious agendas.

When goodness is a "mere add-on" to the concept of God, perhaps he is right. But for devout theists, goodness is essential to God. If we take this idea seriously, the question about what God is like becomes bound up with philosophical questions about morality and the good. If we take goodness as our fundamental datum about God, our basic starting point for all inquiry into the divine, we will naturally resist those so-called prophets who attribute to God motives that fly in the face of our best moral judgment. We will question the literal authority of so-called scriptures that portray God as a "misogynistic, homophobic, racist, infanticidal, genocidal, filiacidal, pestilential, megalomaniacal, sadomasochistic, capriciously malevolent bully" (Dawkins 2006, p. 31). We will resist the fanatic's call for violence.

And yet.

And yet Jerry Falwell, Pat Robertson, and James Dobson claim to worship a God of love, a God who (if not in so many words) fulfills our ethico-religious hope. And there is every reason to suppose they are sincere. Much of what they say about God, and how we should live as children of God, reflects an image of God as a deity worthy of worship – even if they also insist that God struck down a man named Uzzah for the offense of reflexively touching the Ark of the Covenant to keep it from falling, and that God ordered the Israelites to put to death any man who curses his father or mother, who commits adultery, who sleeps with another man . . . and on and on.

It may be that God is, by definition, benevolent – but many theists who embrace this view seem willing to attribute to God behaviors that don't look very benevolent at all. And so the cultured despisers of religion may wonder: what good does the goodness of God really do?

The Divine Command Theory – or,
How to Strip God's Goodness of Significance

My answer is this: when people who claim that God is good are able, at the same time, to attribute moral horrors to God, it is because they have first stripped from the concept of goodness any substantive meaning. They have embraced a framework of belief in which "God is good" doesn't actually say anything about God.

How does this happen? There are at least two ways. The first is by way of something called the divine command theory of ethics. According to this theory, morality is nothing more than a product of divine decree. Moral values and obligations are whatever God says they are, just because He says so. Not many among the greatest Christian thinkers have actually embraced this theory – the medieval theologians Duns Scotus and William of Ockham may be exceptions. Most have rejected it.

The basis for that rejection is vividly captured in the famous words of the great seventeenth-century philosopher, Gottfried Wilhelm Leibniz:

> In saying, therefore, that things are not good according to any standard of goodness, but simply by the will of God, it seems to me that one destroys, without realizing it, all the love of God and all his glory; for why praise him for what he has done, if he would be equally praiseworthy in doing the contrary? Where will be his justice and his wisdom if he has only a certain despotic power, if arbitrary will takes the place of reasonableness, and if in accord with the definition of tyrants, justice consists in that which is pleasing to the most powerful? (Leibniz 1973, pp. 4–5)

The idea here is simple: If morality is just whatever God says it is, then *God's* moral goodness amounts to nothing. To say that God is good is just to say that God approves of Himself. But we all know pompous, selfish bastards who approve of themselves.

This theory turns God into the arbitrary tyrant of superstition. If the whole of morality is just the product of divine decree, then until God has issued his decree on some matter – for example, whether it is right or wrong to torture children for fun – the two alternatives have just as much (and just as little) going for them. God could as readily have commanded child-torture as prohibited it. The divine command theory claims, in effect, that the only thing that would make child-torture bad would be a divine decree to that effect.

But if this is true – if there is nothing morally wrong with child-torture until God has issued a decree, then God's decree would have to be arbitrary. He couldn't have a reason to prohibit child-torture unless there's something about child-torture that makes it worthy of condemnation – something bad about it. I think there is such a thing. But if I'm right, then, to paraphrase Plato, child-torture isn't bad because God prohibits it; God prohibits child-torture *because it's bad*. The only way to stick to the divine command theory is to say that there's nothing bad about child-torture apart from a divine prohibition.

Leibniz's point is that if you accept this theory, then goodness can't be something that helps to make God *God* (since goodness is just whatever God arbitrarily says it is). But goodness is the only thing that can make God worthy of worship. While power might make God worthy of being feared, it doesn't warrant the devotion that defines worship. It might be prudent to fawn over a powerful tyrant. But a tyrant doesn't deserve our love and obedience – not in the way that, say, a wise and compassionate parent does.

I should point out that modified versions of the divine command theory have been proposed that aim to avoid these problems. But to do so, they need to offer a *basis* for obeying God other than fear of a tyrant's power. The most convincing of these modified versions, proposed by Robert Adams (1979), makes God's loving nature that basis.

As I interpret Adams' theory, while moral duties are the result of divine decrees, goodness is not. Love is good in itself, not by virtue of God's say-so. In fact, God's say-so would have no binding power were it not for God's goodness, embodied in His love. God's commands have authority because they are expressions of love, because love is supremely good, and because His commands are issued in the context of a relationship that gives moral authority to loving commands. There is, in other words, this complex set of moral principles by virtue of which God's commands acquire moral authority. It isn't God's commands that give rise to morality. Rather, the nature of morality gives God's commands their moral force. For this reason, I wouldn't want to call Adams' theory a version of the divine command theory at all.

A thorough discussion of Adams is beyond my objective here, which is to call attention to a way of thinking that strips the claim "God is good" of meaning. Adams' theory, whether we call it a divine command theory or not, doesn't do this. Neither does the natural law theory championed by the Roman Catholic Church. According to that theory, God has designed the world with a natural order to it. In much the way that some things you might do to your car would be good or bad for it, based on the car's design and function, there are some things that we might do that are bad or good for the natural order and the organisms (including ourselves) that exist within it. What is bad in this sense is morally wrong, and what is good is morally right. On this natural law theory, morality is not a product of divine decree but a reflection of the nature of things.

Of course, on Catholic theology, created things have the natures they have by virtue of God's creative intentions. And those intentions, in turn, reflect God's nature (which is taken to be love). And so, the natural law theory retains the idea that moral truth is ultimately rooted in God, even if it denies that moral truth is simply a product of God's decrees. The ongoing popularity of the divine command theory may rest on a failure to recognize that there are alternative theories which nevertheless preserve God's status as the ultimate foundation for morality.

If you accept one of these alternatives, God's goodness is not stripped of meaning. But the theory which can really and unambiguously be called a divine command theory – namely, the theory holding that all moral values and obligations are the product of divine decrees – does precisely this. On this theory, God's "goodness" means nothing and His decrees are as arbitrary as a tyrant's. The God that emerges is not one worthy of worship, nor is it one that can fulfill our hope that the universe is fundamentally on the side of goodness.

Just in case these last points are not completely obvious, consider the following. Imagine that you're playing roulette and someone assures you that the roulette ball always lands on a red space, so that betting on red is always a safe bet. And so you put your chips on red. The ball careens across the roulette wheel – and lands on black. "Red wins!" someone shouts. You scratch your head in puzzlement but are glad at least that you're a winner . . . until you see your chips being snatched away.

"But I thought you said that *red* wins," you protest.

"Yes," comes the reply, "but for the purposes of the game, 'red' refers to whatever color the ball lands on."

So . . . does this game essentially favor those who bet on red? Of course not. The game is just as arbitrary as ever, as likely to land on one color as another. The fact that whatever color the ball lands on is *called* red doesn't mean that there is any color in particular that the roulette wheel tends to favor. And if God approves things at random, but whatever He arbitrarily approves is *called* good, it doesn't follow that there is *anything* in the universe that God is essentially on the side of.

If you embrace the divine command theory, you can't meaningfully say, as Martin Luther King did, that because its creator is benevolent, the universe bends towards justice. Instead, it is justice that bends. In the hands of the divine command theory's God, justice and goodness are completely malleable. Were God to decide that it was morally just to inflict eternal torment on the most devoted Christians, then it would be. And there is no reason why He wouldn't decide such a thing, since the existence of any such reason would require a moral standard independent of God's will.

Or consider the following. Conservative Christians who believe that God has revealed his will in the Bible are assuming that God is honest in His revelations. But why believe that? Because honesty is good? According to the divine command theory, moral goodness is just whatever God decides it is. Were God to decide to make *dishonesty* good, it would be. And given this abysmal theory, there can be no reason why God wouldn't decide such a thing.

I could go on but the point should be clear enough: were all moral values and all moral obligations just a product of arbitrary divine will, then God would cease to be a being we could rely on for anything. What hope could such a God fulfill, even if He existed? We are left with a view of divine goodness so vacuous that any "god" could be declared good – the tyrannical *god* of superstition as readily as the *God* of religion.

The Fundamentalist Attack on Divine Goodness

There is another, related way, to strip the claim that God is good of any substance. Imagine the following, fairly routine way of thinking: "Personally, I can't see why it would be morally good for half of humanity to be subordinated to the other half. But I'm a limited creature. And since the Bible clearly supports the systematic subordination of women, such subordination must be good even if it doesn't look that way to me. After all, God knows best."

Let me begin by pointing out where this line of thinking goes *right*. First of all, it is surely right that if God exists, He is wiser than us and has a better understanding of morality than we do. Secondly, there is pervasive biblical support for the subordination of women. This fact might be explained by reference to the patriarchal prejudices of the biblical authors. And our contemporary moral discomfort with this perspective might be explained by the fact that feminist consciousness-raising over the last century has made us aware of how destructive patriarchy is for the life prospects of women – an awareness that the biblical authors did not have. If Christians were reading any other book, that is exactly what they'd conclude: *we are aware of morally relevant facts that these ancient authors didn't see.* But when the doctrine of biblical inerrancy is put forward as an indubitable starting point, they are forced to the opposite conclusion: *the biblical authors are aware of morally relevant facts that we don't see.*

Paradoxically, the very same Bible that fundamentalist Christians defer to so completely offers the following advice: "Beloved, do not believe every spirit, but test the spirits to see whether they are of God; for many false prophets have gone out into the world" (1 John 4:1). And how do you distinguish a true prophet from a false one? "By their fruit you will recognize them" (Matthew 7:16).

This is actually pretty good advice. It is saying you shouldn't believe that some so-called prophet or prophetic writing really is from God just because you have been assured of this (by the prophet or your parents or your pastor). You should investigate the claim. And how do you investigate it? You look at the "fruit" of what the so-called prophet or prophetic writing teaches.

"Fruit" is, of course, a metaphor: You know a tree is healthy if it produces good fruit, and diseased if the fruit is bad. Analogously, we should use our best judgment about good and bad to evaluate the consequences of a so-called prophetic teaching. If it produces bad fruits overall (suffering, broken communities, alienation and despair, bitterness and enmity, etc.), then we should conclude that the prophetic teaching is false.

In short, the Bible itself urges its readers to use their best moral judgment to assess the authority of anyone or anything that claims to speak for God. And so, when fundamentalists claim that every verse of the Bible speaks for God, its readers should follow this advice and test the Bible, verse by verse, according to the light of their best moral judgment, to see if the fundamentalists are right.

So why don't more Christians do this? When following the fundamentalist's theory about the Bible leads to a shattered relationship with a gay son – or, worse yet, drives a gay son to suicide – why don't more Christians say, "Aha! Bad fruit! It's a mistake to treat the Bible, verse by verse, as the infallible Word of God!"

In many cases, the answer is a simple failure to think carefully. And in many cases, this confused thinking has been encouraged by religious leaders who have something to gain from it. They point out that a morally perfect and all-knowing God would have a better understanding of morality than fallible human beings do. And they then insist that, therefore, we can't legitimately question God's judgment just because it doesn't seem right to us. And since God commands the patriarchal subordination of women in the Bible, or the categorical condemnation of homosexual acts (not to mention the execution of those who perform them), we must humbly obey and trust that it is for the best, even though we can't see how.

The reasoning here is thoroughly bad. Even if we accept that God knows what is right and good better than we do, there is an enormous difference between questioning the accuracy of God's pronouncements and questioning of the accuracy of a human theory about the nature of the Bible (or the Koran, or Jim Jones, etc.). It is one thing to question God, something else entirely to question whether the Bible, verse by verse, inerrantly represents God's will. But religious patriarchs often have a vested interest in perpetuating the confusion.

And when that confusion becomes entrenched, ordinary people stop using their good moral judgment to question the teachings of their religious leaders or inherited texts because, out of confused humility, they don't think they're qualified to question God.

The fact is that we cannot escape human judgments. Whenever we attribute some commandment to God, we are making a human judgment to the effect that God actually commanded it. In making that judgment, we can do it foolishly (without any consideration of evidence or opposing arguments) or we can do it wisely – based on a careful, critical, sustained engagement with all of the relevant evidence, especially that offered by our best moral judgment. Either way, we might make a mistake. We're just less likely to make one if we pursue the latter path.

But religious leaders who should know better often convey the message that human judgment *can* be bypassed, that this book or that institution offers an unmediated line to God. And too many people, longing for an unattainable certainty, are sucked in by the lie.

When this happens, the doctrine that *God is essentially good* ceases to be of any value as a critical guide towards deciding whether the teachings of a prophet or church or holy book are to be trusted. If the inerrancy of a given prophetic authority is taken as the starting point for thinking, rather than a claim to be tested in the light of our moral sensibilities, then "good" just becomes whatever your chosen authority says it is. And "God is good" can mean just about anything, since there are self-proclaimed authorities out there that attribute all kinds of crazy things to God.

In short, this kind of thinking eviscerates the meaningfulness of God's goodness in much the way that the divine command theory does. And in so doing, it opens the door to the god of superstition and to the fear-driven extremism this god can inspire.

But notice that belief in God, understood as the fulfillment of our ethico-religious hope, is *not* the cause of the trouble. The cause of the trouble is a fundamentalist insistence that one ought to accept without question that some text or institution or prophetic leader is perfectly artic-ulating the very will of God.

The God Hypothesis needn't be paired with such a disturbing and dangerous doctrine. In fact, when God is conceived as the fulfillment of our ethico-religious hope, the result is that we must take a critical stance towards the revelatory claims of so-called prophetic authorities. We must ask of them the following questions: Do they represent a God worthy of worship? Do they offer a picture of God that could fulfill our deepest moral hopes?

The Problem with Young Earth Creationism

Let me finish this chapter with a concrete case that reveals the implica-tions of asking these questions. I choose one that touches an issue near the hearts of the new atheists: the integrity of science.

One of the most heartfelt passages in *The God Delusion* comes when Dawkins is discussing the fundamentalist subversion of science. Dawkins tells the story of a promising young scientist, a man named Kurt Wise, whose future as a scientist was undermined by "a mind fatally subverted and weakened by a fundamentalist religious upbringing that required him to believe that the Earth – the subject of his Chicago and Harvard geological education – was less than ten thousand years old" (2006, p. 284).

According to Dawkins' account of the story, Wise struggled with the conflict between science and his religious beliefs, and could ultimately find no reconciliation. One day he took scissors to the Bible, "literally cutting out every verse that would have to go if the scientific world-view were true" (p. 284). This exercise left the book a tattered filigree that couldn't be opened without falling apart. So, what did Wise decide based on this exercise? Dawkins quotes Wise himself for the answer:

> I had to make a decision between evolution and Scripture. Either the Scripture was true and evolution was wrong or evolution was true and I must toss out the Bible . . . It was there that night that I accepted the Word of God and rejected all that would ever counter it, including evolution. With that, in great sorrow, I tossed into the fire all my dreams and hopes in science. (Wise 2000, p. 354, quoted in Dawkins 2006, p. 285)

Dawkins culminates his discussion of Wise's case with a quote from Wise that captures the driving force behind his fateful choice. Wise claims that "if all the evidence in the universe turns against creationism, I would be the first to admit it, but I would still be a creationist because that is what the Word of God seems to indicate" (Dawkins 2006, p. 285; Wise 2000, p. 355).

One gets the sense that Dawkins' expressed horror at what happened to Wise is real: He thinks it a tragedy that Wise would throw out a promising career in science out of allegiance to the creationism that biblical literalism seems to demand. He thinks it's appalling that Wise would still embrace biblical literalism and its implications even if "all the evidence in the universe" turned against it.

I am equally appalled. And the chief reason why I am appalled is the nature of my belief in God. I think Wise was, from a scientific standpoint, foolish. But more significantly, I think that out of allegiance to a doctrine of literal biblical inerrancy, Wise unwittingly eviscerated God's goodness.

Wise believes, as all fundamentalist Christians do, that the universe and everything in it were created by God. Let us suppose, for a moment, that the Young Earth Creationists are right, and that the universe was created less than 10,000 years ago. If so, then God designed it to look *as if* it were far more ancient. He designed it to look *as if* our universe had been born in a tremendous explosion billions of years ago, *as if* life originated in the Earth's ocean some three-and-a-half billion years ago, *as if* there were mass extinctions some 250 million years ago and again some 65 million years ago. On this picture of things, God buried in the earth fossilized bones of ancient creatures that never existed. He left signs of ancient peoples who, according to the evidence, would have lived and walked the earth many thousands of years before the world was created.

In other words, God systematically and perfectly designed the world to convey a message about the history of the universe and our world that is false in almost every detail. The entire creation, in almost every nuance, is an elaborate hoax. God designed the universe so that those who diligently examine His creation with the best methods available will get it all wrong.

This is what Young Earth Creationists are committed to. In order to preserve their belief that the literal meaning of the Bible is God's inerrant word, they must commit themselves to the view that what God has revealed in the created order is, to put it bluntly, a big fat lie. Kenneth Miller (1999) makes a similar point, using contemporary astronomical observations of distant phenomena (which, given the speed of light, are actually observations of the distant past, long before Young Earth Creationists claim the world was created). He concludes that the creationists' God must have "filled the universe with so much bogus evidence that the tools of science can give us nothing more than a phony version of reality" (p. 80).

But why would God perpetrate such an elaborate hoax? To test our faith in the Bible? If God is prepared to create the universe so that virtually every message it conveys is false, why believe that He wouldn't do the same in the Bible? Once we accept that God is prone to outrageous deception in His revelatory acts, on what grounds can we possibly trust the Bible, even assuming we know that it is God's Word?

Theists don't have to believe that every passage of the Bible is, in its literal sense, the inerrant word of God. Many don't. But no theist could deny that the universe is the creation of God and that in its most basic elements it is exactly as God designed it to be. If it is ten thousand years old, then no reasonable theist can escape the conclusion that God designed the world to look like something it is not: astonishingly ancient.

Young Earth Creationism is appalling, not just from a scientific perspective, but from a religious one. It forces us to swallow a picture of God that undercuts our capacity to trust God. It represents God as engaging in detailed deception, designing the universe so that the evidence points overwhelmingly in one direction, while the truth is contained in one old book. And then, presumably, it is those who side with the book that God will favor. To those who side with science, we can imagine how God would chide them:

> You *should* have concluded that, when I created the world, I would design it to be *consistently and systematically deceptive*. Instead, you concluded that this ancient book passed down in one part of the world, within the Judeo-Christian tradition, was not literally accurate in every detail. How dare you! What an insult to my majesty! I will go now and reward those who think that in my great act of creation, I designed it all to be a fabulous lie! Those are the ones who clearly love me!

Of course, any God who said that wouldn't be a good God, worthy of our devotion, the fulfillment of our ethico-religious hope. It is one thing to say there's more to the universe than meets the eye, something else entirely to say that what meets the eye is a bunch of hokum. To say the former is to say that there are orders of reality beyond the empirical one, to which a scientific examination of the universe cannot speak. It is to say that, while what we learn from the best empirical observation may be true, it is not the *whole* truth – and perhaps the whole truth will radically reshape our understanding of the truth that is available to the naked eye.

To say the latter, however, is to say that if there is a transcendent reality that is responsible for the world we encounter around us, that reality is messing with us. And so we should approach it not as a source of hope but with suspicion and fear. We are led, once more, to Plutarch's god of superstition.

Concluding Remarks

When we evaluate the moral implications of belief in God, it matters a great deal what we mean by "God." When "God" is defined without reference to moral properties, we are likely to reach very different conclusions about the implications of theism than we'd reach when "God" is defined in terms of such properties. And so by defining "God" as they do, Dawkins and Stenger have preemptively prejudiced the case against theism.

This prejudice is doubly pernicious precisely because so many theists *do* define God in moral terms. For many of us, allegiance to the idea that God is supremely good is more important than any other allegiance – more important, for example, than allegiance to a doctrine of scriptural inerrancy. If it seems that the teaching of some religious authority clashes with our clear moral judgment, the proper conclusion to draw is that the authority does not, in this case, speak for God.

There is more to be said here, of course. Among other things, we need to consider why, if belief in God is not essentially pernicious, it seems so susceptible to pernicious abuse. Why is the god of superstition always hovering so close, ready to muscle the God of religion out of our collective psyches? Why have believers in God been so routinely inspired to wage war in God's name, blow themselves up in public venues in God's name, reject their children in God's name, and parade around the funerals of homophobia victims waving signs that say "Fags Die, God Laughs"?

Before offering my own answer, I must dispel an answer that the new atheists are likely to propose, namely the following: There is not only no evidence for belief in God, but overwhelming reason to suppose that such a being does not exist. Hence, belief in God is irrational. But if so, then to embrace theistic belief in the first place, theists must endorse the legitimacy of believing things in the teeth of the evidence. Once that door is opened, it threatens to become a floodgate.

Perhaps, on some level, religious believers know that if they question their theistic belief, it will crumble. And so they're drawn to philosophies that tell them not to question anything in the religious domain. To preserve their faith, they justify it by reference to an artificial external authority, one that they invest with infallibility. And once they have taken that step, religious extremism is not far away.

I actually think that, for many religious believers, something like this is going on: they immerse themselves in communities of faith that encourage them not to think, not to wrestle with God as Simone Weil encourages us to do. Let others do the thinking for you and you can relax. Don't question their teachings and you can wrap yourself in a comfortable cocoon of certainty.

But it isn't just religious communities that offer such cocoons of certainty. And, despite what some atheists think, not all religious communities offer such cocoons. And I disagree with the judgment that one *must* wrap oneself in false certainty in order to embrace the God Hypothesis. I disagree with this judgment because I don't think the God Hypothesis is as irrational as Dawkins and the other cultured despisers of religion take it to be.

I must turn, therefore, to the crucial question: Can belief in God be rational?

4

Science, Transcendence, and Meaning

What Plutarch meant by "superstition" is not exactly what we mean by it today. For Plutarch, it meant belief in fearful supernatural forces (or gods) that need to be appeased on pain of harsh retribution. But as we use the term today, belief in garden fairies would readily be called superstitious, even were there no quaking terror at the thought of their pixie dust and butterfly wings. A persistent American superstition (which most outgrow in early elementary school) is belief in a jolly gift-giver who rides into town every Christmas Eve on a sleigh pulled by flying reindeer. That Santa is the nicest guy you'd ever meet doesn't change the fact that you never will, in fact, meet him – and *this* fact is what makes belief in him a superstition in the contemporary sense.

It's become almost conventional for atheists today to put God in the same category as Santa Claus and garden fairies. The philosopher Michael Scriven draws out the analogy as follows:

> As we grow up, no one comes forward to *prove* that . . . [Santa Claus] does not exist. We just come to see that there is not the least reason to think he *does* exist. And so it would be entirely foolish to assert that he does, or believe that he does, or even think it likely that he does. Santa Claus is in just the same position as fairy godmothers, wicked witches, the devil, and the ether . . . So the proper alternative, when there is no evidence, is not mere suspension of belief, for example, about Santa Claus, it is *disbelief*: it most certainly is not faith. (Scriven 1966, p. 103)

Scriven's point is roughly this: Belief in the existence of some entity is legitimate only given sufficient evidence for its existence; in the absence of such evidence, the proper stance is disbelief. And so, in the absence of evidence for God's existence, we should treat God just as we treat Santa: as a pleasing fiction.

Hovering over Scriven here is Bertrand Russell's celestial teapot, which Russell introduced in the following passage from his 1952 essay, "Is there a God?"

If I were to suggest that between the Earth and Mars there is a china teapot revolving about the sun in an elliptical orbit, nobody would be able to disprove my assertion provided I were careful to add that the teapot is too small to be revealed even by our most powerful telescopes. But if I were to go on to say that, since my assertion cannot be disproved, it is intolerable presumption on the part of human reason to doubt it, I should rightly be thought to be talking nonsense. (Russell 1997, pp. 547–8)

Richard Dawkins is a fan of Russell's teapot. In 2005, the theologian Alister McGrath wrote a thoughtful, book-length criticism of Dawkins' attacks on religion. The book, *Dawkins' God: Genes, Memes, and the Meaning of Life*, is mentioned only once in *The God Delusion*. If Dawkins is to be believed, he dismisses all of McGrath's arguments by appeal to Russell's teapot. In Dawkins' words, "On page after page as I read McGrath, I found myself scribbling 'teapot' in the margin" (p. 54). But what is the force of this kind of refutation-by-teapot? Dawkins explains it in the following way:

Russell's teapot . . . stands for an infinite number of things whose existence is conceivable and cannot be disproved. . . . The journalist Andrew Mueller is of the opinion that pledging yourself to any particular religion "is no more or less weird than choosing to believe that the world is rhombus-shaped, and borne through the cosmos in the pincers of two enormous green lobsters called Esmerelda and Keith." . . . A popular deity on the Internet at present – and as undisprovable as Yahweh or any other – is the Flying Spaghetti Monster, who, many claim, has touched them with his noodly appendage. (Dawkins 2006, pp. 52–3)

This passage garnered guffaws when I read it to my philosophy or religion class. My wife was so delighted by the doctrine of Esmerelda and Keith that she shared it with her colleagues who have, I'm told, developed a fondness for Esmerelda in particular (perhaps out of sympathy for the nontraditional spelling of her name).

In any event, the point of these examples is to raise what philosophers call the "evidentialist challenge" to theistic belief. The challenge goes like this: "Belief in God is no different from belief in a celestial teapot. In either case, if there is no credible evidence for the existence of this extraordinary entity, you should not merely be agnostic. Even though you can't disprove its existence, you should still *disbelieve*. If you don't, you're as superstitious as those who believe in leprechauns."

For Dawkins, the challenge also targets Stephen Jay Gould, who famously claimed that "science simply cannot adjudicate the issue of God's possible superintendence of nature" (1992, p. 119). Gould elaborates in his now famous NOMA (nonoverlapping magisteria) thesis, which holds that science and religion are two entirely distinct realms of inquiry: science explores "the empirical realm" while religion "extends over questions of ultimate meaning and moral value" (1999, p. 6).[1]

In reply, Dawkins asks, "Why shouldn't we comment on God, as scientists? And why isn't Russell's teapot, or the Flying Spaghetti Monster, equally immune from scientific skepticism?" (2006, p. 55). Dawkins apparently shares Victor Stenger's presumption that if science can find no evidence *supporting* belief in some entity, whether it's a celestial teapot or God, then science has weakly falsified any hypothesis claiming that it exists.

The main point I want to make in this chapter is that Dawkins and Stenger are just wrong about this. When it comes to God, absence of scientific evidence is simply not a reason for disbelief because belief in God is *different in kind* from belief in Santa, orbiting chinaware, or space lobsters.

Religion vs. Superstition

We have aerial photographs of the North Pole, and none have turned up idyllic villages of elves and reindeer. Explorers have walked there and found no hints of Christmas Town. Even if we restrict ourselves to children who celebrate Christmas, it seems logistically impossible for one person in one night to visit every child's home, slide down the chimney, and deposit presents – even with a very fast sleigh. Furthermore, I happen to know that this past Christmas, my wife and I placed gifts for our children under the tree, labeling some "from Santa." In the morning, the only gifts under the tree were those we'd put there.

It would in principle be possible (if prohibitively costly) to install video cameras in every home in which Christmas is celebrated, in order to ascertain whether a gift-toting elf clatters in through a chimney or other point of entry on Christmas Eve. Likewise, we could devote all of NASA's resources to The Great Teapot Investigation and have spacecraft dart about between the orbits of Earth and Mars searching for Russell's elusive teapot. While failure to find it wouldn't decisively disconfirm its presence, it's at least in principle possible that such a search would uncover the stray chinaware. Perhaps, if we're really lucky, what we'll discover instead are two enormous crustaceans, pincers waving in friendly greeting.

There are, in short, at least three properties shared by belief in Santa, the celestial teapot, garden fairies, space lobsters, and the rest. First, they are beliefs that can in principle be tested empirically. While they might not be falsifiable in a strong sense, they are in principle *verifiable* – and can thus be falsified in the weak sense discussed in Chapter 2. Second, given what we know about the empirical world (partly from science), we have no good reason to think these beliefs are true and at least some reason to think them false. Thus, the burden of proof clearly falls on the defenders of these beliefs. Finally, this burden has not been met (as far as I know) with respect to Santa, or Russell's teapot, or garden fairies, etc.

I'd like to suggest that "superstition" in the contemporary sense (rather than Plutarch's) refers to any belief that meets these conditions. Thus defined, it's not just belief in weird *things* that can count as superstitious. So can belief in weird causal laws. In principle, we could test the belief that if you break a mirror you'll experience seven years' bad luck. We could observe a sample group of mirror-breakers over the course of seven years, cataloguing the frequency of paradigmatically "bad luck" events (job loss, death of a loved one, serious illness or accidents, etc.), and then compare with the frequency of such events in a control group.

Given what we know about the laws of nature, it seems unlikely that mirror-breaking would have any impact on the frequency of bad luck events. The burden of proof rests, then, with those who believe it does – a burden that, to my knowledge, has never been met. Hence, what we have here is a superstition in the sense defined above.[2]

On this definition, it is quite possible that many beliefs that have traditionally been labeled as religious will turn out to be superstitions. But even if this is so (and I think it is), it doesn't follow that there is no class of distinctively religious beliefs, as different from superstition as real science is from pseudoscience. And it certainly doesn't follow, without further ado, that belief in God is superstitious.

But what makes God relevantly different from the celestial teapot or Santa or Esmerelda and Keith? I have already argued that, for devoted theists, "God" refers to a being whose existence would fulfill our ethico-religious hope – that is, our hope that the universe is fundamentally on the side of goodness. But the fulfillment of that hope is not found within the empirical world studied by science. The ethico-religious hope is, in the words of William James (1914), the hope that "the visible world is part of a more spiritual universe from which it draws its chief significance" (p. 485). It is the hope that, beyond the world of "pitiless indifference" that science describes, there is a *transcendent* reality – something outside the empirical world (or beyond it – the point is not about location, but about inaccessibility through empirical investigation). And this transcendent reality bestows upon the world we see a new meaning, one it wouldn't have if the empirical world were all that there is.

Distinctively religious beliefs, then, are *meaning-bestowing beliefs* about a transcendent reality. And that is very different from superstition as I've defined it here. With respect to superstition, the absence of scientific evidence is a compelling reason to disbelieve. But when it comes to meaning-bestowing beliefs about the transcendent, things are considerably more complicated.

Virgin Mary Sightings

Consider a remarkable recent trend: the tendency to see images of the Virgin Mary in such things as pancakes and toasted cheese sandwiches (a ten-year-old toasted cheese sandwich with the blessed Virgin's supposed likeness was sold on e-bay for $28,000 in 2004[3]). A *USA Today* report on August 18, 2006, tells the tale of the holy mother's appearance in a gourmet chocolate shop in Fountain Valley, California:

> Kitchen worker Cruz Jacinto was the first to spot the lump of melted chocolate when she began her shift Monday cleaning up drippings that had accumulated under a large vat of dark chocolate.
>
> Chocolate drippings usually harden in thin, flat strips on wax paper, but Jacinto said she froze when she noticed the unusual shape of this cast-off: It looked just like the Virgin Mary on the prayer card she always carries in her right pocket.

"When I come in, the first thing I do is look at the clock, but this time I didn't look at the clock. My eyes went directly to the chocolate," Jacinto said. "I thought, 'Am I the only one who can see this?' I picked it up and I felt emotion just come over me.

"For me, it was a sign," she said.[4]

I must admit that the religious power of this experience is lost on me – although I've seen a photograph of the alleged chocolate virgin and the resemblance to the Virgin of Guadalupe is remarkable. But I also agree with one blogger who thinks the dripping looks like "a hooded Anakin Skywalker, just before he killed the Younglings."[5]

But whatever we think about the chocolate, few would deny that Cruz Jacinto's belief – that this chocolate image was a sign from God – is religious. It's not a religious belief I happen to share. In fact, I think there are reasons to be skeptical of it – but science's role in evaluating this belief is decidedly limited.

Science can say many things about this case. For example, it can explain the tendency to see human forms in natural phenomena (or foodstuffs). Dawkins could offer a handy evolutionary account of this tendency – called "pareidolia" – in terms of the survival advantage of interpreting ambiguous visual impressions as belonging to agents who could affect your life. This doesn't explain how chocolate drippings could acquire a shape amenable to interpretation as a likeness of Mary, but that can be chalked up to chance: there are lots of opportunities for natural processes to generate outcomes open to "pareidolian" interpretation.

Furthermore, scientists could probably demonstrate without much trouble that the shape Jacinto saw on that omen-rich August day is entirely consistent with what might be generated by the natural processes that regulate chocolate drippings.

But Jacinto needn't deny any of this. She is not claiming (or certainly needn't) that anything has happened that defies ordinary natural laws. Rather, she is invoking views about a reality that transcends the empirical world in order to explain the meaning of an ordinary empirical event, not to displace a naturalistic explanation of the causal processes that gave rise to it. This means that Jacinto's belief isn't falsifiable in the strong sense. But it also means that no strictly empirical observation could verify it. And in the absence of any prospect of verification, the failure to find verification tells us nothing.

I do, however, think that empirical observations can play a role in more philosophical assessments of beliefs like Jacinto's. But to develop this idea, we need to look more carefully at the concept of transcendence.

Schleiermacher and the Transcendence of God

By "transcendence," I have in mind the idea that there is more to reality than what we can discern empirically (aided or unaided by scientific instruments). And this is not just a claim about the current limits of science and technology. Transcendent objects are not just inaccessible to empirical observation *in fact* (as the celestial teapot would have been in Russell's day). They are inaccessible *in principle*.

There are several ways to get a sense of how this could be the case. Because the spirit of Schleiermacher hovers over me, I begin with him.

As we've seen, Schleiermacher maintains that we have two basic kinds of experiences: *receptive* ones, in which the world affects us, and *active* ones, in which we affect the world. The former are accompanied by what he calls "the feeling of dependence" – basically, how it feels to be acted *upon*. The latter are accompanied by "the feeling of freedom" – that is, how it feels to *act*.

In the empirical world, every object is one that we can experience in either of these ways: we can passively experience it with our senses, or we can act on it. When I eat an apple, I am active (crunching into it) and receptive (I sense the flavor and texture) in equal measure. When I contemplate the vastness of the universe, I am far more receptive than active – but by choosing to contemplate, I have changed the universe itself, if only slightly.

In the empirical world, there is nothing towards which I am *only* receptive or *only* active. Everything I act on in that world is something that impresses itself upon me through my senses. And everything that impresses itself upon me through my senses is something I can make choices about, if only the very modest choice to focus attention on it or not. But by "the feeling of *absolute* dependence," Schleiermacher means a feeling of being exclusively receptive, without even a trace of the opposing feeling of activity.

And so, if I have this feeling of absolute dependence, the feeling is either delusional or its source lies outside the empirical world. If there exists anything upon which I depend absolutely, it simply can't be anything in the sensible universe. It must be Something beyond it. And the feeling of absolute dependence is the immediate sense of being connected to that Something – what Schleiermacher calls "God."

If all of this is right, then anything that appeared to us through the senses couldn't be God. At one point in *The God Delusion*, Dawkins claims that if God existed "and chose to reveal it, God himself could clinch the argument, noisily and unequivocally, in his favour" (p. 50). Presumably Dawkins has in mind something like a spectacular parting of the heavens. But for Schleiermacher, nothing of the sort could be an experience of God. While God could presumably cause some spectacular sensible manifestation, the judgment to this effect would always be a fallible inference. Someone could deny the manifestation's divine origins by calling it a mass hallucination or the work of space aliens. Contrary to what Dawkins thinks, nothing we encounter through our senses could "clinch the argument" in God's favor.

In other words, the feeling of absolute dependence is not only the primordial religious feeling, but our only direct avenue to God. Because of what God is – that upon which we depend *absolutely* – God can *only* be experienced by some kind of consciousness distinct from our ordinary interactions with the sensible world. I will return to these ideas in Chapter 7. For now, I simply want to stress that if "God" names something we depend on absolutely, then God cannot be part of the world that science investigates. No empirically observable entity – like teapots or space lobsters – could *be* God, because God transcends the empirical world.

Brains in Vats

In considering the implications of God's transcendence, it may help to reflect on a thought-experiment that was popular among philosophers long before *The Matrix* hit theaters. Imagine that a mad scientist has kidnapped you, removed your brain, and placed it in a vat where it is attached to a supercomputer that feeds you perfectly lifelike virtual experiences. All memory of the transition has been erased. Experientially, the virtual world is completely continuous with the real one.

Philosophers often use this thought-experiment to explore questions about our ability to have knowledge of an external world. But my aim is to explore the concept of transcendence. To this end, let's imagine an entire civilization of brains in vats whose collective experience is the product of a computer so sophisticated that it reproduces lived experience in every detail, without any glitches.

Imagine, in other words, that there is no difference experientially between the lives of these brains-in-vats and the non-brain-in-vat lives that we lead (presumably, unless we're brains in vats!). In this brain-in-vat universe, virtual scientists could investigate the whole of virtual reality. They could create subtle (virtual) instruments to detect what is happening in the far reaches of (virtual) outer space. They could investigate the (virtual) subatomic world. And they could uncover the law-like regularities that the supercomputer has programmed into the universe in which these brain-in-vat scientists subjectively exist.

Let us suppose that these natural laws are identical to those in our universe – and hence are too complex for finite humans to fully understand even through generations of collective effort. While this means there will always be gaps in the scientific understanding of the (virtual) world, it does not mean these gaps cannot, in principle, be filled by more investigation. There is no point at which scientists living in this virtual world would need to hypothesize a supercomputer to fill the gaps. The computer is *that* good. It has created a completely coherent and explicable virtual world.

If we grant all of this, there would be no reason for the scientists investigating this world to ever suspect they're just brains in vats. The question of whether they are brains in vats pertains to a reality that falls in principle outside the empirical scope of their science. In our thought-experiment, the supercomputer and the brains are transcendent realities. And when it comes to the question of whether there exists a transcendent reality – that is, a reality science cannot investigate, even in principle – science must, obviously, remain silent.

What Science Can and Cannot Say About
the Transcendent

But there is more to be said here. In *God: The Failed Hypothesis*, Victor Stenger goes so far as to claim that "science has advanced sufficiently to be able to make a definitive statement on the existence or nonexistence of a God having the attributes that are traditionally associated with the Judeo-Christian-Islamic God" (2007, p. 11).

Stenger's argument depends on an insight that Gould, in his bold formulation of NOMA, seems to miss: If there is a transcendent being, there are *some* ways in which that being might interact with the world which, were that being to do so, would affect how the empirical world looked. But as we saw in Chapter 2, in order to make use of this insight for his purposes, Stenger needs to ensure that claims about what God does (and doesn't do) in the empirical world are part of the very definition of God. He then needs to make this definition rigid, so that God ceases to be *God* if His behavior differs from what the definition enshrines. Only then can scientific discoveries be treated as evidence against God, rather than as reasons to refine our understanding of God.

The problems with this strategy don't need repeating. At some points, however, Stenger seems to think scientific evidence can be marshaled against even a *generic* version of the God Hypothesis – one that doesn't make any specific, empirically testable claims about how God interacts with the world. At one point he characterizes God as "a supreme, transcendent being – beyond matter, space, and time – and yet the foundation of all that meets our senses that is described in terms of matter, space, and time . . . The Judeo-Christian-Islamic God is a nanosecond-by-nanosecond participant in each event that takes place in every cubic nanometer of the universe" (pp. 11–12). For Stenger, it's what follows the "and yet" that makes God a proper object of scientific scrutiny. He holds that "God should be detectable by scientific means simply by virtue of the fact that he is supposed to play such a central role in the operation of the universe and the lives of humans" (p. 13).

But quick reflection on our brains-in-vats thought-experiment will show just how wrongheaded this thinking is. The supercomputer in our analogy plays "a central role in the operation of the (virtual) universe and the lives of humans (or brains in vats)." It is a "nanosecond-by-nanosecond participant" in everything that happens in the virtual world. But, as our analogy shows, virtual scientists investigating their world will never discover, in that world, the supercomputer and its work. This is because the supercomputer transcends that world, and because it has created a seamlessly unified virtual reality with perfectly explicable laws. The computer doesn't need to step in to fill gaps in the programming because there are none.

So, what exactly follows from the fact that no scientific explanation of the observable world requires us to posit a divine creator-and-sustainer of the universe? Does it tell us that no such being exists? Hardly. It only tells us that *if* such a being exists, it has created and sustains a seamlessly unified empirical reality with perfectly explicable laws.

And so Stenger is wrong when he claims that the scope of God's supposed role in the world, by itself, entails science should be able to detect Him. What he gets right is that at least some claims about God – claims about how God interacts with the empirical world – should be susceptible to scientific testing. Stenger may have been overeager when he tried to define God in terms of such claims. But the general point has merit.

Let us suppose, for example, that a scientist in our virtual world encounters a cult with some strange beliefs: they think their world is a virtual one, and everyone in it a brain in a vat. The scientist thinks they're crazy. But they have a growing following and so he sets about trying to debunk them.

Let us suppose these cult members believe that the supercomputer routinely suspends the laws of the virtual world in response to petitionary prayer. These suspensions and their correlation with petitionary prayer would be observable. And so, if the scientist investigates the matter diligently and discovers no such suspensions or correlations, the scientist could reasonably conclude that if there is a supercomputer, it does not intervene in this way. But the scientist will have no grounds for concluding that the supercomputer doesn't exist nor for concluding that the supercomputer is not actively engaged in every facet of life in the virtual world.

Likewise, if scientists in our world can discover no suspensions of natural laws correlated with petitionary prayer, that would support the conclusion that if there is a God, He doesn't routinely interact with the world in that way. And this is the one clear way in which science might have something to say about the transcendent. There are some claims that can be made about the transcendent that, if literally true, would have implications for the patterns we'd expect to observe in the empirical world.

Sometimes, however, these implications are not so clear as to allow for straightforward falsification. Instead, what they offer is room for *philosophical* challenge in the light of observation. Consider again Cruz Jacinto's belief that the curious chocolate formation was a sign from God. I've already mentioned that I don't believe it. Here's why: Small children die every summer in Oklahoma because their parents forget them in the car just long enough to cause fatal heat stroke. If God doesn't jog their memories before their forgetfulness turns to tragedy, then I doubt He's hard at work sculpting chocolate. Put simply, if God is the kind of interventionist God who would mess with chocolate drippings to produce likenesses of the Virgin Mary, I'd expect a pattern of intervention that I don't see.

As a philosophical argument, this is incomplete. I can already anticipate objections that might force me to rethink my conclusion. But my point here isn't to refute Jacinto's belief but to highlight a way in which empirical observation can play a role in evaluating some beliefs about the transcendent. Science can make observations about patterns in the empirical world. And sometimes these observations could contribute to philosophical reflections on the plausibility of beliefs about the transcendent.

In doing this, scientists are basically saying that if a transcendent reality exists, it doesn't seem to have such-and-such properties. But even here, scientists need to be cautious. Small children may see a pattern of increased suffering every time they visit the dentist. They may think, "I wouldn't observe such a pattern were the dentist looking out for my welfare" (although probably not in those words; the more likely words would be "She hurts me. She's bad! Bad!"). But the pattern they see is incomplete. Were they privy to the entire pattern, they'd reach a different conclusion.

And if a transcendent reality exists, scientists are necessarily working with only a partial picture of reality. The patterns they discover may be imbedded in a broader one essentially invisible to scientific eyes. And so scientists ought to approach any reflection on the transcendent with a healthy dose of humility.

This insight cuts both ways. For example, consider what would happen if scientists discovered a correlation between petitionary prayers and the suspension of previously observed regularities. This discovery could neither falsify nor verify God's existence. While scientific evidence of the "power of prayer" would be consistent with many religious beliefs, it wouldn't imply their truth. And scientists would likely treat that evidence as justifying new directions in research. Dawkins would doubtless rail angrily (and with some justification) against those who leap to the God-of-the-gaps to explain prayer's efficacy, not giving science the chance to unravel the mystery. Scientists might begin to study the regularities between mental effort and physical events, cataloguing their discoveries in the form of "psychodynamic laws." Theoretical entities analogous to photons might be proposed to provide a unifying framework for understanding these laws (we could call them psychons – a wave or a particle or a wish, depending on how you look at it!).

In other words, science would plod along, determined to construct the appropriate naturalistic account of the power of prayer. The field of psychodynamic engineering would be born, devising new technologies that worked with the observable laws of psychodynamics. Technology-induced psycho-disasters analogous to global warming would surely not be far behind.

The point is this: belief in the efficacy of petitionary prayer is not, as such, a religious belief. The religious belief is that, if there is such a connection in the empirical world, it is the work of a transcendent God. Likewise, it would be a religious belief to hold that whatever the causal laws in the empirical world, they are the work of God. And *that* is a religious belief science cannot touch.

The God of the Chance Gaps

Science is all about finding the consistent patterns by which the empirical world operates. Every event is taken to follow antecedent conditions according to observable laws – although these laws may not always determine a specific consequence. They might, instead, determine some range of possibilities. Which possibility is realized may be a matter of chance.

When science discovers an anomaly – something that conflicts with the pattern of the universe that's been uncovered so far – science will look for a *deeper* pattern that explains *both* the previously observed pattern *and* the anomaly. It will keep going until it succeeds, because it assumes that the universe operates according to predictable rules (although, again, these rules might underdetermine what actually happens, which would then be explained by chance).

Science has become so successful because these assumptions work. If there were no regularities to be found, the discipline of science would never have been born. If scientists didn't have a track record of success in finding deeper patterns to explain anomalies in older ones, scientists would have long ago decided that the kind of unified explanation of the world that science seeks just isn't there to be found.

But science has been successful, and so most scientists operate with the belief – yes, the *faith* – that we live in a universe where everything that happens fits into a consistent pattern that we might eventually map out. If they're right – and I think they are – what room does that leave for a transcendent reality to affect the world?

Suppose God wants to make little Johnny's leukemia go away. Given the antecedent conditions (the kind of leukemia, Johnny's bodily composition, the spread of the disease, the specific course of chemotherapy Johnny's undergoing, etc.), we might think that either Johnny's leukemia was already destined to go away in accordance with the laws of nature, or not. If the former, God wouldn't need to act. If the latter, then it seems God would have to violate natural laws in order to cure little Johnny – in which case the universe would no longer be what science assumes it to be: a universe in which everything fits an observable pattern describable in terms of laws.

Scientists would, of course, like to think that if they study Johnny's case, they can learn something that might help other leukemia patients. But if Johnny's spontaneous remission resulted from a transcendent reality stepping in from the outside in defiance of natural laws, then science *cannot* learn anything helpful in the fight against leukemia.

All else being equal, it seems to me a good God would want the very thing that scientists want. Such a God would want us to live in a predictable world, one that works according to rules that we can come to understand and rely on. God would want us to be able to use that understanding to help others, so that the quest for knowledge could itself become an act of love.

But if God were committed to ensuring that we live in a world like this, the extent of His direct influence on the world would have to be limited. Does that mean God couldn't act on Johnny's behalf?

Two avenues of divine intervention come immediately to mind. On the one hand, the creator of the universe would be responsible for its rules as well as its initial conditions. And so, God could orchestrate everything from the start so that, at the right moment, natural laws would bring about Johnny's cure. This is the kind of solution that the philosopher Leibniz (and also Schleiermacher) would favor – but it's a solution that doesn't leave room for human freedom, or for God to be responsive to our free choices.

Another solution is to suppose that God intervenes only on a spiritual level. One might think that conscious beings like us straddle the divide between the material world and the transcendent spiritual realm inhabited by God. As physical beings, we are subject to the laws of the physical world, but some part of us is transcendent. And this part is one God can act on directly, without violating any physical laws – offering comfort in time of need, as well as courage, wisdom, serenity and perseverance. In short, God can provide every moral and psychological resource necessary to remove the sting from a physical universe that sometimes crushes us bodily. And this, we might say, is enough.

While this solution has some appeal, it seems to undervalue the physical world and its significance for our lives in a way that many (including myself) find objectionable. For those who want to affirm a God who is responsive to our needs as physical creatures in a material world, something more is called for.

Of course, if God interferes with the course of natural events but does so *very* rarely (a "once-a-millennium" affair), it would be possible for God to intervene without significantly undermining our ability to understand and work with the patterns of the world. But there is another solution. If much of what happens in the world is determined, at least from a scientific standpoint, by chance, there is a space in which a transcendent being might act upon the world without violating the laws of nature.

This same space might also offer room for human freedom. Consider again the brain-in-vat analogy. Since the brains in vats are not part of the empirical domain that virtual scientists in that virtual world would study, the influence of these brains will have no place in the scientific picture of what happens. Whatever causal role the brains play in what happens in the virtual world, they are not operating according to the laws of that virtual world. They're doing their own thing in the *real* world (following whatever laws apply there); but what they do in that reality has an effect on the virtual one. In short, these brains are transcendent. They fall outside the scope of the virtual world's science. But they affect the virtual world even so.

If their causal impact isn't going to defy the empirical laws of the virtual world, the brains may need to work entirely in those spaces in which the laws of the virtual world *under*determine what happens – the spaces in which, from a scientific perspective, chance is the only thing that can decide events, since there is nothing else in the virtual world to do the job. There may, in short, be an indeterminacy to the laws created by the supercomputer that keeps them from wholly deciding what happens. *That* may be decided by what happens in the "chance gaps" – and while much of what happens in those gaps may be a matter of chance, some may result from the purposive decisions introduced into those gaps by either the brains in vats or the supercomputer.

Einstein famously declared that "God does not play dice with the universe." He also famously held that there is no such thing as free will. But there may actually be a reason why a good God would play dice with the universe – that is, create a universe whose causal laws underdetermine what happens. Such a universe would create chance gaps that allow *agents* to affect the world for good or ill. And this may be a prerequisite for moral responsibility, as well as for acting in loving ways.

In fact, contemporary physics has concluded that Einstein was, in an important sense, wrong: at the quantum level, science has uncovered a radical indeterminacy. Electrons and other subatomic particles do not behave in accordance with predictable, deterministic laws. At the most basic level of the physical reality studied by science, chance offers the only naturalistic explanation for why things happen – that is, chance is the only explanation to be found within the empirical world that scientists study. If something other than chance is at work, it would be something outside that world – something supernatural or transcendent.

The point here is this: the transcendence of a crucial element of the human person (the "soul") may offer a solution to the puzzle of free agency, but only when combined with something like the space for action that "chance gaps" allow – the very chance gaps that quantum physics confirms as an ineradicable feature of the natural world. But once we make that space for ourselves, we also make it for God.

If there is a transcendent reality affecting the physical world through the chance gaps, would science be able to establish this? Consider an example that Christopher Hitchens (2007, p. 93) tries to use to his own purposes. In *Wonderful Life*, Stephen Jay Gould offers the following remarks on a fossil, found in the Burgess shale, of the *Pikaia gracilens*, arguably the first vertebrate:

> Wind the tape of time back to Burgess times, and let it play again. If *Pikaia* does not survive in the replay, we are wiped out of future history – all of us, from shark to robin to orangutan. And I don't think that any handi-capper, given Burgess evidence as known today, would have granted very favorable odds for the persistence of *Pikaia*.
>
> And so, if you wish to ask the question of the ages – why do humans exist? – a major part of the answer, touching those aspects of the issue that science can treat at all, must be: because *Pikaia* survived the Burgess deci-mation. This response does not cite a single law of nature; it embodies no statement about predictable evolutionary pathways, no calculation of probabilities based on general rules of anatomy or ecology. The survival of *Pikaia* was a contingency of "just history." (Gould 1989, p. 323)

For Gould, the evolution of vertebrates and, therefore, of humans, depended on an historical accident, a bit of chance: that despite the odds, the Pikaia survived. Gould reaches this conclusion because chance is the only thing within the empirical universe that can explain *Pikaia*'s survival.

Posit a transcendent reality, and other explanations become possible – but these would not be *scientific* ones. Is the survival of *Pikaia* the result of chance or of a divine being working in the chance gaps? Can science answer this question? The fact is that every course that evolution might have taken is statistically improbable, just like every deal of a poker hand. For anyone betting on the emergence of rational agents with moral, aesthetic, and religious sensibilities, evolution has dealt a winning hand. But what does this prove? Anyone betting that evolution, by now, would have produced perfect moral agents without any inclinations towards violence would have been dealt a losing hand.

Whether you think the scientific evidence speaks for or against a God working in the chance gaps depends entirely on what goals you think are motivating God. But here, then, is the lesson: unless science can plumb the Mind of God, scientists would be well advised to remain silent on the whole matter.

Before moving on, I should point out that "chance gaps" are nothing like the explanatory gaps God is invoked to fill in the so-called "God of the gaps." For some, every explanatory gap in science is presumed to be a gap in the operation of natural laws that only God can fill. They imagine that God is like a computer programmer who created a virtual world that couldn't run on its own. Occasionally it needs the programmer's direct input. And so they look frantically for something that can only be explained by a "programmer" stepping in from the outside.

The chance gaps I am talking about are nothing like this. The indeterminacy of quantum states is a crucial feature *of* contemporary scientific explanation, not a gap *in* scientific explanations. As Kenneth Miller (1999) puts it, "the uncertainties inherent to quantum theory do not arise because of gaps in our knowledge and understanding." Instead, "the more accurately we measure individual events, the clearer it becomes that the outcomes of those events are indeterminate" (p. 201). It is a conclusion of science that, at the basic quantum level, events occur without any naturalistic explanation other than chance. Put a different way, the best scientific evidence supports the conclusion that, if there is an explanation for these events other than chance, that explanation is not to be found within the natural world. To suppose that a transcendent being might be at work in these chance gaps is not to exploit a shortcoming in scientific explanation, but to piggy-back on the findings of current science.

Furthermore, while explanatory gaps are invoked to prove God's existence, I am using the chance gaps to explain why we shouldn't expect to be able to prove or disprove God's existence scientifically, even if God intervenes in the world.

In short, my view is this: if there is a God, there is no good reason to think He would create a universe that couldn't run on its own according to discoverable laws. But such a world is still a world in which God might be a "nanosecond-by-nanosecond participant" in events. It remains a world in which God might exert significant influence (both by establishing the initial rules and conditions and by working through the chance gaps). It remains a world in which God might be directly linked to the hearts and minds of every person (as the supercomputer is linked to every brain in a vat). If God really is *transcendent*, then it simply isn't true that "God should be detectable by scientific means simply by virtue of the fact that he is supposed to play such a central role in the operation of the universe and the lives of humans."

A Meaningful "God"

But there remain two closely-related challenges to all this talk about transcendence. Both ask whether any such talk is even meaningful.

Those familiar with the philosophical history of the brain-in-a-vat thought-experiment will notice that, up to now, I have left out an important chapter in that history. The philosopher Hilary Putnam (1981) made fruitful use of that very thought-experiment to make a point about the meaning of our concepts. He wanted to argue that in a universe like the one that I described, in which everyone is just a brain in a vat, no one who *claimed* to be a brain in a vat would be speaking the truth.

Basically, Putnam's thinking runs as follows. If we live our entire existence as a brain in a vat, then what we mean by words such as "tree" and "chair" is different from what we would mean had we lived our lives in a world with real physical objects. In the virtual world, the word "tree" refers to the virtual tree, that is, the sensory impression generated by the stimuli from the mad scientist's computer. It does not refer to what, for us (presumably), it refers to – namely, a physical object in the physical world.

But then, of course, "brain in a vat" means something different, too. And, given what "brain in a vat" means for those who are, well, brains in a vat, if any of them were to say, "I am a brain in a vat," they'd be saying something false. Why? Because the term "brain," for them, refers to a virtual brain generated in their awareness by the computer. What else could it mean? Within the virtual world, that is what is picked out by the term. When virtual children are taught the language, they won't have actual physical brains pointed out to them since there are none of those in the virtual world to be pointed out.

"Vat," likewise, refers to a virtual vat. And so when a person in this virtual world says, "I am a brain in a vat," that person is making a claim about the virtual world. And since the person is not a brain in a vat in the virtual world, the statement is false. The people in the virtual world just cannot *say* the true thing that we, as observers who exist in the real world, can say: "They're brains in vats." They can't say it because their language is about the virtual world they experience. What transcends their experience – our world, in which they are brains in vats – also transcends their concepts. They just can't talk about it (Putnam 1981, pp. 1–21).

While this seems mostly right to me, there is a perspective (ours) from which our hypothetical person can be meaningfully said to *be* a brain in a vat. And there is therefore a sense in which the hypothetical person can say, "I am a brain in a vat," and be asserting something true – if the person means to be making a non-literal use of the relevant terms. We can treat the statement as shorthand for something like the following: "I am something analogous to what I mean by 'brain' in something analogous to what I mean by 'vat' at a level of reality that transcends the one in which I experience my life." And the fact that we are able to conduct the brain-in-a-vat thought-experiment shows that we can attach meaning to the idea of one reality transcending another.

While we can't talk literally about such a transcendent reality, that doesn't mean we can't gesture towards it with non-literal language. And some metaphors and analogies may come closer to characterizing the transcendent reality than others. If, in the virtual world of our thought-experiment, someone were to wake up one day with the burning intuition that she was, after all, just a brain in a vat, that physical objects were not solid things out there but just images created by a supercomputer through neural stimulation – well, wouldn't we have to say that this person's intuition was awfully close to the truth? None of it would be literally true given the meaning of words in her language – but in metaphorical terms, she's really hit the nail on the head.

It is interesting that theologians from St Thomas Aquinas to John Hick have held that religious talk involves non-literal – analogous and metaphorical – uses of language. Of course, whatever transcendent reality we are trying to get at with religious language is unlikely to resemble the empirical world as closely as the real world resembles the virtual one in our thought-experiment. And so our non-literal language may not hit the nail on the head quite so perfectly. And so, when theists say that "God loves us like a parent," we can't conclude that God will behave towards us precisely as loving human parents behave towards their children.

And this makes it hard to make predictions based on religious statements, even ones that would have clear implications for the world of experience if we understood them in their literal sense. The non-literal nature of religious language entails that religious beliefs resist empirical falsification. At least in theory, they might be consistent with just about anything we happened to observe.

But this fact leads to another, more important argument against the meaningfulness of religious claims: If the claim that God exists is consistent with anything we might discover about the empirical world, then are we really saying anything meaningful when we say that God exists? This question was forcefully raised by the philosopher Anthony Flew in a symposium discussion first published in an Oxford University undergraduate journal. Flew opens this discussion with a parable:

> Once upon a time two explorers came upon a clearing in the jungle. In the clearing were growing many flowers and many weeds. One explorer says, "Some gardener must tend this plot." The other disagrees, "There is no gardener." So they pitch their tents and set a watch. No gardener is ever seen. "But perhaps he is an invisible gardener." So they set up a barbed-wire fence. They electrify it. They patrol with bloodhounds . . . But no shrieks ever suggest that some intruder has received a shock. No movements of the wire ever betray an invisible climber. The bloodhounds never give a cry. Yet the Believer is not convinced. "But there is a gardener, invisible, intangible, insensible to electric shocks, a gardener who has no scent and makes no sound, a gardener who comes secretly to look after the garden which he loves." At last the Sceptic despairs, "But what remains of your original assertion? Just how does what you call an invisible, intangible, eternally elusive gardener differ from an imaginary gardener or even from no gardener at all?" (Flew, Hare, and Mitchell 2005, p. 463)

In a recap and final comment on the symposium discussion, Flew states the philosophical moral of his parable in the following terms:

> Some theological utterances seem to, and are intended to, provide explanations or express assertions. Now an assertion, to be an assertion at all, must claim that things stand thus and thus; *and not otherwise*. Similarly an explanation, to be an explanation at all, must explain why this particular

thing occurs; *and not something else* . . . And yet sophisticated religious people . . . tend to refuse to allow, not merely that anything actually does occur, but that anything conceivably could occur which would count against their theological assertions and explanations. But in so far as they do this their supposed explanations are actually bogus, and their seeming assertions are really vacuous. (Flew, Hare, and Mitchell 2005, pp. 469–70)

Instead of denying the truth of what Gould would later dub "NOMA," Flew admits from the start that many religious claims fall outside the scope of science. They are unfalsifiable. But this, he claims, creates a grave problem for religious language. It makes it meaningless. When people say that God exists, they aren't saying anything meaningful at all. They might as well say "Shubacabalan" (something my son said recently while pretending to be a baby; when he's older he can correct my spelling of it).

In responding to Flew, the other main participants in the debate offer some interesting reflections. Basil Mitchell points out that theologians have always regarded the variety and amount of evil in the world as a *problem* for traditional theism. This suggests that belief in God *does* have meaning for how we experience the world – a meaning that is in tension with what we actually discover. What Mitchell argues is that theists base their belief on an initial experience that is so powerful as to evoke trust. And this trust leads them to continue to believe in God even when they encounter evidence that counts against God's existence (Flew, Hare, and Mitchell, pp. 467–9).

I think there is much to be said about Mitchell's ideas. But I won't develop them here since I will pursue my own reflections on the problem of evil in Chapter 9. R. M. Hare, however, offers a different response to Flew that warrants consideration here. Hare's idea is that Flew has underestimated the ways in which language can be meaningful. According to Hare, religious language serves a different function than description or explanation.

To make his point, Hare offers his own parable. He asks us to imagine that "a certain lunatic is convinced that all dons want to murder him" (Flew, Hare, and Mitchell 2005, p. 465). The lunatic fits all of his experience into a grand conspiracy theory: the dons are careful, concealing their murderous intent with "diabolical cunning" (p. 465). In effect, the lunatic's view is consistent with *any* empirical evidence that might be put before him – even the fact of his living to a ripe old age.

On Flew's view, the lunatic isn't *saying* anything when he says that all dons are out to get him. Hence, he isn't saying anything false. And yet, we want to say there's a big difference between the lunatic and the rest of us. If the difference doesn't lie in a falsifiable belief to the effect that "things stand thus and thus, and not otherwise," then where does it lie? Hare's answer is that it lies in our "*blik*" (p. 466). A *blik* is, roughly, a *way of looking at things*. For the lunatic, everything a don does will resonate differently than it does for us. It will be sinister. It will be full of significance for his life, rather than of little account. In short, our *blik* is what gives our experience its meaning.

Now Hare is of the opinion that these *bliks* don't say anything true or false about reality. I am not prepared to say this about religious claims. I believe that such claims routinely do say something about reality: they posit the existence of a transcendent reality beyond the world encountered through the senses; and they say some things about that reality, even if the language they use has a non-literal meaning. The brains-in-vats scenario shows us that the idea of a transcendent reality is hardly incoherent. And while we may be able to talk about such a reality only in non-literal terms, we'd still be talking about it. And what we have to say can still fit (or fail to fit) with the way things really are (even if it may be impossible to know how good a fit we've achieved).

But I will admit that, if claims about a transcendent reality have no significance for the world of ordinary experience, then we might as well be saying nothing. Even if religious beliefs are about more than just the world of ordinary experience, they are *also* about that world. If they weren't, they'd be insignificant even if not strictly speaking meaningless.

What Hare does is show how what we say can be significant even if it doesn't make any factual claims about the empirical world, and even if it offers no scientific explanations for why things happen as they do in that world. The fundamental role that religious beliefs play in our lives is not to explain the causal mechanisms by which observable events come about. Superstitions typically play such a quasi-scientific explanatory role – and insofar as they do, they are scientifically testable. But distinctively religious beliefs, rather than offering causal explanations of observable events that compete with scientific ones, serve a different role: to *give meaning* to the world we encounter through our senses. A religious belief is about a transcendent reality – a reality beyond what we encounter in ordinary sense experience – that ultimately explains the meaning and significance of the world encountered through our senses.

Given my working definition of "God," the statement that God exists tells us something very significant about the ordinary empirical world. It tells us that the apparently pitiless indifference of the universe is not the whole story but a false impression created by a picture of reality that leaves out the most fundamental part.

Such a message is hardly meaningless. Like Hare's *blik*, it colors the world in an entirely different way.

The Meaning of Life

Several times now, I have suggested that beliefs about the transcendent can confer *meaning* on ordinary experience. But what exactly does that mean? An account of the meaning of an event is a kind of explanation – but one that's entirely different from the kind science offers.

Consider an example. When a pool player strikes the cue ball, which collides with the eight ball and knocks it into the corner pocket, scientists can explain what happened in terms of scientific laws. What they are doing is showing how the course of events fits with the rules that the empirical world follows. The rules are causal ones, in the sense that they tell us what *will* happen given certain antecedent conditions, what *might* happen, and what *won't* happen. The aim of science is to lift such causal explanation to the most abstract level possible by looking for a model in which the smallest possible set of basic elements or forces are seen to follow predictable laws.

Explaining, in these terms, why the eight-ball clunked into the corner pocket would involve showing how this event follows from antecedent conditions according to the observed laws by which the universe operates. The antecedent conditions can themselves be explained in the same way, in a chain of causation that, at least in theory, could move from the twitching of muscles in the pool player's arm to the firing of neurons in her brain and, ultimately, all the way back to the Big Bang.

Nowhere in this explanation would we find the following ordinary account of what happened: "The pool player intended to put the eight ball in the corner pocket because she wanted to win the game." That is a different kind of explanation. It explains, not the causal mechanisms whereby the events occurred, but the *purposes* behind them.

It has always been a challenge to fit human purposes into the scientific picture of the world because that is not the kind of explanation that science gives. One might try, of course, to explain away human purposes. One might argue that they are nothing but the predictable, law-governed consequences of antecedent conditions – nothing more than side-effects of physical brain processes, "epiphenomena" that don't *do* anything. Human motives and aspirations might then be absorbed into the simple, mechanistic operation of the basic elements of the universe that science has posited. And if you follow that course, what you've done is strip the universe of meaning.

An explanation that confers meaning is one that tells us why something happened in terms of the purposes or intentions behind it. The scientific picture, because it only looks for mechanistic causal explanations in terms of antecedent conditions, sees a universe without ultimate purpose, without driving intentions, without meaning.

Religion says that, beyond this world of causal explanations, there are explanations in terms of purposes. Instead of explaining away human purposes by appeal to the mindless operation of mechanistic forces, religion posits a transcendent realm in which these mechanistic forces are themselves explained by appeal to purposes.

There is an enormous difference between invoking a transcendent God to answer questions about meaning and purpose and invoking God to offer *causal explanations* of observable phenomena. The latter is the "God of the gaps," who fills in the explanatory gaps that science has (so far) left us. The thing to keep in mind is that, whenever God is invoked to fill in the explanatory gaps left by science, God is being used to offer explanations of the same kind that science offers.

This "God of the gaps" is a competitor with science. As such, this is a God that science can investigate, a God for which Gould's NOMA makes no sense. When an evolutionary biologist offers a naturalistic explanation of some complex biological system that Michael Behe claims can only be explained by the supernatural intervention of an intelligent designer, the biologist has refuted Behe's claim.

But when religion offers purposive explanations for what we encounter in experience, it is not competing with science. It is offering a different kind of explanation about which science has, in principle, nothing to say. This may have been what Gould was trying to say when, in articulating his NOMA thesis, he claimed that "religion extends over questions of ultimate meaning and moral value."

Critics of Gould, including Dawkins and Stenger, have tended to jump all over the "moral value" clause, arguing that religious *texts* don't play much role in shaping moral beliefs, that atheists can be moral, and the like. Their points are generally accurate but they miss the deeper truth. We may not need religion to *know* what is right and wrong, or to have a personal sense of right and wrong. And if Kantians are right that morality is grounded in reason alone (a view I'm drawn to but have doubts about), religion may not be necessary in order for moral claims to be true (or false) according to some non-arbitrary standard.

But it may still be the case that if our moral lives are to be more than obedience to a cold duty disconnected from our deepest aspirations, we need a vision of the world that includes a transcendent reality – one that says "yes" to goodness at every point that the blind mechanisms of nature say "I don't care."

Religion, in its truest forms, may be about conferring upon the universe a meaning that makes morality *matter* in a way that it wouldn't otherwise. It may be that what the God Hypothesis says to us is that, beyond the world that science sees, there lies an order of reality that invests our moral lives with abiding significance.

This hypothesis isn't scientifically testable but it isn't meaningless either. And it surely isn't in the same category as belief in celestial teapots.

Concluding Remarks

I have argued here that science cannot determine whether a transcendent reality exists. Science might be of some use in debunking naive literal claims about the properties of a transcendent being, but this usefulness is limited, and scientists should approach the task with caution.

These insights go a long way towards refuting the claim that the absence of scientific evidence for God's existence gives us reason to disbelieve. But the absence of such evidence surely doesn't provide any reason to *believe*, either. At best, we are pointed towards agnosticism. Unless, of course, we have resources other than science.

Do we? Absolutely. We have philosophy, and we have religious experience. And while neither of these resources *forces* theism upon us, taken together they make theistic belief eminently reasonable. Or so I will argue in the chapters to come.

5

Philosophy and God's Existence, Part I

How are books born? The one you're reading now was born when a colleague gave me a photocopied page from a book, without identifying information, and asked me to evaluate it as I would a student's paper. The page offered "summaries" of the first three of St Thomas Aquinas' five arguments for God's existence (popularly called the "Five Ways"). The writer of the passage got the arguments wrong – and then objected to them at precisely those points *where* he got them wrong.

The writer was Richard Dawkins. The book was *The God Delusion*. The photocopied passage, had Dawkins turned it in to me for a grade, would have earned him a whopping "D." And for many people, this D-level work may be their only exposure to Aquinas' arguments for God's existence.

And so I bought Dawkins' book. And as I read it, I was taken in by the author's *swagger*. Dawkins is clearly confident, writing as if he knows what he's talking about. The only problem is that, as often as not, he has no idea what he's talking about.

Mangling Aquinas

Here's how Dawkins summarizes the first of Aquinas' Five Ways: "Nothing moves without a prior mover. This leads us to a regress, from which the only escape is God. Something had to make the first move, and that something we call God" (2006, p. 77).

This is a misreading, albeit an understandable one for a novice with no grasp of Aquinas' technical language and little training in following philosophical arguments. Arguably, Dawkins is precisely such a novice. And so his mangling of Aquinas is understandable, even if his pretense of expertise is not.

But what does Aquinas *really* say?[1] First of all, for Aquinas "motion" means "change," and "change" means "reduction of something from potentiality to actuality." When Aquinas says that something "moves," he means that something changes from being only *potentially* such-and-such (say, potentially hot), to being *actually* such-and-such (actually hot). And he thinks nothing can be the cause of its own change. You need something that is *already* actually hot to heat up what is only potentially hot.

So, anything that changes needs to be changed by something else. If that "something else" also undergoes change, then it needs to be changed by something else again. But Aquinas doesn't believe an infinite regress here is coherent. If stone A is heated by stone B, which is heated by stone C, and so on *forever*, Aquinas doesn't think we'd have any explanation for why any of these stones are hot.

To explain this wave of heat moving from stone to stone, you need something to start the wave. And something that *gets* hot only by the influence of another hot thing won't do the trick. That just shifts the burden of explanation back one level. It would be like explaining the movement of one train car by saying that it's pulled by the one ahead of it, which is pulled by the one ahead of it . . . and so on forever. Since no train car in this entire infinite series moves by itself, where is this movement coming from? The mere fact that the train goes on forever does not eliminate the need for a locomotive.

And so Aquinas thinks we can't have an infinite regress. We need a starting point, something that initiated the whole series of changes. But what would such a "starter" have to be like? First of all, to change other things it would have to possess already the property it produces in others. But if at some point it acquired this property from something else, then we'd be back in the regress. So, in order to end the regress, we need something that doesn't change, because it has always been fully actualized – something that, by virtue of what it is, has *eternally* possessed the properties that other things only *come* to possess.

Presumably, each property that things come to possess could have its origin in a different eternal thing: an eternal flame for heat, an eternal genius for intelligence, etc. But Aquinas has a simpler view. He proposes to explain "motion" by reference to a single source, something whose power to move other things flows from itself, rather than from an outside source. And what would such a being have to be like in order to have such power by virtue of its own nature? It would have to be a lot like God.

By similar means, Aquinas seeks to establish that an uncaused cause must exist. His idea is that everything that comes into existence must have a cause. To prevent an infinite regress of causes, we must suppose that there exists something that doesn't come into existence and hence something that is not in need of a cause.

Contrast this compact statement of Aquinas' "Second Way" with Dawkins' equally compact one: "Nothing is caused by itself. Every effect has a prior cause, and again we are pushed back into regress. This has to be terminated by a first cause, which we call God" (2006, p. 77). What Dawkins misses is Aquinas' point that everything *of a certain kind* – namely, that which *comes* into existence – requires a cause. In order to avoid an infinite regress of causes, we need the chain of causation to be started by something of a *different* kind – namely, something that *does not* come into existence (something that exists from eternity).

By a somewhat different argument, Aquinas seeks to show that there needs to be a *necessary* being (one that could *not* have failed to exist) in order to explain all of the *contingent* beings in the world (things that *could* have failed to exist). Dawkins offers the following gloss on this Third Way: "There must have been a time when no physical things existed. But, since physical things exist now, there must have been something non-physical to bring them into existence, and that something we call God" (p. 77).

This is just wrong. First, it confuses the distinction between contingent and necessary beings with the distinction between physical and non-physical things. More significantly, it leaves out crucial details of Aquinas' argument. In this argument, Aquinas asks us to imagine an infinite past. If the past is infinite, then why couldn't every contingent thing be explained by a preceding one, stretching back forever?

Aquinas' answer seems to be this: everything that is possible will eventually happen given infinite time. If everything that exists could, possibly, not have existed, then it is possible for there to be a time when nothing exists. Given an infinite past, *that* possibility would be *actual* at some point. But since nothing can come from nothing, it follows that nothing would exist *now*. So, if we tried to explain the existence of contingent things in terms of antecedent contingent things, eventually we'd hit a point in the past where nothing existed – even if we posit an infinite past.

And so, to explain why anything exists, we need a necessary being.

Following traditional terminology, each of these three arguments is a version of the "cosmological argument" for God's existence. What they have in common is this: Each holds that to explain the existence of the world we know – a world of finite, limited things – there needs to be something that gave rise to it all which *isn't* finite and limited.

In his "Five Ways," Aquinas supplements his versions of the cosmological argument with two arguments of a different sort in order to show, first, that there must be something that maximally embodies all the positive qualities found in the world, and second, that the universe must be the product of purposive intelligence. I will not consider the "Fourth Way," since my understanding of Aquinas' metaphysics isn't deep enough to assess its merits.[2] The Fifth Way is a variant on the "argument from design," which I will look at later in this chapter.

In any event, Aquinas seems to employ something like Ockham's razor when reflecting on these arguments. What they show, he thinks, is that the existence of the world we know requires an unmoved mover, an uncaused cause, a necessary being, something that maximally embodies all positive qualities, and a purposive intelligence. And it just makes sense to suppose, for simplicity's sake, that it is the *same thing* that performs all these functions. And this thing is what we call God. In subsequent sections of his enormous *Summa Theologica* (and also in the *Summa Contra Gentiles*), Aquinas pursues the task of showing that this one thing that we call "God" has the properties attributed to God in the Judeo-Christian tradition: omniscience, omnipotence, perfect goodness, and the like.

The Five Ways, in short, are intended to focus our attention on *that which explains the world as we encounter it.* They appear in the First Part of the *Summa Theologica*, which is organized in terms of 119 Questions, each containing numerous articles. The first 43 of these "Questions" focus on the existence and nature of God. The Five Ways are offered early on – in the third article of Question 2. What follows is an exhaustive series of questions and arguments aimed at establishing that this unmoved mover, uncaused cause, etc., has the properties that Christians traditionally have attributed to God. The articles through Question 26 focus on the general concept of God shared among Christians, Jews, and Muslims. The rest focus on the uniquely Christian idea that God is one divine essence in three Persons (the doctrine of the Trinity).

With all this in mind, let's consider how Dawkins criticizes the first three of Aquinas' Five Ways. To start off, Dawkins claims that "All three of these arguments rely upon the idea of a regress and invoke God to terminate it. They make the entirely unwarranted assumption that God himself is immune to the regress" (p. 77).

But this is confused. That "God himself is immune to the regress" is hardly an *assumption* in Aquinas' arguments. As we've seen, Aquinas identifies what something needs to be like in order to end the regress. He argues that if the existence of the world as we know it is to be explained, the regress needs to be ended. And so he concludes that, to explain this world, something must exist that has the regress-ending features. He calls this being "God." Exactly how does this translate into *assuming* that God is immune to the regress?

Dawkins commits the crude logical blunder of treating the conclusion of Aquinas' argument as if it were an assumption. But let's move on, because Dawkins isn't done yet. "Even if we allow the dubious luxury of arbitrarily conjuring up a terminator to an infinite regress and giving it a name," he says, "there is absolutely no reason to endow that terminator with any of the properties normally ascribed to God: omnipotence, omniscience, goodness" (p. 77).

Readers should immediately see what's wrong with this thinking. The Five Ways appear in the second of 43 topical sections devoted to establishing that the regress-ending being is also the theistic God. But Dawkins has neither the time nor the inclination (nor, it seems, the philosophical ability) to work his way through all 43 topical sections of the First Part of the *Summa Theologica*. Far easier just to foist on Aquinas the false view that the Five Ways *by themselves* are supposed to prove that God is omnipotent, omniscient, and the rest – and then point out that they don't do that.

Aquinas' arguments for God are hardly immune to philosophical challenge. I am personally unconvinced by Aquinas' view that an infinite regress of ordinary causal explanations is impossible. And so, when I return to the cosmological argument in the next chapter, I will defend a version that does not suppose the impossibility of an infinite regress. In defending that argument, I will consider several substantive objections that, while in my view unsuccessful, are philosophically important.

No important objections, successful or not, come from Dawkins. Instead, he offers a cavalier attack on a caricature, in which swagger replaces careful thinking.

So how are books born? There are many answers – but this book was born because I felt the need to counteract a wave of popular attacks on religion in which careless thinking and intellectual laziness are masked behind bluster and bravado. Dawkins' mangling of Aquinas is a perfect example of this wretched trend.

The Argument from Design

Dawkins is much better when he targets a different argument for God's existence, namely the argument from design (also called the teleological argument). Roughly, this argument says that the universe exhibits organized complexity that is best explained by positing an intelligent designer who made it all.

In fact, I share Dawkins' judgment that as a stand-alone argument for God's existence, the argument from design is unconvincing. But there are many failed arguments for God's existence, just as there are enormously many bad arguments that could be devised for any belief. It's not how many bad arguments there are that matters but whether there are any good ones. If the argument from design is unconvincing, what we should conclude is that it fails to give us good reasons to believe, not that there is no God.

Although I think the argument from design fails, I want to look at it carefully because Dawkins' argument against God's existence builds on his critical assessment of the design argument. He tries, in jujitsu fashion, to turn this argument against the theists who invoke it, in an effort to show that God's existence is "highly improbable." To see whether he succeeds, we need a basic understanding of the argument from design.

This argument is based on an important observation about the natural world, namely, that it contains complex *teleological systems.* "Teleological system" is a technical term for an organized system whose parts work together to achieve one or more ends. A telephone is an example: its parts work together to enable people to communicate over long distances.

There are obvious examples of teleological systems in nature: livers, immune systems, and, of course, entire living organisms. And some thinkers argue that the universe *taken as a whole* is such a system. This is sometimes referred to as the "fine-tuning" argument: it imagines that the possible laws of physics are like an enormous range of frequencies on a radio dial in which only one narrow band will "tune in" life. And it just so happens that the laws of physics are "tuned in" just right.[3]

But what does any of this show? The argument from design relies on two observations about teleological systems. First, they appear to be highly improbable. The likelihood that chance would generate precisely the systems we see is very low. But by itself, this improbability tells us nothing. Deal a five-card poker hand. Suppose you are dealt a three of clubs, a seven of spades, a queen of hearts, a four of hearts, and a ten of diamonds. The likelihood of being dealt that hand is very low. But it is also just about as useless a poker hand as you could imagine. And so, even though it is improbable that you should be dealt that particular hand, you don't look for any explanation other than chance. After all, *any* poker hand is unlikely, and you have to be dealt something.

But suppose you were dealt four aces and a king. Of all the unlikely hands you might have been dealt, you're dealt one that almost can't be beat (only a royal flush would beat it). In addition to being highly unlikely, it has value.

You might still chalk it up to luck, of course. But suppose you played an entire poker tournament and unfailingly received winning hands – different hands every time, but always winning ones.

In this case, you'd think with good reason that someone's fixing the deck. This is true even though the series of hands you were dealt is, strictly speaking, no more or less likely than any other series of hands you might have been dealt. What is so unlikely is that all of the hands in the series are winning ones. That is what suggests an intelligent agent at work.

Consider a different example. Suppose there is sand spread across the bottom of a tray, lying in something like a half-moon shape with a bulge on one side and a tapering tail on the other, with smaller blobs of sand here and there. That the sand would fall into *that* particular shape is highly unlikely. Shake up the tray a hundred thousand times and you'd be unlikely to see that exact design ever again. But you wouldn't conclude that someone had deliberately pushed the sand into that shape.

But then suppose the sand is shaped to exactly match the Abraham Lincoln profile on a standard penny. In that case, you'd assume intelligent agency. And this is true even if the likelihood of the grains of sand falling into this arrangement were the same as the likelihood of them falling into the earlier one. What requires an explanation beyond mere chance is that, of all the trillions of highly unlikely arrangements, what we have before us is one that exactly matches a well-known image.

Now suppose I take a bunch of small electronic components filched from Radio Shack's dumpster, put them into a container, and shake them up while spraying molten solder in through a hole in one side. Suppose I open the container and find a jumbled mess. The chances that this *exact* mess would have been produced is, of course, astonishingly low. But there's nothing that happened that can't be chalked up to chance.

But then suppose that what I pull out of the container is a functioning transistor radio and it's picking up my favorite radio station. In that case, I'd blink in dumb incomprehension. In that case, what resulted was a *teleological system.* Teleological systems are like successive winning poker hands or Lincoln's profile in sand. Of all the unlikely things that might have happened, if what *did* happen was a teleological system, that needs some kind of explanation beyond mere chance.

Teleological systems look as if they were put together for a purpose. Their parts look as if they were arranged in order to achieve a functional unity. They look, in short, as if an intelligent designer were at work – someone to get all the soldered connections just so for the purposes of converting radio frequencies into the voice of Freddy Mercury singing *Bohemian Rhapsody*.

And so, if chance is insufficient to explain a teleological system, the alternative that leaps to mind is *intelligent design*. After all, intelligent design *is* what explains the existence of machines like my Citizen Eco-Drive watch. And so, if chance is the only alternative explanation, intelligent design seems the more reasonable option.

And this is the basic idea behind the argument from design. Although there are numerous ways to lay it out, one way would be as follows:

1   In the natural world (that is, the world of things not designed or built by human beings), there exists T (where T refers to a teleological system or a collection of such systems).
2   Chance does *not* provide a satisfactory explanation for T's existence.
3   Intelligent design *does* provide a satisfactory explanation for T's existence.
4   Chance and intelligent design exhaust the possible explanations for T's existence.
5   Therefore, in order to satisfactorily explain what we find in the natural world, we must posit an intelligent designer.

Why the Argument from Design Fails

So, what's wrong with this argument? That all depends on what we plug in for T. If T stands for complex biological organisms or their component systems – dogs and people, or cameric eyes and immune systems – then the problem lies with premise 4. Put simply, Darwin showed that chance and intelligent design do *not* exhaust the possible explanations for such biological systems. There is a third alternative: gradual development through random variation and natural selection over an extraordinary stretch of time. As Dawkins puts it,

> natural selection is a cumulative process, which breaks the problem of improbability up into small pieces. Each of the small pieces is slightly improbable, but not prohibitively so. When large numbers of these slightly improbable events are stacked up in series, the end product of the accumulation is very very improbable indeed, improbable enough to be far beyond the reach of chance. (Dawkins 2006, p. 121)

To understand Dawkins' point, we need an overview of how natural selection works. Natural selection operates on organisms that reproduce – either those that make nearly identical copies of themselves, such as amoebas, or those that, through sexual reproduction, pass on key elements of themselves to their progeny.

Imagine that you have 10,000 amoebas in a pool. Suppose all of them are identical but one. This oddball, because of some random mistake in the mitosis of its predecessor, is slightly more complex than the others. But this increased complexity is written into its DNA so that, when it reproduces itself, its progeny will preserve the random increase in complexity. Now suppose that a chemical deadly to ordinary amoebas, but not to the oddball, gets dumped into the pool.

What will happen? The oddball will survive while the others die. And then the oddball will reproduce, and its offspring will reproduce, etc. Eventually there will be a pool with thousands of amoebas once more – all of them slightly more complex than amoebas in the pool used to be.

A *slightly* improbable increase in complexity, because it was adaptively advantageous, was preserved through replication and became dominant in the population. And now, lo and behold, another slightly improbable increase in complexity happens by chance, and the process continues.

Somewhere along the line, imagine that a mutation causes an amoeba to fail to complete the process of replication. Instead of making a copy of itself that floats off into the water, the copy gets stuck to the original. And this keeps happening until the cluster forms an S-shape whose curvature overcomes the tendency for the new "amoebas" to stick to the old. At that point, the new amoebas break free – and they do the same thing, forming S-shaped clusters. And then suppose these clusters survive more effectively than their single-celled cousins.

If this process continues long enough, we could very well end up with a rather complex multi-celled critter with various organs for navigating successfully through the hostile pool of water. This complex teleological system couldn't have just come about by chance – it's just too complex, and that complexity is just too advantageous for its survival. But it *didn't* come about by chance. A gradual process of incremental increases in complexity, all of which *can* be explained by chance, are preserved and cumulatively added to one another through natural selection.

The point, of course, is that chance and intelligent design do *not* exhaust the possible explanations for complex teleological systems. Such systems might also result from a gradual accumulation of chance changes preserved through self-replication and adaptive success. And extensive empirical observation of the natural world shows that such a process of evolving complexity *actually happens*. So, what we have is a known process that we see at work in nature, one that can explain the existence of complex teleological systems. Surely a process *known* to occur, one that *can* explain complex teleology, offers a *better* explanation than a *hypothetical* intelligent designer.

Now, when *T* in the argument from design stands for complex biological organisms or their components, this Darwinian response is strong. There are challenges, of course. The most celebrated comes from biochemist Michael Behe (1996) who argues that some organic systems are irreducibly complex. His idea is that some biological systems, to achieve their function, need to be exactly put together just as they are, with each component in place just so. Behe and his allies argue that such systems couldn't have evolved gradually from simpler ones because the simpler systems wouldn't have any survival value. The simpler systems don't do anything, and so natural selection wouldn't keep them around long enough to acquire the incremental increases in complexity that would finally give rise to a useful system.

But Behe's challenge to Darwin's theory is hardly decisive. The fact is that many of the complex organic systems Behe trots out as examples of irreducible complexity *have* been explained in evolutionary terms.[4] And this gives us reason to be suspicious of other so-called "irreducibly complex" systems. Just because *we* can't see how they could be preserved through the course of evolution doesn't mean there is no such explanation. As Dawkins puts the point, "Those people who leap from personal bafflement at a natural phenomenon straight to a hasty invocation of the supernatural are no better than the fools who see a conjuror bending a spoon and leap to the conclusion that it is 'paranormal'" (2006, p. 129).

Science seeks out the unexplained and then tries to explain it in naturalistic terms. Just because a particular organic system has yet to be explained in terms of natural selection doesn't mean it can't be done. So long as evolutionary biologists are continuing to make steady progress in explaining the mysteries of evolution, the continued existence of some mysteries is no reason to reject the comprehensiveness of Darwin's theory. On the contrary, the enormous success the theory has had so far in unraveling mysteries gives us reason to think that, with enough time, scientists will unravel the new mysteries as well. We shouldn't leap to the conclusion that only an intelligent designer can explain improbably complex organisms.

But none of this entails that the argument from design is dead and buried. The thing about Darwinian evolution is that it can't get off the ground unless there are molecules that replicate themselves – molecules like DNA. These self-replicating molecules need to be able to store information about their structures, and they need the tools to recreate these structures from available surrounding materials. Even the simplest of them are miraculously complex teleological systems – and Darwinian evolution, because it *presupposes* their existence, cannot explain their origins.

And this means we can refurbish the argument from design. Go back to my outline for it, and instead of plugging in "organisms and their component systems" for *T*, plug in "self-replicating molecules." Since Darwin's theory presupposes their existence, it can't explain them.

With our new version of the argument in place, it seems we have rehabilitated our premise that chance and intelligent design exhaust the possible explanations for complex teleology (premise 4 in my outline). But this new version is not immune to challenges. Dawkins gestures towards one kind of challenge by calling Darwin's theory a "consciousness raiser" (pp. 114–19). His idea is this: Darwin's theory should call to our attention the possibility of alternatives to chance and intelligent design. Even if we don't *know* of any "third alternative" to explain the origin of DNA, there might be one.

This response, however, is speculative. Natural selection is a known process that could explain the origins of complex organic systems, and that is what makes it a better explanation than a hypothetical intelligent designer. But when we pit a hypothetical intelligent designer against a hypothetical process that no one knows anything about, we are pitting something that we know from experience *can* produce teleological systems against *something-I-know-not-what*, its features a mystery and its capacity to generate teleological systems equally mysterious. Given these alternatives, surely it isn't unreasonable to go with intelligent design.

But Dawkins also invokes a better response to our rehabilitated argument. When it comes to the origins of DNA or some progenitor self-replicating molecule, chance isn't such a bad explanation after all. Why? Because even the most staggeringly improbable coincidences become likely with enough *opportunity*. If I shuffle a deck and deal you five cards, the likelihood that I'll deal you a royal flush is low. But if I kept dealing for twenty years, it wouldn't be at all surprising if at some point I dealt a royal flush.

Dawkins' point about the origin of self-replicating molecules is this: *it only had to happen once* (p. 135). Once it's happened, the molecule will reproduce itself, making copies, organizing the basic materials around it into more and more self-replicating molecules. Evolution will be off and running. So, what's the likelihood that, among all the planets in the universe with the right conditions and building blocks, in all the trillions of years the universe has existed, a self-replicating molecule might be formed . . . once?

It's hard to establish the odds, of course. But the idea that chance might be responsible seems less than nutty, given the immense opportunity the universe provides. And, as Dawkins argues, we shouldn't be surprised that the fortunate event happened *here*, where there are people to take notice of the fact. That there are people around to take notice of the fact is a *consequence* of the fact that it happened here (p. 138). Had it happened elsewhere, evolution might have given rise to rational beings there who would have taken notice of it there.

Perhaps defenders of the design argument would do better to formulate it in terms of the "fine-tuning" of the universe. The fine-tuning argument, sometimes also called the anthropic argument, proceeds from the observation that if the basic physical constants of the universe (such as the gravitational constant) had been significantly different from what they in fact are, life as we know it could not have emerged, and we would never have existed. As Kenneth Miller (1999) puts the point, it's almost as if "the details of the physical universe have been chosen in such a way as to make life possible" (p. 228).

On the assumption that there is only one universe, this "fine-tuning" argument has considerable power. But if there are, as some physicists suggest, multiple universes (perhaps even an infinite number), then the immensity of opportunity might explain fine-tuning just as it does self-replicating molecules.[5]

But even if there is only one universe, there may be reason to question just how convincing the fine-tuning argument is. After all, we could imagine a universe much more conducive to life than the one in which we live. As Stenger puts the point, "any huge, random universe, regardless of its properties, will naturally develop at least a few tiny pockets of complexity within a vast sea of chaos, which is just what we see in our universe. We do not need either a designer or multiple universes to account for such rare deviations as are consistent with chance" (2007, p. 163). I am far from expert enough in physics to say whether Stenger is right that *any* "huge, random universe" would develop "pockets of complexity" (by which I assume he means stable environments in which complex organisms like ourselves endure over time). I suspect that, among reputable physicists, you wouldn't find anything near unanimous agreement on this point.

But the main lesson here is that the argument from design is hardly decisive. There is too much uncertainty to say with authority that the universe as a whole is a finely-tuned teleological system directed towards the creation of life (or some other improbable goal). This was a point that David Hume made centuries ago with regard to the argument from design (1989, pp. 32–3). And even though we know more about the cosmos than we did in Hume's day, the basic point still stands.

No matter how much we know about the world, there will always be more to know. What we have accomplished with our limited intellects is remarkable. But every new discovery brings us closer to another paradigm shift – another radical change in our understanding akin to what Copernicus achieved when he proposed that the Earth revolves around the sun, or what Darwin achieved when he proposed that complex organisms could evolve gradually through natural selection.

Our scientific understanding of the universe is a work in progress and so any conclusions we reach about intelligent design are always susceptible to revision. Two hundred years ago, complex biological organisms seemed to be a knock-down argument for the existence of an intelligent designer. Then along came Darwin. Will the newest directions in physics make an intelligent designer of the universe seem more likely, or less? Stenger thinks that given the current scientific picture of the cosmos, the supposition of a designer is entirely unneeded. Perhaps so. But if a new discovery in fifteen years offers a picture of the cosmos that is hard to explain by reference to chance alone, and if no naturalistic mechanism analogous to Darwin's theory presents itself, what is Stenger likely to say then? Probably the same thing Dawkins says in reply to intelligent design theorists who trot out examples of supposedly irreducible complexity: *Science is still working on it. Don't jump to conclusions.*

But why couldn't the same be said in reply to Stenger's judgment that the observed universe looks just as we'd expect were there no God? *Science is still working on it. Don't jump to conclusions.*

While science today may uncover a naturalistic explanation for what had before seemed inexplicable in naturalistic terms, thus silencing those heralding proof of a supernatural agent, science tomorrow may discover a new mystery that defies naturalistic explanation. Neither shift in the scientific terrain really tells us anything about the transcendent. The real lesson to be drawn here is that a provisional scientific picture of things – and every scientific picture is provisional – just shouldn't be invoked one way or another when it comes to the existence of the transcendent.

As Alister McGrath (McGrath and McGrath 2007) recently put the point, nature "can be interpreted in atheist, deist, theist and many other ways – but it does not demand to be interpreted in any of these" (pp. 45–6). This "conceptual malleability" of the empirical world may explain an observation that Stenger finds "rather amusing" – namely, that defenders of theism will routinely offer "two contradictory arguments for life requiring a creator." The first of these, the fine-tuning argument, holds that "the universe is so congenial to life that the universe must have been created with life in mind." The second argument holds that "the universe is so *uncongenial* to life that life could not have occurred by natural processes and so must have been created and be sustained by the constant actions of God" (Stenger 2007, pp. 163–4).

The reality is that however the facts are arranged, it is possible to interpret them in theistic *or* atheistic terms. And what this means is that both theists and atheists should probably stop trying to defend their interpretation by appeal to purely empirical evidence. Scientific pictures of the empirical world just don't offer much evidence either way concerning the existence of realities that transcend that world.

If I am right about this, then we should set the design argument aside. When it comes to whether it is reasonable to believe in a transcendent being that fulfills our ethico-religious hope, we need to look elsewhere.

Dawkins' Case Against Theism

But before we can look elsewhere, we need to consider Dawkins' case against God's existence which seeks to turn the key assumptions of the design argument against theistic belief. The idea behind Dawkins' argument isn't new. It was succinctly stated in the late 1970s by George Smith in his book, *Atheism: The Case Against God*. Smith notes that the design argument assumes that a complex, ordered system cannot be the result of chance and requires a designer. He then poses his challenge as follows:

> Who designed God? Surely, nothing as complex and intricate as a super-natural intelligence can be the result of mere "chance." Therefore, there must be a super-designer who designed God. But a super-designer would require a super-super-designer, and so on *ad infinitum*. Thus, by the premises of the teleological argument, we are led to an infinite series of transcendental designers – a "solution" that leaves much to be desired. (Smith 1979, p. 259)

Dawkins takes this thinking a bit further than Smith. Smith is simply trying to show that the design argument fails because it leads to an infinite regress. But Dawkins aims to show that the existence of God is highly *improbable*, and that the ultimate explanation of things must instead be what he calls a "self-bootstrapping crane" (2006, p. 155). By this, Dawkins means a system that follows the same basic pattern as Darwinian evolution: a simple system that operates mechanistically on simple elements to create more complex products. As more complex things emerge, they operate as elements in the system to generate ever-increasing levels of complexity.

Dawkins' objection to the God Hypothesis can be summed up as follows. He thinks that, for an intelligent creator of the universe to explain the enormously complex universe we live in, that creator would need to be enormously complex too. And so, when we explain the universe in terms of the creative efforts of a God, we have only shifted what needs to be explained back one level. In Dawkins' terms, "any God capable of designing a universe, carefully and foresightfully tuned to lead to our evolution, must be a supremely complex and improbable entity who needs an even bigger explanation than the one he is supposed to provide" (p. 147).

Dawkins does think that the complexity found in our universe needs to be explained. But explaining it in terms of an intelligent designer just leads to a regress. The only way out of the explanatory regress, in Dawkins' view, is to posit a "self-bootstrapping crane" as the ultimate explanation. "The first cause we seek," Dawkins insists, "must have been the simple basis for a self-bootstrapping crane which eventually raised the world as we know it into its present complex existence" (p. 155).

Since "self-bootstrapping cranes" do not need to be explained by reference to anything but chance, they can end the explanatory regress in a way that God cannot, since God is necessarily so complex that "His existence is going to need a mammoth explanation in its own right" (p. 149). According to Dawkins, "To suggest that the original prime mover was complicated enough to indulge in intelligent design . . . is tantamount to dealing yourself a perfect hand at bridge" (p. 155). And so, Dawkins concludes, "If (which I don't believe for a moment) our universe was designed, . . . the designer himself must be the end product of some kind of cumulative escalator or crane, perhaps a version of Darwinism in another universe" (p. 156).

If this line of argument is sounding familiar, it's probably because it has the very same formal structure as Aquinas' First and Second Ways. Just as Aquinas did, Dawkins notes that a certain kind of explanation leads to an infinite regress. He insists that an infinite regress explains nothing. And so he concludes that there needs to exist a regress-ending explanation of a different kind.

Dawkins' failure to fairly represent Aquinas is rendered all the more disturbing when we see that Dawkins' own thinking has precisely the same form. If Dawkins accepts the logical validity of his own reasoning, he should accept that of Aquinas.

And the most crucial feature of Aquinas' argument is the assumption that everything needs to be explained. The significance of Dawkins' implicit embrace of this assumption will be discussed in the next chapter. For now, I simply want to point it out and move on to critiquing Dawkins' case against theism.

A Fundamental Difficulty with Dawkins' Atheistic Argument

I have two main objections to Dawkins' case against theism. The second will emerge in the next chapter in the light of assessing the cosmological argument. My first objection, which I will consider here, challenges Dawkins' claim that *any intelligent being capable of designing, creating, and sustaining the entire universe would need to be exceedingly complex*. For ease of reference, let's call this the Principle of Necessary Complexity. If there is no good reason to embrace this principle, then Dawkins' atheistic argument collapses.

So, why does Dawkins think an intelligent designer of our universe *must* be complex? One might think this if one believed that the explanation for any complex thing must itself be complex. But this cannot be Dawkins' view. He thinks Darwin's theory has shown us how something simple can fully account for astonishing complexity.

For Dawkins, the trouble lies with the idea of an *intelligent designer* being simple. He thinks that any entity with the intelligence to design and create something else has to be complex . . . and the more complex the creation, the more complex the intelligent designer would have to be.

But why think that? Dawkins might claim that the scientific evidence supports this view. But would he be right about that? He surely could point out that, among biological species, a more complex brain seems to be a necessary, if not a sufficient, condition for more complex designing activities. But to move from this observation about biological phenomena to the judgment that this is a necessary truth about any conceivable entity would be a decidedly unscientific leap.

God, if He exists, is not a biological organism with a brain. He transcends the physical world and is usually said to be pure spirit. Does a pattern that seems to hold for physical entities also apply to spiritual ones? In a scathing review of *The God Delusion*, Alvin Plantinga (2007) points out that, by the definition of "complexity" proposed by Dawkins himself in *The Blind Watchmaker*, God wouldn't be complex at all. To quote Plantinga:

> According to (Dawkins') definition . . . something is complex if it has parts that are "arranged in a way that is unlikely to have arisen by chance alone." But of course God is a spirit, not a material object at all, and hence has no parts. A fortiori (as philosophers like to say) God doesn't have parts arranged in ways unlikely to have arisen by chance. Therefore, given the definition of complexity Dawkins himself proposes, God is not complex. (Plantinga 2007)

The basic lesson is this: when we're talking about God or another spiritual thing, "complexity" can't mean what it means when we're talking about physical objects. So what does Dawkins even mean when he says that God is complex? The inference from what is true of physical objects to what is true of spiritual ones cannot be straightforward, especially with respect to complexity.

Assuming we can overcome this problem, a scientific approach to the matter would, on the basis of what has been observed in the domain of biology, offer a hypothesis along the following lines: "*All* entities (including nonphysical ones) that use intelligence to design other things increase in complexity in proportion to the complexity of what they design." But a scientific approach would then seek to test this hypothesis. Scientists would be especially interested in determining whether the supposed correlation holds for entities that are different in kind from those in which the correlation has previously been observed. If a medicine is proven safe in rats, that would lead scientists to hypothesize that it might be safe for monkeys, too. But they wouldn't leap to the conclusion that what is true for rats has *got* to be true for monkeys or people. That hypothesis needs to be tested.

And if Dawkins' hypothesis about increasing complexity should prove to be untestable for the class of entities to which God belongs then, with respect to that class of entities, science would have nothing to say.

Now, I'd be more than surprised to hear that Dawkins has submitted a grant proposal to the Royal Society (the United Kingdom's national academy of science) to fund a scientific study assessing his complexity hypothesis with respect to the "transcendent class" of entities to which God belongs. After all, Dawkins doesn't believe this class exists. And even if he did believe in such a class, I doubt he'd be able to write into his grant proposal a convincing research methodology. After all, the "transcendent class" is nothing other than the class of things that fall *outside* the empirical world that science studies. Good luck getting the Royal Society (or any other granting institution) to fund a scientific study of *that* class.

In short, when Dawkins endorses the Principle of Necessary Complexity, it can't be on the basis of any science because this principle, as a general law pertaining to all entities including God, falls outside the scope of science. On such matters, critical inquiry must rely on something other than empirical observations – such as, for example, philosophical reflection.

Among the philosophers who have reflected on the complexity of God, we find St Thomas Aquinas, in the *Summa Theologica*, devoting an entire section to making the case that God must be wholly and altogether simple. Fully understanding his case for this view would require that we delve into his metaphysical system, but it is not my aim to devote such sustained attention to this question. Rather, I want to point out that Aquinas did not treat God's simplicity as self-evident but rather as an implication drawn from other conclusions already reached about God – for example, that God is the unchanging cause of change in other things. Aquinas concludes from this fact that there can be no distinction in God between what is actual and what is only potential since the unchanging source of all change must be fully actualized. He likewise concludes that other distinctions cannot apply to God. Since complexity requires distinctions, God cannot be complex.[6]

Dawkins offers nothing of this sort in defense of his contrary claim that God *must* be complex. Rather, it just seems intuitively obvious to him. At the root of Dawkins' thinking is a powerful intuition that an intelligent designer who designed the entire universe would just *have* to be complex (in *some* sense), even if that designer were non-physical and thus fell into a class entirely beyond the scope of his experience.

Let me say that I don't think there is anything intrinsically wrong with reasoning on the basis of strong intuitions. In fact, with some important qualifications, I think we should trust our deepest and clearest intellectual intuitions unless we encounter compelling reasons to question them. But if we can't say more in defense of a principle than that *this is my strong intuition*, we shouldn't expect to convince those whose intuitions differ from our own.

And the fact is this: reasonable people have different intuitions about things. All else being equal, there may be nothing unreasonable about Dawkins' endorsement of the Principle of Necessary Complexity, even if all he can say in its favor is that it just seems obvious to him. But someone with a different intuition isn't thereby unreasonable.

Rationality isn't as simple as that. Reasonable people can disagree, even on basic matters. I am not suggesting that you can believe just anything and be reasonable. But perhaps the difference between theists and atheists is that they have different basic intuitions – intuitions that are just as undefended, but just as reasonable, as Dawkins' intuition that intelligent designers need to be complex.

6

Philosophy and God's Existence, Part II

Why is there something rather than nothing?

When I first heard this question, I was a floundering college sophomore majoring in biology. In a real sense, it was this question that sparked my passion for philosophy. It struck me as the sort of vital question whose answer would ripple through your entire view of life, fundamentally shaping your sense of what it all means.

And as I explored the question, I couldn't help but stumble across an answer that's become increasingly popular in modern times: *No reason.*

I shook my head. I couldn't accept that answer. It didn't just strike me as absurd. It struck me as making *life* absurd. At the foundation of reality and the richness of life, there is . . . nothing.

The cosmological argument begins with the intuition that such an answer is untenable. And if you share this intuition, then the cosmological argument – at least in the version championed by Gottfried Leibniz and Samuel Clarke – will lead you to conclude that there is a transcendent reason for it all, beyond what science can see, something that sounds awfully like God.

Or so I will argue in this chapter.

The Cosmological Argument of Leibniz and Clarke

In an essay from 1697 entitled "On the Ultimate Origination of the Universe," Gottfried Wilhelm von Leibniz offered the following argument:

> Let us suppose a book entitled *The Elements of Geometry* to have existed eternally, one edition having always been copied from the preceding: it is evident then that, although you can account for the present copy by refer-

ence to the past copy which it reproduces, yet, however far back you go in the series of reproductions, you can never arrive at a complete examination, since you always will have to ask why at all times these books have existed, that is, why there have been any books at all and why this book in particular. What is true concerning these books is equally true concerning the diverse states of the world, for here too the following state is in some way a copy of the preceding one (although changed according to certain laws). However far you turn back to antecedent states, you will never discover in any or all of these states the full reason why there is a world rather than nothing, nor why it is such as it is.

You may well suppose the world to be eternal; yet what you thus posit is nothing but the succession of states, and you will not find the sufficient reason in any one of them, nor will you get any nearer to accounting rationally for the world by taking any number of them together: the reason must therefore be sought elsewhere . . . Hence, it is evident that even by supposing the world to be eternal, the recourse to an ultimate cause of the universe beyond this world, that is, to God, cannot be avoided. (Leibniz 1965b, pp. 84–5)

The similarity between Aquinas' first three Ways and Leibniz's argument here is obvious, which is why all are considered versions of the cosmological argument. But there are important differences. In each of his arguments, Aquinas points to a regress of explanations, insists that an *infinite* regress is impossible, and concludes that a regress-ending entity must exist.

Leibniz, however, grants for argument's sake that you can always explain the present state of things by appeal to a preceding one that gives rise to it according to certain laws. In short, he grants that an infinite regress of *scientific* explanations – in terms of antecedent conditions and observable laws – is possible. His point is that even if we grant this, we still need "an ultimate cause of the universe beyond this world" in order to explain why this infinite chain of contingent states exists at all.

In a brilliant work of compact argumentation called *The Monadology*, Leibniz lays out this argument more formally. He notes that it presupposes what he calls "the principle of sufficient reason" (hereafter PSR), which he expresses as follows: "no fact can be true or existing and no statement truthful without a sufficient reason for its being so and not different; albeit these reasons most frequently must remain unknown to us" (1965c, p. 153). The last clause of this principle reveals something important: Leibniz isn't referring to the reasons people *have* for believing such-and-such, but to reasons "out there" to be discovered – the things that, if only we knew them, would explain why the world is as it is. By a *reason* Leibniz means, roughly, what makes a truth true.

Leibniz observes that there are different kinds of truths and they need to be explained in different ways. Logically necessary truths (or "truths of reason") explain themselves. You analyze a logical theorem into its component ideas and you see that those ideas are related to each other in precisely the way the theorem says they are. And that's what makes it true. But matters of fact are different. What makes it true that Sally is at the café eating hummus? Nothing about the meaning of "Sally" and "café" and "hummus" makes it true. Were she in her office sheepishly eating Skippy peanut butter from the jar, *that* would be true. And, knowing Sally (name changed to protect the innocent!), that might just be the truth.

Matters of fact *could* have been different than they are. They are contingent rather than necessary. And so we need to look outside of them for their explanation. But, according to Leibniz, looking to *other* contingent facts won't do the job, because then those facts will need to be accounted for too, "so that nothing is gained by such an analysis" (p. 153). He goes on: "The sufficient or ultimate reason must therefore exist outside the succession or series of contingent particulars, infinite though the series may be. Consequently, the ultimate reason of all things must subsist in a necessary substance . . . this substance is what we call *God*" (pp. 153–4). Further on, he summarizes his main point as follows: "For the sufficient and ultimate reason for these [contingent beings] can lie only in the necessary being *which has in itself the reason for its existence*" (p. 155).

This phrasing is helpful for understanding Leibniz's argument. The crucial fact about contingent beings is that the reason for their existence lies *in something else*. The crucial fact about a necessary being is that the reason for its existence lies *in itself*. If everything needs to have a reason for its existence, then these options exhaust the possibilities: a thing's existence is explained either by something else or by itself.

Samuel Clarke, a contemporary of Leibniz, formulated essentially the same argument but, instead of the language of contingency and necessity that Leibniz inherited from Aquinas, Clarke used the terms "*dependent* being" (a being whose existence is explained by something else) and "*self-existent* being" (one whose very nature explains its own existence, such that it could not have failed to exist).[1]

Clarke argues that even if every dependent being is explained by a previous one in an infinite regress, we still need to explain the whole collection of dependent beings. Since no member or subset explains itself, there is nothing *in* the collection that explains the whole. And so, to explain the existence of the entire collection of dependent things, we need something that isn't part of that collection – in other words, something beyond the universe of dependent things that can explain *both* itself *and* everything else. In short: we need a self-existent or necessary being.

To better see the point Clarke and Leibniz are making, it may help to borrow an example from one of their critics, Paul Edwards (1959). Following Hume, Edwards challenges the claim that, even if every dependent thing is explained by a preceding one, we still haven't explained the whole. Edwards wants to deny this.

How does he do it? He asks us to imagine a group of five Eskimos standing on a street corner in New York City. Suppose you ask why this group is in New York, and I tell you that the first Eskimo was fleeing the cold northern climes, the second is the wife of the first, the third is their child, the fourth came to audition for a TV gig, and the fifth is a private detective keeping tabs on the fourth. Since I've explained why *each* Eskimo is in New York, haven't I thereby also explained why the *group* is in New York? Edwards thinks so, and he draws the following conclusion: if you've explained each member of a set, then you've explained the entire set. And so he concludes that, if every dependent being is explained in terms of another one, then the whole collection of dependent beings has been adequately explained (Edwards 1959, pp. 71–2).

But is he right? Suppose you asked me why the five Eskimos were in New York and I gave you the following answer: "Eskimo 1 followed Eskimo 2, who followed Eskimo 3, who followed Eskimo 4, who followed Eskimo 5. And Eskimo 5 is in New York because he followed Eskimo 1."

On hearing this answer, would you say, "Aha! It all makes sense now"? Of course not. Because this answer *doesn't explain anything*. So what's the difference between Edwards' explanations for the Eskimos' presence in New York and mine? In Edwards' case, the presence of Eskimos 1 and 4 is explained by something *outside* the group. In my case, all the explanations are *internal* – that is, the presence of each Eskimo is explained exclusively by reference to the presence of another one. And in no case is the presence of any Eskimo *self*-explanatory. To explain the group, we need at least one *external* explanation. If we have nothing but *internal* explanations, then nothing's been explained.

And when every dependent being is explained in terms of another one in an endless regress, what we have is a case analogous to every Eskimo's presence in New York being explained by the presence of another one.

The explanations are all internal and no member of the set explains itself.[2]

And so the insight of Leibniz and Clarke holds good: an infinite regress of explanations in terms of other contingent beings *doesn't explain anything.* If there is to be a reason for the existence of the universe, we need something that has the explanation for its existence somehow in itself.

Such a being would be like nothing in ordinary experience. If this argument succeeds, it shows that the existence of every contingent thing is explained by a mysterious reality beyond the world of contingent things encountered with our senses. It shows, in short, that there exists something that is both *transcendent* (it falls outside the empirical world) and *fundamental* (it explains the existence of everything else).

The cosmological argument tells us nothing about the character of this reality and hence falls short of proving *God's* existence. In order to establish the existence of God – conceived as a being that fulfills our ethico-religious hope – we'd need to show that there exists a fundamental reality beyond what science sees *that says yes to goodness.* At best, the cosmological argument shows that there exists a fundamental reality beyond what science sees.

But this conclusion is hardly trivial. It's an important step in the direction of God. Before we can embrace it, however, we must consider some objections.

Ontological Arguments and the Concept of a Necessary Being

For Leibniz, a necessary being is one that "has in itself the reason of its existence." It is a being "whose essence implies its existence, that is, to which it suffices to be possible in order to be actual" (Leibniz 1965c, p. 155).

I must admit I cannot imagine what such a being would be like. But David Hume didn't just express perplexity about such an idea. He claimed that the idea of something that *has* to exist makes no sense. In his *Dialogues Concerning Natural Religion,* he reasons as follows: Anything that I can imagine to exist I can also imagine *not* to exist. And if I can imagine it, it's possible. Non-existence is therefore never impossible, and existence is never necessary. And so there is no being whose existence is necessary (Hume 1989, pp. 74–5).

But perhaps Hume is operating with a faulty principle here. Perhaps the human capacity to imagine things is not a perfect measure of what's possible.

Let me explain. Hume believed that empirical experience is the basis of everything we can think or believe. *All* our ideas, he thought, are derived from sense impressions. We can break these ideas down into their simplest components and recombine them in our imaginations – for example, we can combine the idea of a horn with that of a horse to generate the idea of a unicorn. But we can have no ideas whose basic elements aren't derived from sense experience. For him, to *conceive* or *imagine* something just means to take the basic elements of sense experience and recombine them into a picture of how empirical reality *might* be arranged.

But maybe there are realities that we just can't imagine in this way at all. What's true of everything we can imagine may not hold for realities we can't imagine. And so defenders of the cosmological argument might respond to Hume in the following way: That everything we can *imagine* as existing is also something we can imagine as non-existent doesn't tell us anything about those entities that *defy imagination*. And what the cosmological argument shows us is that, in order to explain why there is something rather than nothing, there must exist precisely this sort of thing: *something that defies imagination*. Even if we can't imagine what a necessary being would have to be like in order to *be* necessary, we nevertheless must conclude that such a being exists.

This strikes me as an important answer to Hume. Since the cosmological argument concludes that there must exist something that defies ordinary imagination, it would amount to question-begging to blithely assume that the only things that can exist are those we can imagine in Hume's sense.

Furthermore, imagination in Hume's sense may not be the only way to get at an idea. When Hume says there is nothing we can conceive of as existing which we cannot also conceive of as non-existent, he is deliberately dismissing the great medieval theologian and philosopher, St Anselm. Anselm thought, contrary to Hume, that our intellects can grasp the idea of a being whose existence is necessary, even if we can't *imagine* what this being is like in Hume's sense.

And what idea is this? It's Anselm's concept of God: *the being than which none greater can be thought.* And what does that mean? More power is greater than less, and so God would have infinite power. More knowledge is greater than less, and so God would be all-knowing. More goodness is better than less, and so God would be perfectly good. We can't imagine infinite greatness in Hume's sense, any more than we can picture in our heads an infinite series of numbers. But we can have *some* concept of an infinite series because we can count upwards and then say, *and so on*. A similar move can give us *some* concept of infinite greatness, even if we can't imagine it.

Anselm famously argues that one thing we can know about such a being is that it exists. Why? Because a being that exists is greater than one that doesn't. And so the greatest conceivable being wouldn't be the greatest conceivable being unless it actually existed. A being whose essence is maximal greatness would possess every "great-making quality" or "perfection" – including existence. And so a being with that essence *has* to exist (Anselm 1998, pp. 87–8).

Anselm's argument here, dubbed the *ontological argument* for God's existence, has generated enormous controversy since he first introduced it in the eleventh century. The argument just seems too easy. How could you possibly prove that God exists just by reflecting on the concept of God? But however fishy the argument seems, it isn't easy to pin down just what the problem is.

One thinker who thought he'd done it was Kant. He argued that existence cannot be part of the concept of anything, let alone God, because to say that something exists is just to say that a concept has an instance in the real world. It doesn't add anything *to* our concept. In Kant's terms, existence is "not a real predicate" (Kant 1958, pp. 282–3).[3]

The philosopher Norman Malcolm (1960) expresses Kant's objection as follows:

> The doctrine that existence is a perfection is remarkably queer. It makes sense and is true to say that my future house will be a better one if it is insulated than if it is not insulated; but what could it mean to say that it will be a better house if it exists than if it does not? (p. 43)

When you say a house has hardwood floors or is two stories tall, you've added to the idea of the house. You've described it. But when you say it exists, you haven't *described* the house. You've just said that a house *as described* is found in the world. And so existence doesn't add anything to our idea of something, let alone make it the idea of something better. In Malcolm's terms, existence isn't "a perfection."

Dawkins relies on this passage from Malcolm in his cursory attack on Anselm – but fails to point out that the passage comes from the very article in which Malcolm identified and *defended* a second version of Anselm's argument (which appears alongside the first version but was historically overlooked). Since Dawkins got the quote from an internet encyclopedia article, he apparently doesn't know this.[4]

So what is this second version of Anselm's argument? Instead of arguing that the concept of God contains the concept of *existence*, the second version holds that it contains the concept of existing *necessarily* rather than contingently. While Malcolm agrees with Kant that *existence* is not "a perfection," *existing necessarily* is a different matter (p. 46). To say that God exists necessarily rather than just contingently is to *describe* God, not just say that a being fitting God's description is found in reality. It tells us that if God is found in the world, it's because God is found in every possible world. Saying that God exists may not add anything substantive to our idea of God, but saying that His non-existence is impossible surely does.

In studying the *Proslogion*, Malcolm finds Anselm arguing that existing necessarily is part of the concept of a "greatest conceivable being" – or, in Malcolm's terms, the concept of an "absolutely unlimited being" (p. 47). Malcolm agrees, arguing that as a matter of definition an unlimited being would exist under *all possible circumstances* – that is to say, necessarily. Why? Think of it this way. Suppose an unlimited being existed under some possible circumstances but not others. If so, we'd need to ask why the being doesn't exist in some circumstances. Is it because something is missing from those circumstances which the being *needs* in order to exist? Is it because there is something in those circumstances which *prevents* it from existing? Either answer supposes a limitation or constraint and hence is inconsistent with the idea of an *unlimited* being (p. 47).

The inconsistency here arises only when you say that an unlimited being is possible but not actual. To exist under some conditions, it must exist under all – since only then would it be an unlimited being. But no comparable inconsistency arises if you deny that such a being exists under *any* possible conditions. What this means is that an unlimited being is either necessary or impossible (p. 49). Grant that such a being is possible and you've conceded that it exists under all possible conditions, including those that obtain in the real world.

Leibniz seems to have something like this version of the ontological argument in mind when he discusses the essence of God. He explicitly claims, in the *Monadology*, that God's *possibility* would be sufficient for God's *actuality*. And he goes on to argue that "nothing can hinder the possibility of the substance which contains no limit, no negation, and hence no contradiction" (Leibniz 1965c, p. 155).

This final statement is a rich argument in its own right and is mirrored centuries later by Malcolm (1960, p. 50). The idea seems to be that the only things that are impossible are things that involve a contradiction and that the concept of an infinite being *cannot* involve a contradiction since contradictions require that something be both affirmed and negated, and negations are only true of limited beings. So, an unlimited being is possible and therefore has to exist.

This line of thought is admittedly controversial. But my aim here is not, ultimately, to defend its soundness. Rather, it is to explore the idea of a necessary being. The conclusion of the cosmological argument is that, in order to explain the existence of the universe, we must posit something that exists necessarily, whose very nature implies existence. What the ontological argument offers us is at least one approach to understanding what kind of nature or essence could *do* this: an essence stripped of all the limitations and restrictions that accompany our concepts of more ordinary things.

The idea of a necessary being remains mysterious. The ongoing controversy surrounding the ontological argument reveals, if nothing else, that it's hard for us mere mortals to wrap our brains around the infinite. In my judgment, the ontological argument really amounts to a plea for humility when confronting the infinite since so many of our commonsense assumptions break down in the face of it. Just because, for every *limited* being I can imagine, I can conceive of it as existing or not, it doesn't follow that this is true of an *infinite* being. If Malcolm (following Anselm) is right, either this concept names something impossible, or it names a being that exists necessarily.

And so, if you think an infinite being might be possible (and to insist confidently that it's impossible is just the kind of intellectual arrogance we should be cautious of when dealing with the infinite), then such a being would be a good candidate for the necessary being that, according to the cosmological argument, must exist in order to explain the world.

None of this is to say that a necessary being is something our minds can conceptualize in such a way as to provide an understanding of why its existence is necessary. But even if it is impossible for us to imagine what something would have to be like in order to exist necessarily, there may still be good reasons to conclude that there *is* such a being. The limits of what the human mind can fathom might not track the limits of reality. "Unimaginable" does not mean "incoherent." If the cosmological argument is sound, then the fact that its conclusion posits something that defies human understanding shouldn't be treated as a reason to reject that conclusion since doing so amounts to unjustifiably supposing, in a question-begging way, that the limits of what we can imagine *do* track reality's limits.

Before moving on, I want to make good on a promise. In the last chapter I promised a second objection to Dawkins' argument against God's existence. We now have the insights needed to lay it out. Dawkins claims that God's existence is highly *improbable* since any intelligent creator of the universe would have to be exceedingly complex and anything exceedingly complex is also highly improbable.

But here's the problem. For Leibniz and Clarke, "God" names the necessary being that has to exist in order to explain the universe. But while you might think that such a being is impossible, you cannot say that it's improbable. The existence of a *contingent* being with the power to design and create the universe might coherently be called improbable; but it makes no sense to make such a claim about a *necessary* being.

In short, Dawkins pursues the question of God's existence as if God were a being of the same kind as the contingent beings in the universe that scientists study. He never takes seriously the foundational premise of theism, namely, that there is a different order of reality, something radically unlike anything in the empirical world, a reality that explains itself, in relation to which our mundane ways of thinking just don't apply.

Why Not a Self-Existent Universe?

I turn now to another important objection to the cosmological argument. Once again, David Hume offers a seminal statement of it. He asks "why may not the material universe be the necessarily existent Being . . . ? We dare not affirm that we know all the qualities of matter; and for aught we can determine, it may contain some qualities which, were they known, would make its non-existence appear as great a contradiction as that twice two is five." He goes on to observe that, if God is necessary, it's by virtue of qualities inconceivable to us. But then, "no reason can be assigned why these qualities may not belong to matter. As they are altogether unknown and inconceivable, they can never be proved incompatible with it" (Hume 1989, p. 75).

Daniel Dennett raises essentially the same objection in *Breaking the Spell*. "What caused God?" he asks. "The reply that God is self-caused (somehow) then raises the rebuttal: If something can be self-caused, why can't the universe as a whole be the thing that is self-caused?" (Dennett 2006, p. 242)

Dennett leaves the argument at that. Apparently, he thinks such a hand-waving dismissal is sufficient to dispense with the likes of Leibniz – who, by the way, invented the infinitesimal calculus that revolutionized mathematics and the sciences. A gesture of dismissal is apparently enough to do away with one of the greatest geniuses in history.

But is Dennett right? Does this Humean objection undermine the Leibniz/Clarke version of the cosmological argument? Recall that their argument makes a case for something that has the explanation for its existence internal to its own nature. Such a being is mysterious. As Hume himself observes, nothing in our ordinary experience, nor anything we can piece together from ideas derived from that experience, has this property of self-existence. So what, exactly, is Dennett proposing when he suggests the universe *itself* might be self-existent?

The proposal amounts to this: there is something about the universe that transcends empirical experience and is thus essentially mysterious. For the universe to explain its own existence, there needs to be more to it than meets the empirical eye. The universe must have a *supernatural* side to it that's inaccessible to science.

But those with a lofty view of science may balk here. If there's something about the universe that makes it self-existent, why assume that such an element must be essentially outside the scope of empirical investigation?

The answer comes from Hume himself, in his first objection to the cosmological argument. Science is rooted in empirical observation. It begins by finding observable regularities, posits theories to explain those regularities, and then tests those theories against the observable world. And as Hume points out, the observable world is one in which the question of *existence* is always separable from the *idea* of a thing. No matter how much we combine and recombine the basic ideas derived from sense experience, even with the help of mind-bending mathematical models, we'll never come up with something which could not have failed to exist.

The world of sense experience – the world that science investigates – is a world of contingent realities. And so, if the existence of the universe *is* necessary, it is so by virtue of something non-empirical, something outside the realm of science. And so Dennett's retort to the cosmological argument amounts to claiming that there is a supernatural dimension to the universe.

But perhaps I am missing something here. Victor Stenger argues that science may already have answered the question that motivates the cos-

mological argument – namely, why there is something rather than nothing. His reasoning runs as follows:

> many simple systems of particles are unstable, that is, have limited lifetimes
> as they undergo spontaneous phase transition to more complex structures
> of lower energy. Since "nothing" is as simple as it gets, we cannot expect it
> to be very stable. It would likely undergo a spontaneous phase transition to
> something more complicated, like a universe containing matter. The tran-
> sition from nothing-to-something is a natural one, not requiring any agent.
> (Stenger 2007, p. 133)

Stenger seems to think that the reason for the universe's existence can be
found within the regularities that science observes. Science has observed
that simple particles and structures are unstable and tend towards more
complex things. This natural tendency would operate on nothingness – the
simplest of all things – to create the universe.

If Stenger is right, we might not need a mysterious element inaccessible
to science in order to explain how the universe could explain its own
existence. It explains itself by virtue of being naturally more stable than
nothing.

But there are so many problems with Stenger's thinking here that I hardly
know where to begin. First, there's his claim that nothingness is the
simplest of all things. This is a category mistake. *Things* are simple or complex. *Nothingness* is neither simple nor complex. There's nothing there to
be simple or complex.

Second, the principle that simple things are unstable is an observed regularity in the universe. It's a law *of* this universe, if you will. Suppose Stenger
has in mind an existing universe – an expanse of space-time regulated by
laws – but one that happens to have nothing in it. And suppose he imagines that one of the laws regulating this empty universe is that vacuums
are unstable and hence spontaneously resolve into matter and energy. If
that is what he has in mind, then he hasn't explained the origins of the
universe at all. What he's done is offer a scientific account of how an already
existing universe, complete with physical laws, would – in accordance with
those laws – move from being empty to containing matter and energy.

But where did this empty space, governed by these laws, come from? He
hasn't explained *that*. But perhaps I've misunderstood him. Perhaps he
means that this law – that nothingness spontaneously resolves into matter
and energy (rather than into, say, immaterial spirits) – is some fundamental
law *beyond* the universe, according to which universes come into being.

But if this is what he means, then isn't he positing the existence of a transcendent realm beyond any universe and saying that there is this law operative in that realm? Is it legitimate to apply observations made about *our* universe to some realm *beyond* our universe – and so infer a transcendent law that brings material universes into being?

But let us set these problems aside. The fact remains that even if there is some law discovered by science which holds that nothingness in the truest sense is unstable, we can still ask: why is this so? We could certainly imagine nothingness being stable. It doesn't seem necessary that nothingness is unstable.

And if the instability of nothingness is a contingent fact, then Stenger's odd little argument hardly brings us to a self-existent reality that explains itself. The fact is that whenever science says that something is necessary, they always mean that it is necessary relative to some more basic rule or principle. But anything that is necessary in this sense is necessary only dependently: it gets its necessity from something else. We are back to the cosmological argument. We need something to end the regress: something that gets its necessity from itself. And such a thing is fundamentally mysterious.

And so, if the universe is self-existent, it is by virtue of some fundamentally mysterious element that falls outside the scope of science as we know it.

What Dennett and Hume get right is this: If the cosmological argument shows anything, it's that underlying the world of contingent and dependent things encountered in ordinary experience, there's a different kind of reality – one that's self-existent or necessary. It doesn't tell us what this necessary or self-existent reality is *like*.

But Leibniz and Clarke know that. What they think the argument establishes is the existence of a necessary or self-existent being. This conclusion does not rule out, in advance, the hypothesis that the self-existent being is identical with the universe – at least not so long as we add the qualifier that there has to be more to the universe than any empirical investigation can discern.

In short, what the cosmological argument shows, if anything, is that there needs to be a dimension to reality that is, in an important sense, religious: an element that is fundamental (it explains the existence of everything else) and transcendent (it lies outside the scope of normal empirical investigation). Theism identifies this element with a personal God. Pantheism identifies it with the universe itself but only by holding that there is more to the universe than the surface reality that science can see.

Of course, Leibniz and Clarke both reject pantheism, but their reasons are not that the cosmological argument as such rules it out. They have other arguments. If Dennett and Hume want to know why anyone would think that the necessary cause of the universe should be identified with a personal God (rather than with some pantheistic deity continuous with the universe), they should at least look at what Leibniz and Clarke and others have to say on that subject. Their arguments may be unconvincing. But it's unfair to foist upon those who advance the cosmological argument the false view that this argument is supposed to tell us more than what it's intended to prove.

In any event, I doubt that when Dennett sets out to challenge the cosmological argument, he means to make a case for pantheistic religion. If the cosmological argument succeeds in showing that either theism or pantheism is true, it has accomplished something remarkable. Its conclusion may not be that a personal and loving God exists but it's a major step in that direction: it points to a religious reality.

In Chapter 4, we saw that science cannot exclude the possibility that there's a realm beyond the empirical one in which our ethico-religious hope might find fulfillment. What the cosmological argument does, if it succeeds, is show that there *is* such a realm.

But before we can say this conclusively, we must consider one more objection.

The Contestable Principle of Sufficient Reason

By far the most important objection to the cosmological argument attacks the principle that underlies it: the principle of sufficient reason, or PSR. Put simply, PSR says that *for everything that is the case, there is a sufficient reason why it, rather than something else, is the case.*

If we reject this principle, we can always hold that the existence of the universe is just a "brute fact." We could hold that there is no explanation for the universe, no *reason* why there is something rather than nothing.

And why shouldn't we hold this? We can certainly imagine things just popping into existence for no reason at all. And, as David Hume argued, if we can imagine it, then it's not logically impossible. So, the principle of sufficient reason isn't a logically necessary truth since we can imagine things happening that defy it.

And there is no compelling empirical basis for embracing it. As John Mackie points out in *The Miracle of Theism*, "Even if, within the world, everything seemed to have a sufficient reason, that is, a cause in accordance with some regularity, with like causes producing like effects, this would give us little ground for expecting the world as a whole, or its basic causal laws themselves, to have a sufficient reason of some different sort" (Mackie 1982, p. 85).

Mackie's point is this. Suppose we conclude on the basis of our observation of the universe that every event and state of affairs in the empirical world can be explained in terms of scientific laws and antecedent conditions. Even if this is true, there wouldn't be any reason to infer that the world as a whole needs to be explained in what would have to be some very different way. As Bertrand Russell once put it, the fact that every person has a mother is not a reason to conclude that humanity as a whole has a mother (Copleston and Russell 1964, p. 175).

And so, we're not required to accept PSR as a matter of logic and we can't infer it from empirical observations about how the world works. So why accept it at all? Why not just say that the existence of the universe as a whole is an unexplained brute fact?

I want to begin my reply in what might be a surprising way. I want to say that, on one level, this objection succeeds. It calls into question the view, rather common in earlier ages, that we're rationally *required* to accept PSR. But it might still be reasonable to accept PSR even if we aren't rationally required to accept it. It might be one of those principles that reasonable people have every right to accept. If so, then it's also reasonable to accept what follows from PSR – namely that a self-existent being exists.

Put simply, the cosmological argument may not *prove* to the skeptic that there is a self-existent being since that skeptic might reasonably deny PSR. But the argument may still show that it is entirely *reasonable* to believe in such a being, so long as PSR is a reasonable principle. And it may show, furthermore, than anyone who in fact accepts PSR ought to accept that a self-existent being exists.

As I pointed out in the last chapter, it certainly looks as if Dawkins accepts PSR as part of his case against religion. If that's true, then unless he's prepared to change his basic assumptions, he'll have to accept the conclusion of the cosmological argument – that there exists an extraordinary reality that transcends the world of ordinary experience.

Of course, I might be misreading him, or Dawkins might be misstating his own position. And if PSR isn't the kind of principle that a reasonable person could accept, then the implications of Dawkins' assumptions don't much matter. If he's being unreasonable in accepting PSR, then he should change his views on that matter, and no one else should follow his lead.

And so the crucial question becomes whether PSR is a principle that one could reasonably accept (even if one could also reasonably reject it). That some of the greatest thinkers in history – such as Leibniz – have accepted it is significant but hardly decisive. Even the greatest among us might be selectively unreasonable.

But before we can evaluate how reasonable it is to accept PSR, we need to look more closely at the principle itself. As stated by Leibniz, the principle seems all-encompassing. It covers every true statement, every matter of fact. But wouldn't PSR, stated in such sweeping terms, rule out things happening by chance?

In fact, there are numerous competing formulations of PSR. This is true, in part, because many who accept the idea that there is, in some sense, an explanation for everything *also* believe that many things happen by chance. Similar difficulties arise when we reflect on free choices: can my choice be free if there is a sufficient reason why I chose *this* rather than something else?

One way to avoid these problems is to understand PSR as a principle about the existence of things. What needs to be explained, on this view, is why things exist. If the existence of everything needs to be explained, we're still left with Clarke's alternatives: either a thing's existence is explained by something else (a dependent being), or by itself (a self-existent being). And so, for example, Norman Kretzmann (1999) states PSR as follows: "Every existing thing has a reason for its existence either in the necessity of its own nature or in the causal efficacy of some other beings" (p. 65). Conceived in this way, PSR leaves room for chance events (so long as they involve things that already exist) and free choices (which are events that take place *in* existing agents).

But I want to propose a somewhat different way of thinking about PSR. Suppose I toss a coin and it lands heads up. Why did it land heads up? If I answer, "Chance," most people would probably find that a perfectly good explanation. But how could chance be an explanation? The answer lies, I think, in the fact that sometimes the laws of nature and the existing conditions, instead of determining what will happen next, determine the probability of various outcomes within a range of possibilities. These laws and conditions basically make it true that no specific outcome from within this range *has* to happen. That is, they make it true that (barring a transcendent influence) chance must settle the matter.

The tossed coin seems like such a case. There's no reason why the coin landed heads rather than tails. That was just chance. But there *is* a reason why chance had to settle the matter.

Consider an example that touches on the issue of free choice (a full treatment of freedom goes far beyond what I can do here). Specifically, consider a case of choosing arbitrarily. I'm at a restaurant and there are two things on the menu that look delicious: the roasted duck with the brie soufflé and dried cherry chutney, and the grilled salmon on a bed of couscous with a dill hollandaise sauce. My waitress tells me both are wonderful.

And I'm stuck. I just can't decide, but I can't keep putting the waitress off. After all, my wife and I are on our first date since our second baby was born and we don't want to miss the start of *Spamalot*. And so I choose . . . arbitrarily.

If you asked why I chose the duck, I wouldn't say, "No reason." What I'd say is this: "I had to choose something. I was hungry. The duck and salmon both looked good. I knew I'd be happy with either one. It was time to decide. And so I flipped a coin in my head, and it landed duck-side up."

In other words, the arbitrary choice happened for a reason, even if there's no reason apart from arbitrariness why I settled on the duck.

In my view, the most plausible version of PSR is not one that rules out chance events (or arbitrariness) but one that fixes such events *within a broader framework of explanation*. That is, it is a version of PSR which holds that when things happen by chance, there is a reason why things happen by chance. And when that's true, we tend to accept chance as part of the explanation of why things are as they are rather than some other way.

And so, when we say there's a sufficient reason for why things are as they are, we don't mean to rule out chance events (or arbitrary choices) but to say that, when things do happen by chance, there is a sufficient reason why they do. We might formulate this version of PSR as follows: *For everything that is the case, there is either a sufficient reason why it (rather than something else) is the case, or a sufficient reason why the precise determination of what is the case must be a matter of chance (or arbitrariness).*[5]

What PSR in this form rules out is having chance events where there is no reason why things happen by chance. And this means that chance cannot be the "ultimate" explanation. If you ask me why the coin landed heads up, "chance" seems to be the best answer. But if you ask me why there is something rather than nothing, "chance" doesn't seem like any answer at all. It's not that chance seems *unlikely* to be the reason why there is something rather than nothing (the way that it seems unlikely to be the reason why armadillos exist). Instead, "chance" is no answer to the question. It amounts to saying, "Your question has no answer." When chance is offered as an *ultimate* explanation that isn't fixed within a broader explanatory framework, it basically does away with explanation altogether.

What PSR in my form holds is that even if randomness exists, that randomness is explicable because it occurs within a broader framework that's explicable. It implies, in short, that despite the randomness in the world, there really are explanations. And that simply wouldn't be true if the universe itself has no explanation.

Let's reflect on this last point. If everything in the universe is "explained" in terms of law-like regularities and antecedent conditions, even at the most general level, but the most general regularities themselves are not explained (why *these* regularities rather than some *other* ones?) and the existence of the universe is not explained, then nothing has really been explained. Rather, all we have done is trace out the pattern of things at the most general level.

It would be like looking at a Norwegian sweater, describing its pattern, and then saying, "See, the reason why there is black yarn on this spot is because that is what the pattern calls for. White yarn would break the pattern." This may *sound* like an explanation but it's really just a *description*. If we give up on PSR, what we've really done is embraced the view that we can describe the universe (hopefully in the most general conceivable terms) but cannot explain it – not because of some limitation in our capacities but because there just is no reason out there why anything is as it is.

So the question comes down to this: could a reasonable person accept PSR (in a form that allows for chance events)? Or must every reasonable person do away with PSR altogether and say that "no reason" is the ultimate answer to our most basic questions?

I can think of only one plausible argument for the latter. It comes from science. Recent discoveries in quantum physics have led to the conclusion that what are called "virtual particles" can pop in and out of existence spontaneously. Richard Morris describes these discoveries in the following way:

particles can come into existence for short periods of time even when there is not enough energy to create them. In effect, they are created from uncertainties in energy. One could say that they briefly "borrow" the energy required for their creation, and then, a short time later, they pay the "debt" back and disappear again. Since these particles do not have a permanent existence, they are called virtual particles. (Morris 1990, p. 24)

It could be argued that these discoveries count against PSR because they tell us that something can come into existence from nothing, spontaneously, for no reason at all.[6]

But does the empirical evidence here really count against PSR? If you're committed (as a matter of faith?) to the view that nothing exists beyond what can be observed in the empirical world (a view sometimes called *naturalism*), then the spontaneous emergence of virtual particles in a vacuum would lead you to conclude that things can come into existence without any reason – from nothing. And so you might reject PSR. But if you're committed to PSR, then the scientific evidence would lead you to conclude that there needs to exist an otherworldly explanation for the origination of virtual particles. And so you would reject naturalism.

So, on the basis of this evidence, those who accept PSR would reject naturalism and those who accept naturalism would reject PSR. The science alone doesn't point to either conclusion. As always, science is silent on matters of the transcendent.

So how do we decide whether to believe a principle like PSR when we can't decide based on either logic or empirical evidence? My answer is this: *rational intuition*. That is, reflect on the principle. Be sure you clearly see what accepting it and rejecting it imply. And if, after such reflection, it just seems right to you, and if open-minded inquiry reveals no compelling reason to be suspicious of your intuition, then the most reasonable thing to do is to follow that intuition. For those whose rational intuitions endorse PSR, belief in a transcendent reality is therefore the most reasonable belief.

Of course, people have differing intuitions on matters of this sort. But what that means is that reasonable people can differ. What the cosmological argument ultimately does is force each of us to make a choice: either we accept the principle of sufficient reason, which then forces us to accept a transcendent cause of the world; or we deny any such transcendent cause and thereby also deny that there is ultimately *any* explanation for things at the most basic level. All we can do is reflect on these alternatives and decide which seems more intuitively plausible.

Speaking for myself, I'll go with God.

Concluding Remarks

Of course, "going with God" isn't precisely the option that the cosmological argument offers. What it offers is something vaguer, if no less significant: a mysterious transcendent reality upon which everything else depends. While the traditional God fits this description, He goes beyond it. The cosmological argument, at least in the form I've laid out here, takes us a step closer to God – but it doesn't take us all the way there.

Other philosophical arguments may take us farther. Leibniz and Clarke both thought so, as did Aquinas before them and Hermann Lotze after. And their philosophical arguments are not without merit.

But those who believe in a personal God don't typically do so on the basis of any of these arguments. In fact, Schleiermacher dispensed entirely with traditional arguments for God's existence (which is why we haven't heard from him recently). Schleiermacher looked beneath the surface of creeds and theological disputations to the heart of religious practice and what he found was a kind of *consciousness*. This, he thought, was the real birthplace of both religion and theistic belief.

Personally, I think that an underdeveloped version of the cosmological argument is at work in the religious lives of many theists. They cross the threshold of the church because they think there's got to be a reason for it all. On some level, even the most unschooled among us are philosophers pondering the ultimate nature of reality. What the cosmological argument does, I think, is develop a line of thinking that often lurks beneath the surface of ordinary theistic belief.

In this chapter, I've tried to look at this thinking more carefully than most people do (but less rigorously than professional philosophers have done in their technical works). What I've tried to show is that this line of thinking *doesn't* take us all the way to God, but *does* open a space which God might fill.

And this is significant. If all rational arguments pointed towards a view of life in which the only reality is what scientific investigation encompasses, then an experience of the divine should probably be dismissed as delusional. But reason *isn't* so thoroughly on the side of Dawkins' reductionistic view of the world. For those whose intuitions say there must be a reason for it all, a reason why there is something rather than nothing, religious experiences can and should be treated as more than just the result of neural misfiring. If we experience in our lives a presence that feels at once personal and ineffably vast, as if we've come into the presence of an ultimate loving reality sustaining the world – well, why shouldn't we treat that as experiential evidence for a personal God?

7

Religious Consciousness

In *The God Delusion*, Dawkins touches on religious experience only briefly. The thrust of his argument is captured in the following passage:

> You say you have experienced God directly? Well, some people have experienced a pink elephant, but that probably doesn't impress you.... Individuals in asylums think they are Napoleon or Charlie Chaplin, or that the entire world is conspiring against them, or that they can broadcast their thoughts into other people's heads. We humour them but don't take their internally revealed beliefs seriously, mostly because not many people share them. Religious experiences are different only in that the people who claim them are numerous. (Dawkins 2006, p. 88)

I'm tempted to respond with something snide. I might say, "So you say you've experienced your daughter directly? Well, some people have experienced a pink elephant, but that probably doesn't impress you. Experience of your daughter's existence differs from the experiences of lunatics only in that people who claim to have met your daughter are more numerous."

As a case for the veridicality of religious experience, this response is weak. But my point is that Dawkins' case *against* the veridicality of such experience is equally weak. His argument amounts to this: "Many people have hallucinations. Therefore, anyone who thinks they've directly experienced God is hallucinating." Plug in "George Bush" for "God" and you can see just how bad this reasoning is. The fact that people hallucinate tells us nothing about whether any *particular* experience is delusional.

But maybe Dawkins has something more subtle in mind. Schleiermacher's characterization of religious consciousness as a *feeling* is apt in that, like feelings, religious experiences are essentially private. Although different people across different times and cultures report religious experiences that are surprisingly similar, these experiences remain personal and internal: they are not part of the world of shared empirical experience, in which what we observe can be corroborated by multiple witnesses. If I hear a loud ringing sound, others in the vicinity with normal hearing should hear it, too. If they don't, I might consider having my hearing checked. But if I have a deep sense of God's presence in a moment of grave danger, there's no reason to suppose that those around me will share the experience. So why not treat religious experiences in the same way we treat a sound no one else can hear? Why think that religious experiences are any different from the occasional report of some lunatic who claims to see a pink elephant while the surrounding crowd sees nothing?

The difference, of course, lies precisely in the following fact: pink elephants, if they exist, are part of the empirical world – the world in which empirical objects are located in time and space, ready to be observed by anyone with normal senses who is in the right place at the right time. If a lone witness reports a pink elephant's presence at a time and place where others are positioned to observe it but don't, this suggests that the lone witness is probably delusional.

But God names a transcendent being, a reality that falls outside the empirical world. If such a being exists, it won't be empirically observable. Schleiermacher, as we saw, defines God as a being upon which we are absolutely dependent, and argues that if there is such a being it would be impossible in principle to encounter it in the empirical world. Experience of it would come, if at all, in an entirely different way.

As we saw in the last chapter, the cosmological argument points us to a transcendent, necessary being, one upon which all merely contingent beings depend absolutely. In this chapter, I will argue that putative religious experiences – especially those of so-called mystics – are distinctive in precisely the ways we'd expect were they experiences *of* such a being. And this means it's unreasonable to cavalierly dismiss them as Dawkins does.

In the current crop of atheist bestsellers, Harris's *The End of Faith* is the only one that offers an account of religious experience. But Harris's account is based entirely on his favored brand of Buddhism. He ignores the full scope of religious experience and refuses to consider seriously the possibility that these experiences can reasonably be interpreted in ways different from the Buddhist one he favors.

In general, when the new atheists take on religious experience, their arguments betray a deep ignorance of their subject. To avoid such ignorance, we need to reflect on religious experience in terms of actual examples. I begin with the case of Simone Weil.

Simone Weil: The Philosophical Mystic

Simone Weil is among the most fascinating intellectuals of the twentieth century. Born in France in 1909 of secular Jewish parents, she suffered all her life from debilitating headaches and ill health – and yet, despite living only 34 years, she left an astonishing legacy. In that brief life, she was a philosopher of stunning originality, an unconventional school teacher, a labor organizer, a factory worker, a volunteer in the anarchist militia during the Spanish Civil War, and a religious mystic. At the time of her death at the height of World War II, she was serving in London under De Gaulle's French government-in-exile – the closest she could get to France after her family pressured her to flee with them to America in advance of the Nazi invasion.[1]

A contributing cause of her early death was her refusal, while in exile from France, to eat more than the official rations of those under Nazi occupation. Her commitment to share in others' suffering, to allow herself no luxury not enjoyed by the least among us, expressed itself spiritually when she said that "every time I think of the crucifixion of Christ I commit the sin of envy" (Weil 1951, p. 83).

In the midst of her tumultuous life, Weil produced a body of profound writings reflecting two passions: the needs of the afflicted, especially the working poor; and the nature of the divine, especially as expressed in the crucified Christ (whose image wedded God to affliction in a way that Weil found irresistible).

Her religious passion only came towards the end of her life, and it came as a surprise. Raised a secular Jew and drawn to Marxism early in life, Weil never intended to become a religious mystic. Thus, Leslie Fiedler writes,

> The particular note of conviction in Simone Weil's testimony arises from the feeling that her role as a mystic was so *unintended*, one for which she had not in any sense prepared. An undertone of incredulity persists beneath her astonishing honesty: quite suddenly God had taken her, radical, agnostic, contemptuous of religious life and practice as she had observed it! (Weil 1951, pp. 4–5)

Although her mystical experiences led her to a deep affinity for the image of the crucified Christ, she refused to join the Church despite persistent urgings from Catholic friends – most notably her confidante, the Reverend Father Perrin. She mistrusted all attachments to communities that created insider–outsider distinctions, fearing that belonging to such a community would alienate her from the mass of humanity – a fact that led Lesley Fiedler to dub her "the Outsider as Saint" (Weil 1951, p. 3).

And so she remained an outsider, self-exiled from ordinary human communities while attaching herself with fierce empathy to the sea of suffering humanity. And in her last years, seized by headaches, sickly and refusing to enjoy privileges others lacked, this secular Jew wrote some of the most potent mystical reflections on the Christian God ever recorded.

Pivotal to these reflections was a series of experiences, born amidst suffering, which lifted her out of her anguish into the arms of the transcendent. In a letter to Father Perrin, dubbed her "spiritual autobiography," Weil describes the conditions leading up to her first such experience. She'd discovered a poem entitled "Love," by the poet George Herbert, which she found so beautiful she learned it by heart. Weil goes on:

> Often, at the culminating point of a violent headache, I make myself say it over, concentrating all my attention upon it and clinging with all my soul to the tenderness it enshrines. I used to think I was merely reciting it as a beautiful poem, but without my knowing it the recitation had the virtue of a prayer. It was during one of these recitations that, as I told you, Christ himself came down and took possession of me.
>
> In my arguments about the insolubility of the problem of God I had never foreseen the possibility of that, of a real contact, person to person, here below, between a human being and God. I had vaguely heard tell of things of this kind, but I had never believed them. In the *Fioretti* the accounts of apparitions rather put me off if anything, like the miracles in the Gospel. Moreover, in this sudden possession of me by Christ, neither my senses nor my imagination had any part; I only felt in the midst of my suffering the presence of a love, like that which one can read in the smile on a beloved face. (Weil 1951, pp. 68–9)

Weil was totally unprepared for this experience. She "had never read any mystical works," a fact for which she thanked God: "God in his mercy had prevented me from reading the mystics, so that it should be evident to me that I had not invented this absolutely unexpected contact" (p. 69).

But it wasn't until several years after this initial encounter that she pursued any sort of spiritual practice. A reluctant mystic all the way, she resisted prayer, "afraid of the power of suggestion that is in prayer" (p. 70). But eventually she came to see prayer in a new light, as a way of focusing the *attention*. And she began to recite the Lord's Prayer much as she had Herbert's "Love":

> I have made a practice of saying it through once each morning with absolute attention. If during the recitation my attention wanders or goes to sleep, in the minutest degree, I begin again until I have once succeeded in going through it with absolutely pure attention. . . . The effect of this practice is extraordinary and surprises me every time, for, although I experience it each day, it exceeds my expectation at each repetition.
>
> At times the very first words tear the thoughts from my body and transport it to a place outside space where there is neither perspective nor point of view. The infinity of the ordinary expanses of perception is replaced by an infinity to the second or sometimes the third degree. At the same time, filling every part of this infinity of infinity, there is silence, a silence which is not an absence of sound but which is the object of a positive sensation, more positive than that of sound. Noises, if there are any, only reach me after crossing this silence.
>
> Sometimes, also, during this recitation or at other moments, Christ is present with me in person, but his presence is infinitely more real, more moving, more clear than on that first occasion when he took possession of me. (Weil 1951, pp. 71–2)

Weil began to see her spiritual practice as a way of forming in her consciousness an empty space for the divine to enter in. She saw the imagination as a chief impediment to creating such a space. In her words, the imagination "is continually at work filling up all the fissures through which grace might pass" (1952a, p. 62).

She was especially concerned about gods of the imagination – that is, images of the divine that we create for ourselves. In the grip of such images, we make it impossible for the true God to enter. "Of two men who have no experience of God," she said, "he who denies him is perhaps nearer to him than the other" (1952a, p. 167).

Thus, she believed atheism could be a kind of spiritual "purification" (p. 168). Always fond of paradoxes, Weil saw her religious experience and her devotion to its object as entirely compatible with atheism in a certain sense. "I am quite sure," she said, "that there is not a God in the sense that I am quite sure nothing real can be anything like what I am able to conceive when I pronounce this word. But that which I cannot conceive is not an illusion" (p. 167).

This is the point where Weil parts company so sharply with conventional atheists. She insists on *the reality of the inconceivable*.

But it would be a mistake to conclude that Weil thought nothing could be meaningfully said of God. Weil never doubted the appropriateness of calling the object of her mystical experiences *God*. It felt like an encounter with something transcendent, something that couldn't be "conceived" using the building blocks of ordinary experience; but it also felt like a "person to person" contact, as if she'd become the object of an astonishing love.

And this was enough to name it God, even if further attempts to describe God using human concepts amounted to little more than hand waving.

The Varieties of Religious Experience

To reflect on the significance of Weil's experiences, it may help to situate them in the broader stream of religious experience. One of the most famous studies of religious experience (and still one of the best) is William James's *The Varieties of Religious Experience*, published in 1902, in which James seeks to characterize and organize these experiences according to similarities and differences, and to assess their significance.

He notices, for example, that religious experiences adopt a different form for optimistic personalities than for pessimistic ones. All religious experiences share the sense "that man has a dual nature, and is connected to two spheres of thought, a shallower and a profounder sphere, in either of which he may learn to live habitually" (James 1914, p. 97). But for the optimistic religion of the so-called "healthy minded," the reality of the profounder sphere serves only to validate a pre-existent optimism, a sense that worldly evils are nothing really to worry about.

The "sick soul," by contrast, is fixated on evil. The sick soul knows that suffering is rampant and that death swallows up *everything* in the end. And so it all seems pointless. The sick soul flails after some meaning to life beyond absurdity. James sees the sick soul as, in a sense, more honest about the state of the world.

For James, while such despondent attention to evil precludes the optimistic faith of the healthy minded, it does not preclude religion. In fact, the vivid awareness of evil may itself become a pathway to religious life – one that takes the sick soul through what James calls a "second birth" (p. 157).

The religious experience of the sick soul begins with an unvarnished consciousness of evil but then *redeems* it – typically in a sudden conversion experience. The moment of change is experienced as a "self-surrender" to "forces seemingly outside the conscious individual" (p. 211). Redemption bursts through in a moment – typically when the conscious mind has become so exhausted from wrestling with the misery of life that it goes on strike (p. 212). And then a new view of life floods in.

Such conversions do not turn "sick souls" into "healthy-minded" ones. Earthly goods are still seen as trivial compared to earthly evils. Redemption comes from a transcendent order. Examining the experiences of Henry Alline, James notes that Alline's conversion, like that of other sick souls, was a redemption "into another universe than this mere natural world, and life remained for him a sad and patient trial" (p. 220).

The final part of James's statement here is actually misleading. Consider the final section of Alline's conversion account:

> in an instant of time, my soul seemed awake in and with God, and surrounded by the arms of everlasting love. About sunrise I arose with joy to relate to my parents what God had done for my soul, and declared to them the miracle of God's unbounded grace. . . . I so longed to be useful in the cause of Christ, in preaching the gospel, that it seemed as if I could not rest any longer but go I must and tell the wonders of redeeming love. I lost all taste for carnal pleasures, and carnal company, and was enabled to forsake them. (James 1914, pp. 219–20)

These are not the words of someone whose life is "a sad and patient trial" but of someone who takes joy in life but draws that joy from a different source than the satisfaction of worldly desires.

If ever there were a "sick soul," Simone Weil was one – and her first religious experience has much in common with Alline's. Although she judged her grueling headaches to be trivial compared to the sea of suffering in the world, they were nevertheless hers and in their grip she knew a crushing misery. And yet that misery was suddenly, unexpectedly redeemed. Her suffering did not dissipate but was put into a context in which it no longer had the appearance of ultimate reality.

But despite these surface similarities, Weil's religious experience was crucially different from Alline's. Part of that difference stems from Weil's fiercely intellectual nature. She resisted simply embracing the experience. As she put it, what resisted was "not my love but my intelligence" (Weil 1951, p. 69).

But there's a more basic difference. Alline was raised in a devout Christian home and his conversion took the form of attaching himself with new enthusiasm to this faith. His internal struggles against depression culminated in an act of surrender to the God of his forbears. The essence of his experience was a sudden emotional and attitudinal shift which he interpreted in the light of his inherited faith. In these ways, Alline's experience was typical of what James discovers in his study of conversions.

James is aware that conversion experiences have been offered as evidence for God: in the wake of an act of surrender, a person's personality and worldview abruptly change – and it feels as if the change is initiated by a higher power (James 1914, p. 228). Don't such experiences give us reason to think that there *is* a higher power?

For James, an early psychologist, it isn't a very good reason, because we can explain sudden conversion in purely psychological terms. Both psychology and religion agree that conversion takes place when forces outside the conscious self take charge, transforming a person's outlook on life. But James notes that "psychology, defining these forces as 'subconscious,' and speaking of their effects as due to 'incubation,' or 'cerebration,' implies that they do not transcend the individual's personality; and herein she diverges from Christian theology, which insists that they are direct supernatural operations of the Deity" (p. 211).

James explains that conscious strivings can often generate "subconscious allies behind the scenes" that better understand what the psyche needs than does the conscious mind (p. 209). The conscious mind actually becomes an impediment; and when it falters in exhaustion, the subconscious bursts forth to reorder the psyche. While the conscious mind experiences it as an abrupt transformation brought on by external forces, it's really the work of subliminal ones.

According to James, the empirical evidence supports this psychological account since those most susceptible to conversion are those with the most active subconscious (p. 240). But he doesn't think this fact rules out a higher power at work. "[I]t is logically conceivable," he says, "that *if there be* higher spiritual agencies that can directly touch us, the psychological condition of their doing so *might be* our possession of a subconscious region which alone should yield access to them. The hubbub of the waking life might close a door which in the dreamy Subliminal might remain ajar or open" (p. 242).

But given how easily sudden conversions can be explained in terms of known psychological forces, the fact that people have such conversions provides no special reason to suppose that a higher power is at work.

But Simone Weil's experience is more than one of conversion. Alline's experience, typical of sudden conversions, is chiefly characterized by two things: an act of self-surrender and a sudden, astonishing change in outlook. For Weil, the key fact about her experience was neither of these things. Rather, it was "the presence of a love, like that which one can read in the smile on a beloved face." For her, the experience was not one of conversion, but an experience whose substance inspired, despite intellectual resistance, a new view of life.

Weil's experience fits better into a different class of religious experiences, the class that James calls "mystical." And unlike conversion experiences, James attaches a special authority to mystical ones. For him, mystical experiences are "absolutely authoritative over the individuals to whom they come" (p. 422). While this authority does not extend to non-mystics, James thinks that "the existence of mystical states absolutely overthrows the pretensions of non-mystical states to be the sole and ultimate dictators of what we may believe" (p. 427). For James, the reality of mystical states gives us rational "permission" to believe in a transcendent order.

Mysticism, its Varieties, and its Authority

James defines mystical experience in terms of four general features:

1 *Ineffability* – that is, mystical experiences defy expression in ordinary language, and can only be inadequately captured with metaphors and analogies.
2 *Noetic quality* – that is, mystical experiences include a sense of being in direct contact with truth, of having an immediate experiential encounter with reality.
3 *Transiency* – that is, mystical experiences can't be sustained for long; details may be hard to remember, although effects on the mystic's life may persist.
4 *Passivity* – that is, mystical experiences feel as if they are happening *to* the mystic; even if the mystic may take steps to bring it about, during the experience the will is "in abeyance" and the mystic feels "grasped . . . by a superior power." (James 1914, pp. 380–2)

To the extent that the content of experiences possessing these features can be described, James finds several common themes. First, ordinary sense experience is swamped by what seems more fully real than anything the senses can grasp. Second, the experience has an intense emotional content that is unambiguously positive. It is joy, love, even ecstasy (p. 412). The message is unswervingly optimistic: the fundamental reality encountered during a mystical state is not grim or evil, but wondrous (p. 416).

Most importantly, the experience is, in James's terms, *monistic*: the mystic has a sense of union with an ultimate reality, in which the sense of self breaks down. In James's words, "This overcoming of all the usual barriers between the individual and the Absolute is the great mystical achievement. In mystic states we both become one with the Absolute and we become aware of our oneness" (p. 419).

Of course, James would be the first to admit that these common themes are accompanied by diversity of detail; but James explains most of this diversity by the fact "that the mystical feeling . . . is capable of forming matrimonial alliances with material furnished by the most diverse philosophies and theologies, provided only they can find a place in their framework for its peculiar emotional mood" (pp. 425–6). Just as Alister McGrath (McGrath and McGrath 2007) claims that "the natural world is conceptually malleable," so does James see mystical experience as conceptually malleable.

The line between experience and interpretation is always thin, even for sense experience. Several years ago, I attended a conference where one speaker had a computer generate ten sounds and then asked the audience what we heard. Like the rest, I heard five "P" sounds followed by five "B" sounds. The speaker informed us that the difference between these two sounds is the interval of time between the "popping of the lips" and the onset of vocalization. If the interval is small, it sounds like a B. If longer, it sounds like a P. What the computer had done was generate ten *different* sounds by incrementally increasing the interval between "pop" and vocalization.

But we hadn't *experienced* ten different sounds. Why? Because our language had only two "phonemes" – categories for organizing vocalizations – in which to place them. Our minds automatically put each sound into one category or the other: P or B. Someone whose native language had different phonemes might hear three sounds, or only one.

This is a difference at the level of experience, not conscious interpretation. But it's a difference created by the cultural categories we bring to bear on experience. In a sense, we experience the world through the lens of these categories.

James recognizes that different categories for organizing experience may lead to differences in the content of mystical experience – and this fact may explain the variations he finds. But amidst these variations, there remain common themes.

James's choice of terms in expressing these themes may, however, betray his own prejudices – especially when he calls mystical states *monistic*. Monism is a philosophical perspective that denies metaphysical differences and in religious contexts usually means that all the things in the world, including ourselves, are not just *dependent* on but *identical* with God. All difference is illusion. The only truth is God. Since the world is thus identified with God, James also tends to use the term "pantheistic" to describe the character of mystical states (p. 422).

But only some mystics, mostly Eastern ones (such as Shankara), describe their experience as one of *identity* with God. Others (such as some Buddhists) leave God out of the picture altogether and simply speak of a loss of self in the field of experience (or a re-conception of self as nothing but a stream of conscious states). But theistic mystics such as Simone Weil describe their experience as a loving union with God in which the self, while swamped by God's presence, remains a distinct reality.

These differences have led R. C. Zaehner (1957) to distinguish between three kinds of mystical experience: *nature mysticism*, which involves a loss of the sense of distinction between self and other in the field of experience; *monistic mysticism*, which involves the sense that the self of ordinary experience is an illusion being cast off, and that what is discovered beneath the illusion is that one *is* God, and that all distinctions between God and not-God are illusion; and *theistic mysticism*, which involves a sense of loving union between the self and God (pp. 28–9).

Zaehner argues that these three forms of mystical experience should not be treated merely as different conceptualizations of the same experiential material. In fact, Zaehner excludes nature mysticism from the class of genuine *religious* mysticism altogether, since it doesn't involve any sense of encountering a value-laden reality beyond the ordinary field of consciousness. Nature mysticism is just an immersion in the field of experience resulting in a loss of the usual sense of self. It can be brought on by many sources (including drugs), and it takes account "of neither good nor evil" (pp. 109 and 202).

While monistic and theistic forms of mysticism have in common a sense of union with a God who transcends ordinary experience, combined with some sort of loss of self, they are fundamentally different. Zaehner expresses the difference as follows:

it is the unbridgeable gulf between all those who see God as incomparably greater than oneself, though He is, at the same time, the root and ground of one's being, and those who maintain that soul and God are one and the same and that all else is pure illusion. For them Christian mysticism is simply *bhakti* or devotion to a personal god carried to ludicrous extremes, whereas for the theist the monist's idea of "liberation" is simply the realization of his immortal soul in separation from God, and is only, as Junayd pointed out, a stage in the path of the beginner. (Zaehner 1957, p. 204)

The final suggestion here comes closest to expressing Zaehner's own view: the classes of mystical experience are stages in an unfolding insight into the truth about God.

Zaehner makes a strong case when he distinguishes nature mysticism from the two religious types. The religious types can and do produce "a total transformation and sanctification of the character" (p. 105) in the mystics who have them. Nature mysticism, being indifferent to good and evil, has no such consistent tendency (as drug-induced mysticism reveals). Nature mysticism seems to involve immersion in the field of experience leading to a loss of the usual sense of self. But religious mysticism seems to be an experience of something *different* from what is found in the field of ordinary experience. The former is a *new way* of experiencing the world. The latter is an experience of *something new*.

But Zaehner is on more controversial ground when it comes to his division between monistic and theistic mysticism. He is absolutely correct that monism and theism are profoundly different philosophies, and that a monistic account of the relationship between the self and God is entirely incompatible with the theistic one. And he is certainly correct that the subjective character of monistic and theistic experience differs. But how much of this difference can be traced back to the objective content of the experience and how much to the concepts and ideas that mystics bring to their experience? Walter Stace (1960) finds enough in common between them to conclude that the differences are on the level of interpretation. He would agree with James's view that the basic experiential material is the same and that the difference lies in "matrimonial alliances with material furnished by the most diverse philosophies."[2]

What this controversy reveals, of course, is the difficulty of disentangling what we bring to an experience from what the experience brings to us. That difficulty is endemic to all experience (as the phoneme example shows). But it's a difficulty that explains why James is unwilling to say that mystical experiences speak "distinctively in favor of any special belief, such as that in absolute idealism, or in the absolute monistic identity, or in the absolute goodness, of the world." Instead, for James, mystical experience is "only relatively in favor of all these things" in the sense that it points "in the direction in which they lie" (James 1914, p. 426).

But even if we adopt James's caution, mystical experiences do convey a distinctive message. Their optimistic character speaks *against* viewing ultimate reality as evil or as "pitilessly indifferent." The sense of union with a more fundamental reality speaks *against* reductive materialism. Mystical experience may not tell us what the ultimate reality is like in rich detail. But it does more than just gesture to something utterly generic. It speaks in favor of a realm that is transcendent, fundamental, and good.

But why grant mystical experience even that much authority? Why not treat it as pure delusion? Mystical experiences might be just that. But James makes several points in favor of granting these experiences the authority outlined above. The first is just how *absolutely authoritative* mystical experiences feel to those who have them. "Our own more 'rational' beliefs," James says, "are based on evidence exactly similar in nature to that which mystics quote for theirs." These more "rational" beliefs are based on the assurances of our senses, but "mystical experiences are as direct perceptions of facts for those who have them as any sensations ever were for us" (pp. 423–4).

Here, James anticipates a line of argument that has been advanced forcefully in recent years by the philosopher William Alston (1983, 1991, 2004). Why do we believe that what we encounter with our senses is real? The answer is just this: it feels that way.

Critics of religious experience are quick to point out that sense experience is *corroborated*. Others see what we see, and when they don't, we're inclined to mistrust our senses. But Alston asks us to consider how in the world we come to believe that others are seeing what we see.

They tell us, of course. That is, we *hear them* tell us. We trust our senses which inform us that there exist other people out there who are seeing and hearing what we are seeing and hearing. In short, this corroboration of our senses' reliability is circular: it appeals to sense experience. All it shows us is that our sense experience is internally consistent. But the mystical experiences of Simone Weil are internally consistent, too. And were she to look to corroboration from others who have had similar experiences, she could do so. Her ordinary sense experience would inform her (in a *non*circular way!) that other people have mystical experiences similar to hers. But how much weight should we give to such corroboration? James himself calls this an "appeal to numbers" that has "no logical force" (p. 424). Alston agrees (2004, p. 140).

What it comes down to is this: the reason we generally trust our sense experience is because it feels like an authentic encounter with reality. But mystical experiences *also* feel like such encounters, with one important difference: for mystics in the grip of them, they feel *even more real than sense experience.* And so, if we are justified in trusting our sense experiences, even though we cannot come up with any noncircular argument for doing so, why shouldn't mystics trust that their mystical experiences are veridical as well? Alston answers that mystics *should* trust them so long as they have no compelling reasons to doubt them – what Alston calls "rebutters" (2004, p. 138).

To these considerations, James adds another one. He notices that mystical experiences, because they are about something other than the world of ordinary sense experience, "merely add a supersensuous meaning to the ordinary outward data of consciousness." They do not *contradict* ordinary sense experience. "It is the rationalistic critic," James says, "who plays the part of denier in the controversy, and his denials have no strength, for there never can be a state of facts to which new meanings may not be truthfully added, provided the mind ascend to a more enveloping point of view." He thinks mystical states may well be "such superior points of view, windows through which the mind looks out upon a more extensive and inclusive world" (James 1914, pp. 427–8).

Finally, we can reflect on the veridicality of religious experiences in the light of broader philosophical ideas. In the last chapter, I invoked the cosmological argument of Leibniz and Clarke to argue that it's reasonable to believe in an essentially *mysterious* reality that is both *transcendent* (it falls outside the empirical world of contingent things) and *fundamental* (it explains why there is something rather than nothing, and is thus the ultimate reality on which all other things depend). If such a reality exists, we wouldn't encounter it through ordinary empirical experience. But does that mean it's inaccessible through *any* kind of experience?

If human beings did have experiential encounters with such a reality, what would those experiences be like? Since this divine reality is essentially mysterious – a self-existent or necessary being unlike anything we can conceive of – we should expect an experience of that reality to be ineffable, impossible to adequately characterize in terms of our normal concepts. Since this reality is transcendent, we should expect it to manifest itself in a mode of experience clearly distinct and distanced from the empirical mode. It would be as if empirical experience were in abeyance, or shunted to the periphery of our consciousness. And since this reality is fundamental, we should expect it to feel like an encounter with a truth somehow more real than anything in ordinary experience. Finally, since this reality is the necessary being on which we and all other contingent things depend absolutely, we should expect – as Schleiermacher noted – to feel totally passive in the face of it.

In other words, the mystical experiences of Simone Weil and others are precisely the sorts of experiences that we would expect from a human encounter with the divine – that is, an encounter with the transcendent and fundamental reality in which, if my arguments from the last chapter are sound, it is reasonable to believe. And if it is reasonable for me to believe that such a reality exists, and if I hear reports of experiences of this sort – or, better yet, I have such experiences or glimmerings of them – would it be irrational for me to take these to be an encounter with the very religious reality in which it is reasonable to believe?

Of course not. But let's not take this conclusion too far. Whether a religious skeptic should be compelled to believe on the basis of reports of religious experience is a different issue. While I have argued that it's reasonable to believe in a transcendent and fundamental reality, I have also argued that it can be reasonable not to so believe – based on differences in our fundamental intuitions. One might argue that the existence of religious experiences offers independent reasons to favor the conclusion of the cosmological argument – precisely because these experiences so closely match what we would expect to find were that conclusion true; but I will not pursue that argument here. The fact is that just as a reasonable person can reject the force of the cosmological argument by denying the widespread intuitive appeal of the Principle of Sufficient Reason, so can a reasonable person explain away religious experiences as nothing but the by-product of misfiring in the brain.

My point is that it is at least as reasonable to think otherwise. While some researchers (Persinger 1987) claim to have found a region in the brain that, when stimulated in the right way, produces religious experiences, what does that show? If my visual cortex is stimulated in the right way, I'll experience bright light. Does that mean the experience of light is just a by-product of neural misfiring and there really is no sun? Of course not.

When I read Simone Weil's spiritual autobiography, I find in her religious experience a vivid account of something I've sensed myself in a more remote way. And my intuitions *do* endorse the Principle of Sufficient Reasons and thereby what it implies. So why not treat Weil's experience as a close-up eyewitness account of something I've seen at a distance? As I read her account, I don't just get the sense that *she* found the experience veridical. Her experience resonates with dimensions of my own, in a way that leads *me* to find them veridical.

And these experiences add something to what philosophy teaches. The mysterious, transcendent, fundamental reality of philosophical reflection turns out to be something else, too: it is *good*. It resonates with my ethico-religious hope. Out there, beyond the boundaries of ordinary sense experience, there is a presence like the smile on a beloved face.

Yes, absolutely. That's *my* experience of the world. So am I deluded, or is Richard Dawkins blind?

Sam Harris on Spiritual Experience

In *The End of Faith*, Sam Harris devotes a chapter to "Experiments in Consciousness" in which he maintains that a particular kind of experience "has been at the core of human spirituality for millennia" (2004, p. 219). He identifies this experiential core with the Buddhist "no-self" doctrine rather than with any experiential encounter with the transcendent, and he thinks this experience arises whenever one pays sufficient unbiased attention to the contents of consciousness.

As Harris puts it, "If you persistently look for the subject of your experience . . . its absence may become apparent, if only for a moment. Everything will remain – this book, your hands – and yet the illusory divide that once separated knower from known, self from world, inside from outside, will have vanished" (p. 219). According to Harris, this experience of "oneness" with the field of experience is the outcome of *empirical* observation, when such observation is turned towards consciousness itself.

Zaehner would point out that what Harris is describing is *nature* mysticism, which is very different from the *religious* mysticism that offers the experiential foundation for religious life. As Zaehner puts it, the theistic mystics describe their experience as "a direct apperception of God" in which "all the veils of sense" are "stripped aside" (Zaehner 1957, p. 21). In other words, there is a loss of contact with ordinary empirical experience, not an immersion in it of the sort Harris describes. We can rightly ask, along with Zaehner, "Why should we be asked to believe that a vision of nature transfigured in any way corresponds to the vision of God Himself?" (p. 21).

But Harris thinks he's captured the experience at "the core of every religion" (2004, p. 204). The problem, as Harris sees it, is that this experience is clouded by "the venom of unreason" (p. 204): doctrinal commitments that interfere with the ability to objectively appreciate experience. Even when they have "spiritual experiences" – which, for Harris, are never anything more than the collapse of the "subject–object" distinction he describes – traditionally religious people misinterpret what they see. Harris insists that there is "no greater obstacle to a truly empirical approach to spiritual experience than our current beliefs about God" (p. 214).

Harris's idea seems to be this: When theistic mystics have genuine spiritual experiences, the distorting effects of religious dogma lead them to mistake what they are experiencing – namely, the dissolution of the illusory self into the field of consciousness – for an encounter with God.

Harris doesn't see himself as interpreting spiritual experience in the light of doctrinal commitments. He sees himself as describing what a careful examination of consciousness reveals. It is the theistic mystics who are misperceiving things through the lens of dogma.

Is he right?

If he is, then Simone Weil's experience (and others like it) can be explained away as a misinterpretation of something Harris has succeeded in describing correctly. Harris might argue that Weil stumbled accidentally into the sort of spiritual practice that Buddhists call "meditation." In fixing her attention on the poem "Love," she was clearing her mind of other thoughts. She was therefore able to "recognize thoughts *as thoughts*" (p. 218). In Harris's view, it is the failure to do this that "gives each of us the feeling that we call 'I,' and this is the string upon which all our states of suffering and dissatisfaction are strung" (p. 218). As soon as Weil freed herself of the illusion of being a *subject* of experience, her suffering fell away – but, apparently, she mistook that relief from suffering for "the presence of a love, like that which one can read in the smile on a beloved face." She personified it and named it Christ.

There is no doubt that Weil did stumble into a method of focusing the attention also found in established meditation practices. But can we infer from this fact that the content of her experience should be dismissed as misinterpretation, while the content of Harris's "spiritual" experience, resulting from deliberate attempts to follow the meditation techniques of Buddhists, should be embraced as honest description?

Let's consider the question more closely by considering what Harris says about meditation. When he first characterizes meditation, he refers to it as "techniques of introspection that aim at uncovering the intrinsic properties of consciousness" (p. 217). But then he defines it in terms of specific results. He says that "meditation" means "any means whereby our sense of 'self' – of subject/object dualism in perception and cognition – can be made to vanish, while consciousness remains vividly aware of the continuum of experience" (p. 217). And so, any introspection that achieved a different outcome (such as, say, an immediate awareness of *absolute dependence* on a fundamental reality beyond oneself) wouldn't be meditation in Harris's sense.

I mention absolute dependence because, of course, Schleiermacher shared Harris's commitment to "techniques of introspection that aim at uncovering the intrinsic properties of consciousness." But Schleiermacher didn't discover the same things in consciousness that Harris does. Why not?

Perhaps Harris is better at empirical examination of consciousness than Schleiermacher was. Or perhaps he's worse at it. Or perhaps there are different things to discover in consciousness and a complete picture will come only when these different discoveries are brought together. Or perhaps the empirical facts about consciousness are amenable to various interpretations, so that what we discover through introspection is shaped by the philosophical and theological commitments we bring to the task. Perhaps Harris isn't so free from beliefs not based on evidence as he claims. Perhaps this is because such freedom is impossible.

So, is Harris truly as objective as he claims? Simone Weil came to her spiritual exercises unintentionally, while Harris deliberately followed in the footsteps of Buddhist predecessors. He tells us that mysticism, "to be viable, requires *explicit* instructions, which need suffer no more ambiguity or artifice in their exposition than we find in a manual for operating a lawn mower" (p. 217).

And so Harris picks up his Buddhist instruction manual. Unlike Weil, who forged her way through the uncharted wilderness looking about in surprise and wonder, Harris followed a path laid down by others, and he *saw what they told him to look for*. Buddhists before him concluded that the "self" in the traditional sense, as a unified substance, is illusory. And Harris, upon engaging in what he takes to be objective introspection, discovers (surprise!) that the self is illusory. This, he claims, is the result of unbiased empirical investigation into the nature of consciousness. Setting sarcasm aside, we may ask if he's right.

Harris *is* right, I believe, to say that if we turn our attention to the field of consciousness, we won't discover a subject of consciousness *in that field*.

But to move from this to the conclusion that there is no self is too quick. Consider an analogy borrowed from Wittgenstein (1961, pp. 57–8): Is my *eye* in its field of vision? Clearly not. To get it into its own visual field, we'd need to pluck it out and put it in front of itself – but then, of course, it wouldn't be there any more to do the looking.

Likewise, the subject of experience cannot be in its own experiential field *even if it exists*. And so the fact that we don't *find* it in the field of experience tells us nothing about whether it exists or not – unless you embrace (on faith?) the doctrine that the only reality is what is part of the ordinary experiential field.

Of course, the fact that we cannot directly experience something doesn't mean we can't infer its existence. If we look at our experience, we discover that it's *unified*. What unifies it, in my view, is that it's all mine. Experience thus points towards a subject, even if that subject cannot be experienced directly. The self, the subject of experience, transcends experience – but there is evidence in experience that makes the existence of a unified self seem, to most, blatantly obvious.

The great German philosopher Hermann Lotze notes that we often have experiences in which "we so lose ourselves in the content of a sensation, an idea, a feeling, or an effort, that we (so to speak) are for a time nothing but this" (Lotze 1886, pp. 41–2). But Lotze goes on to argue that all of these conscious states "in which we thus lose ourselves, are after all never thinkable except as states of a definite, self-identical and separate spiritual subject" (p. 42). These feelings, sensations, etc., do not have any unity in themselves. And so, in order to be experienced as unified, they need to be united *in* something – they need to be the conscious states of a *self*.

There's no doubt that a characteristic feature of mystical states is the collapse of the subject/object dichotomy and a loss of our ordinary sense of self. But the Buddhist "no-self" doctrine is an interpretation of these features. Another interpretation is that the self is capable of identifying with other things, such that they become included within the sense of self. Such identification, which emerges out of genuine attention to the other, is a kind of love. And it might be argued that when we begin to love the world in this way, we become connected with the ultimate reality, whose essence is love. And so, the first stage of mystical consciousness – the stage of "nature mysticism," which Harris is stuck at by virtue of his doctrinal beliefs – can give way to a higher stage, a direct experiential encounter with *love itself*, that is, with God.

This alternative interpretation has some advantages. It allows us to take Weil's experience on its own terms. It explains the variety of mystical experiences as different stages in a process, rather than squeezing all spiritual experience into a narrow interpretive box.

And there are advantages to acknowledging the inevitability of interpretation. What we discover when we introspect may depend greatly on what we're looking for. Inspired by his Buddhist guides, Harris looks for the collapse of the subject/object dichotomy, and sure enough finds it. But are there *other* things worth looking for?

Schleiermacher thought so. And in his introspective study of consciousness, he uncovered things Harris never thinks to look for. If his discoveries are sound, then Schleiermacher has uncovered something important: the mystical experiences of Simone Weil and others, rather than being foreign to most of our experience, may be the realization of something that exists as a glimmering in the consciousness of people everywhere.

Schleiermacher on the Essence of Religious Experience

We've already sketched out what Schleiermacher found in his introspective examination of consciousness, but I want to return to it now in greater detail. As we've seen, for Schleiermacher our experience is accompanied by two contrasting feelings: the feelings of *dependence* and *freedom*. The feeling of dependence is the sense I have of something outside of me affecting me. The feeling of freedom is the sense I have of doing something by my own volition.

In ordinary experience, everything feels like either *something happening to me* or *something I am doing*. In Schleiermacher's terms, it is the contrast between *receptivity* and *activity*, dependence and freedom. Sensory experience is accompanied by the feeling of dependence because, whenever I sense something, I have the accompanying intuition that *something outside of me is acting on me*. It doesn't feel as if I am inventing the blueness of the sky, but as if something external is producing the experience in me.

But when I investigate the world with my senses, I have the feeling that I am *doing* something. I *look* at the sky and see its blueness. The experience of blueness feels as if it comes from something external, but the *looking* feels as if it comes from me. When I close my eyes and imagine a grassy hill, I don't for a minute believe the hill is real. Why? Because the feeling that accompanies the imagined hill is one of freedom, not dependence. The main reason why I believe in real hills out there in the world – why I don't believe I'm just making it up – is because so much of my experience is accompanied by the feeling of dependence rather than freedom.

Likewise, the feeling of freedom is the main reason I believe in free will. When I drag myself out of bed in the morning, it doesn't feel like something that's *happening* to me (the mechanistic result of physical laws regulating neural firings in my brain) but like something I have freely (however grudgingly) chosen to do.

One of these two feelings accompanies every ordinary experience. We might say that experience comes in two flavors. And because there are two flavors, Schleiermacher can call each to our attention by contrasting it with the other. But Schleiermacher thinks there's a more basic feeling that underlies all experience – and this, of course, is the feeling of absolute dependence. If freedom and dependence are the flavors of honey and molasses, then the feeling of absolute dependence is the sweetness they share.

But if everything tasted sweet, it would be difficult to get at the concept of sweetness. There would be no contrasting flavor to call it to our attention. And so, since everything *is* flavored by the same feeling of absolute dependence, that feeling is elusive.

So how can we get at this feeling that underlies every experience? Schleiermacher tries to call attention to it by identifying what the feelings of dependence and freedom have in common. Underlying them both is something analogous to what underlies those experiences that we think of as receptive. That is, all of our experience is accompanied by something like the feeling of dependence – except that it is a feeling of dependence *unaccompanied by any reciprocal feeling of freedom*.

As we've already seen, we can be *both* receptive *and* active in relation to everything in the empirical world. In relation to the world encountered with our senses, we never have a feeling of *absolute* freedom. What we experience and what we do is never wholly in our control, because we are acting on a world that comes to us as a given. Likewise, in relation to the physical world encountered in the senses, the feeling of dependence is never absolute. As Schleiermacher puts it,

> If we consider our relations to Nature, or those which exist in human society, there we shall find a large number of objects in regard to which freedom and dependence maintain very much an equipoise: these constitute the field of equal reciprocity. There are other objects which exercise a

far greater influence upon our receptivity than our activity exercises upon them, and also *vice versa*, so that one of the two may diminish until it is imperceptible. But neither of the two members will ever completely disappear. (Schleiermacher 1928, p. 15)

In short, anything we can see or hear or feel is something over which we exert *some* control, and so will not be something upon which we depend absolutely. If there is such a thing, it's not to be found in the empirical world.

But Schleiermacher thinks we do have a feeling of absolute dependence. And he calls this feeling to our attention in part by pointing out our inability to have a feeling of absolute freedom, even when we are engaged in entirely inward activity such as exercises of the imagination. In these cases, we are not dependent on the physical world, *but we are dependent on our own existence as a being that can act.* We do not call ourselves and our power to choose into existence by our choices. Instead, our existence is a precondition for any free activity at all. Likewise, it is a precondition for our capacity to be receptive (pp. 15–16).

When we focus on this fact of our existence and turn our attention inward to the experience of it, what we immediately encounter is a feeling of dependence unaccompanied by any feeling of freedom. And that very feeling, lurking at the root of *every* experience, points us beyond ourselves. It is "the consciousness that the whole of our spontaneous activity comes from a source outside of us" (p. 16). When we become truly conscious of it, it is a self-consciousness that Schleiermacher can only describe as the sense of being *purely* receptive, not even *remotely* active, in relation to *Something.*

But why trust this feeling? As noted above, the real reason I believe in an external world is because my sensory experience feels receptive. I believe in free will because I have experiences that feel active. Why, then, shouldn't I believe in a transcendent reality beyond the empirical world, given that my experience, at bottom, *feels* utterly dependent on such a reality?

At the root of experience, in our awareness of our own existence, there is a seminal awareness of a transcendent reality upon which our entire being depends. For most of us, most of the time, we remain unaware of this "feeling" because, being a constant in every part of our experience, we fail to notice it. But Schleiermacher believes we *can* notice it. And when we do, why should we doubt its veridicality any more than we doubt our other feelings? When we don't doubt it and focus our attention on its object, a rich vista of insight opens up as surely as when a scientist trusts her senses and begins to explore the empirical world.

One of the virtues of this analysis is that it provides an understanding of both ordinary religiosity and its more extraordinary forms. The mystical consciousness of Simone Weil is, on this analysis, a full flowering of a bud that resides in us all. Religious experience is not some alien thing that only the most rigorous practitioners can enjoy. It's present in everyone. We bring it with us into religious worship and may hope to have it bloom a little fuller as we strive with others to inhabit the feeling more fully. And our efforts to expand this "God-consciousness" can benefit from the teachings of those mystics who dwell in it more often and more completely than we – much as all of us can benefit from scientists who have honed their observational skills in the empirical realm.

In the *Speeches*, Schleiermacher gives his clearest indication of when our religious consciousness is most likely to become vivid. It does so when we are neither "knowing" nor "doing" – that is, when we stop trying to understand the world or to act on it. Instead of conceptualizing it or responding to it, we can just be present *in* experience (1958, pp. 43–6). And in that quiet space, when feelings of relative freedom and *relative* dependence become quiescent, the single constant of experience – the sense of absolute dependence that is the experience of our relationship to God – is laid bare.

What he is describing here sounds a great deal like *meditation*. But the outcome isn't the Buddhist no-self doctrine. It's the theistic doctrine of God. Is one doctrine more true to the lessons of introspection than the other? Is one a misinterpretation, the other honest description?

If you're aware of your self as wholly dependent and passive in the face of a transcendent reality, such awareness might be mistaken for the self vanishing away. After all, it's the active side of experience that calls attention to the self. We identify ourselves with our active strivings. We're *agents*, first and foremost. If our awareness turns to a place in consciousness where there is no feeling of agency, where our feeling of dependence is *absolute*, we could easily confuse this with the self's absence.

In short, Schleiermacher could explain away Buddhist mystical experience as a misinterpretation, much as Harris wants to explain away Christian experience. So, who is confused about what's going on in mystical states? Harris? Schleiermacher? Who has misinterpreted the content of spiritual introspection by an ideological allegiance to religious dogma? Can any of us get out of our own conceptual presuppositions enough to give a wholly objective answer?

Perhaps Harris and Schleiermacher are seeing different sides of a wondrous field of experience that transcends the ordinary. Perhaps the proper attitude is not to choose sides but to adopt a "beautiful modesty" (p. 54) which recognizes that religious experience carries with it "a feeling of man's utter incapacity ever to exhaust it for himself alone" (p. 149). And so the Buddhists and Christians and Muslims and Jews should attend to each other's accounts of religious experience with an eagerness to learn rather than with the fanatic's zeal for insisting that other faiths have gotten it wrong.

We can't do that if we don't let each other have our respective accounts. We need to leave room for interpretation, for speculation beyond what the bare bones of the experience reveals. We should have our own interpretations without attaching ourselves to them fanatically.

And yes, Sam Harris, I'm accusing you of voicing the zealot's cry of heresy. It's not a typical vice of Buddhists – but there are, it seems, exceptions.

8

The Substance of Things Hoped For

In the last two chapters, I've argued that it is reasonable to believe in a religious realm – that is, an order of reality which is both transcendent and fundamental. The philosophical reasoning we looked at takes us only to this very general conclusion, but religious experience takes us further. It not only supports the existence of a religious realm but gives us reason to be optimistic. The vivid experiences of the mystics, as well as the vaguer glimmerings of more ordinary religious consciousness, point us towards a hopeful conclusion: the world is better that it seems to merely scientific eyes.

But my aim in this book is to defend the reasonableness not only of those with an utterly generic religious consciousness but of those who want to wed their religious experience to a theology that interprets it in a distinctive way: as an encounter with *a personal God who cares about the good*.

Many mystics do report such encounters, but this is hardly a universal feature of mystical experience or of religious experience generally. And we may never know the extent to which the content of religious experience derives from the interpretive concepts brought to bear on it. This is as true for those who report an encounter with a loving God as it is for those who report the transcendent oneness of all things. And so, while religious experience is *consistent* with theism (theists can coherently interpret it as an encounter with God), it no more points *decisively* to theism than does the cosmological argument.

And, as we've seen, it's not irrational to reject the cosmological argument or to question the veridicality of religious experience, even if reasonable people may embrace both. My argument is that theists do not *defy* reason and evidence when they believe in a personal God. But that is not to say the weight of reason and evidence demands such belief. It does not.

There *are* philosophical arguments to support the idea that a fundamental, transcendent reality would have to be *personal*. One of the best was offered by the great nineteenth-century German philosopher, Hermann Lotze (1886, pp. 55–69). Unlike most earlier arguments for a personal God, Lotze developed his with an appreciation and respect for science, as well as for the burgeoning materialist worldview that many were starting to advocate. Lotze recognized that the world discovered by science *could* be interpreted in materialist terms. But he argued that such an interpretation did not do justice to key features of our own lived experience as conscious beings with values and feelings. Materialism leaves the most intimate dimensions of our lives a mystery (since it is hard to see how consciousness can be produced by inanimate matter, no matter how complex its organization). More significantly, perhaps, such materialism turns the part of our experience that is most significant – the conscious life of the mind – into a mere by-product of things that are essentially mindless and dead.

And so Lotze argues that the ultimate reality is best understood as a unified being that is both spiritual and personal because such a view fits better with the totality of our human experience than any alternative view.[1]

But even if Lotze's arguments work, they aren't why theists in general believe in a personal God. Most theists have never heard of Lotze, and I embraced such a God long before reading him. It's true that beliefs are often formed in accord with underdeveloped arguments that philosophers subsequently make explicit. In my own case, amateur philosophizing in my youth implicitly tracked the path of the cosmological argument, contributing profoundly to my sense that there's more to reality than meets the eye.

Something like this might be going on with respect to arguments for a personal God. But I suspect not. When I first read Lotze, it didn't feel as if someone were finally laying out with care a path of reasoning I'd been implicitly following all along. Instead, it felt as if I'd encountered a rational argument for something I'd always believed on *different* grounds.

And what are those grounds? While reasoning and experience may point me towards a religious realm, the further step to belief in a personal God is a matter of *faith*. And, of course, if you ask most theists why they believe, faith will likely be their answer.

But for the cultured despisers of religion today, "faith" is just another name for intellectual and moral irresponsibility. Are they right?

The New Atheist Attack on Faith

In *The End of Faith*, Sam Harris defines religious faith as "unjustified belief in matters of ultimate concern – specifically in propositions that promise some mechanism by which human life can be spared the ravages of time and death" (2004, p. 65). Dawkins understands faith in the same general way. In response to those religious leaders who condemn extremists for *perverting* the faith, Dawkins asks, "But how can there be a perversion of faith, if faith, lacking any objective justification, doesn't have any demonstrable standard to pervert?" (2006, p. 306). He goes on: "Faith is an evil precisely because it requires no justification and brooks no argument. Teaching children that unquestioning faith is a virtue primes them – given certain other ingredients that are not hard to come by – to grow up into potentially lethal weapons for future jihads or crusades" (p. 308).

The new atheists are quick to trot out examples of evils motivated by this irrational dogmatism they call faith. Hitchens, a widely traveled journalist, has no trouble providing contemporary cases. Historical ones are equally easy to find. Dawkins, for example, shares the story of a Jewish boy in nineteenth-century Italy, Edgardo Mortara, who was abducted from his parents by the Roman Catholic Church.

The details of the case are disturbing. A well-meaning Catholic nanny, fearing for the infant boy's health and, in Dawkins' words, "brought up in the stupor of belief that a child who died unbaptized would suffer forever in hell" (p. 311), performed an impromptu lay baptism in the back of the boy's house. The priests of the Italian Inquisition, upon hearing of the case a few years later, invoked Church laws still in force in Bologna at the time – laws that forbade a baptized Christian from being raised in a Jewish home, even if it was the home of his own parents. Some five years after the irregular baptism, Edgardo Mortara was seized in the night and taken to Rome to be raised at a Catholic institution.

In the face of burgeoning international protests, Pope Pius IX took a personal interest in the boy and resisted all pressures to return him to his family. But the case didn't die; in fact, it was among the events that helped turn the tide of opinion against allowing the Catholic Church to continue wielding secular political authority in Italy.[2]

Commenting on this case, Dawkins emphasizes "the presumptuousness whereby religious people *know*, without evidence, that the faith of their birth is the one true faith, all others being aberrations or downright false"

(p. 314). More significantly, there is the insensitivity of the kidnappers to the basic human needs and emotional welfare of a child ripped from his loving parents. For Dawkins, this is "an insensitivity that comes all too easily to a mind hijacked by religious faith" (p. 315).

Dawkins thinks this case is an *exemplar* of what happens to minds "hijacked by religious faith." Apparently, human beings who embrace such faith become ticking time bombs, awaiting the influence of "certain other ingredients that are not hard to come by" to be turned into kidnappers (or murderers) for God.

To say you believe on faith just means, for the new atheists, that you believe something *for no reason at all*, but that you believe it really, really strongly for no reason at all, that you won't change your mind no matter what the evidence, and that you are willing to do anything implied by the belief, even things that would be judged horrific by ordinary moral sensibilities.

Now if this is what religious faith is, the game is up. "Faith" in this sense is clearly pernicious. And no one can really deny that there are cases – both historical and contemporary – in which people who call themselves religious do horrible things based on beliefs that are hermetically sealed from critical scrutiny. There's no doubt that "faith" has been invoked, historically and today, in ways that no reasonable, morally sensitive person should endorse.

But that's hardly the end of the story. Not every case of *believing what cannot be proved* is the sort of blind dogmatism the new atheists have in mind. Faith in their sense, while not exactly uncommon in religious communities, is hardly the only sense of faith which plays a significant role in religious life.

In my own experience teaching in the Bible Belt, I've found that only a minority of my religious students have faith in Harris's and Dawkins' sense. For most, faith appears to be a decision made when reason and evidence can take them no further, a decision to live in hope, a hope that calls them to trust in a God of love.

Fides and *Fiducia*

In Christian history, the term "faith" has had two important and distinct ranges of use, corresponding to two Latin terms: *fides* and *fiducia*.[3] *Fides*, which we can translate as "belief-faith," refers to an act of *assent* to religious *teachings* that cannot be rationally proven (because they are about matters that transcend what human reason can know). This is the primary sense of faith discussed by both St Augustine and St Thomas Aquinas and through their influence has become the dominant sense in Roman Catholicism.

Fiducia, by contrast, refers to an act of *trust* in *someone*. Hence, we can translate it as "trust-faith." Religious faith in this sense means placing one's trust in a divine person – in Christianity, it means trusting God or Christ. Emphasis on faith in this sense was a defining feature of the Protestant Reformation, especially in the teachings of Martin Luther and his followers. Philip Melanchthon, in his great work of dogmatic Protestant theology, *Loci communes*, followed his co-reformer Martin Luther in defining faith as *trust in Christ as savior* (1965, pp. 158–9). On this view, Christians who trust Christ put their lives and destinies in Christ's hands, rather than trying to save themselves through their own works.

"Faith" as Dawkins and Harris define it appears to be a species of belief-faith, *not* trust-faith. At first glance, then, one might think their objections to faith only apply to *fides* and have no bearing on *fiducia*. But this would be premature, because *fides* and *fiducia* are related. If you trust someone, you're more likely to believe what they say – even if you can't prove for yourself that they're right. Trust-faith might therefore be a *basis* for belief-faith. Furthermore, when you trust someone, you typically do so based on beliefs you have about them. These beliefs might come from various sources but one possibility is that they're a matter of belief-faith.

In Christianity, belief-faith and trust-faith have been connected in both of these ways. In the Protestant tradition the emphasis has been on *trusting* God. But this trust has often been invoked as a basis for believing things that reason cannot verify – and hence for having a kind of belief-faith.

For example, Christian fundamentalists invoke trust in God as a reason for believing whatever the Bible says. Of course, there are gaps in the thinking here. To move from trusting God to trusting the Bible, we must first accept that the Bible inerrantly expresses the "Word of God." But why believe *that*? Because God has told us so? Where? When? Is there some source of divine revelation *outside* the Bible that assures us that the Bible is revelatory? If so, on what basis do we believe that this other source is revelatory?

Another problem arises when we ask why we should believe that God exists at all, let alone is trustworthy. These beliefs are presupposed in the act of trusting God and so cannot coherently be the *result* of that trust.

In short, matters get tricky if you try to rest *all* your religious beliefs on trust in God. Inevitably, there will be beliefs that need to have their source in something other than that trust. The most significant are those beliefs you need to affirm in order to trust God (for example, that God exists). We might call beliefs of this kind "grounding beliefs." Other beliefs, which I'll call "revelatory beliefs," make claims about where, when, and how God has revealed Himself to humanity. An example would be the belief that the Bible is God's Word, a belief whose difficulties have already been highlighted. Revelatory beliefs piggy-back on our trust in God, but cannot be based on it.

So where do all *these* beliefs come from?

One possibility is that they come entirely from reason and evidence. Consider an analogy. Suppose you receive a note from a friend that says, "Please show up at the high school parking lot tomorrow at 3:30. I can't tell you why, but it will be worth your trouble." Suppose you have excellent reasons to trust your friend (she's proven reliable in the past and seems to care deeply for you). If so, your *grounding* beliefs (the beliefs that lead you to trust her) are rational. And suppose that, upon investigating the note, you recognize your friend's handwriting and see that it's written on stationery you gave her. And so your "revelatory" belief – that the note really comes from your friend – is rational.

You have no reasons apart from your trust in your friend to think there's any value in driving to the high school parking lot tomorrow at 3:30. If you go, you're acting *on faith*. But since your grounding and revelatory beliefs are supported by sound reasons, it's not irrational to go.

So long as you have excellent reasons to believe both that God is credible and that some doctrine really is revealed by God, the new atheists would have little room to complain about believing the doctrine *on faith*. Even though you have no reasons of your own (*internal* reasons) that show you the doctrine is true, you have good *external* reasons for believing it: you know it to come from a credible source.

In fact, faith in this sense is practically essential for living in the world. To get on in life, we need to trust teachers, scholars, and other credible sources. And doing so clearly *is* a virtue – which is why, for example, I think creationists should shut up and listen to Dawkins when he says that life on Earth has been evolving through natural selection for millions of years. Even if they don't have the resources to independently investigate the matter, there's ample reason to believe that, on this issue, Dawkins knows his stuff. And so it would be a virtue to have faith in Dawkins here (even if no sensible person should trust what he has to say about Aquinas).

And so, belief-faith clearly can be rational – *if* it's based on the trust we place in a credible authority. The question is whether religious faith can be understood in this sense.

The Catholic Church has argued that it can.

Catholic Faith

Traditional Catholic thinkers argue that there is compelling rational evidence to believe that the Roman Catholic Church is God's chosen vessel for preserving and communicating divine truth to the world through the ages. The Church is not just a credible authority on divine matters, but *the* authority, whose credibility comes from a sacred commission entrusted to the Church by God.[4]

The argument for this view typically begins with the claim that, were there a God, He would not only reveal Himself and His will to the world but would do so through a *reliable* and *enduring* vessel – one which would manifest its divine commission not merely by claiming to speak for God (although it would do that), but also through other clear signs. For example, its message would be consistent over time and logically consistent with what reason and evidence teach (even if it transcends them); and it would exhibit obvious outward signs of holiness and goodness.[5]

Were we to look into the world and find something fitting this description, the discovery of such a thing would be evidence, first of all, that there is a God, and secondly, that He's revealed Himself through the vessel we've identified.

And is there something that fits this description? According to traditional Catholic thinkers, there is: the Catholic Church itself. In the words of the first Vatican Council, "the church herself by reason of her astonishing propagation, her outstanding holiness and her inexhaustible fertility in every kind of goodness, by her catholic unity and her unconquerable stability, is a kind of great and perpetual motive of credibility and an incontrovertible evidence of her own divine mission" (Tanner 1990, pp. 807–8).

Catholic thinkers will usually say that the evidence for the Church's credibility is not *irresistible* and that the decision to base one's life on Church teachings is a matter of *will*, not intellectual necessity. In the Catholic view, this further act of will is usually thought to be motivated by God's grace.

This is in keeping with Aquinas' definition, according to which faith is "an act of the intellect assenting to the divine truth at the command of the will moved by the grace of God."[6] In defining faith in this way, it is Aquinas's intent to ensure that faith is "subject to the free-will in relation to God" and hence can be judged "meritorious" (1952 II–II, q. 2, art 9), and also to ensure that divine influence is an essential element of faith.[7]

But even if we set aside any supernatural influence, there are good reasons for making commitments *stronger* than the weight of the evidence. Sometimes, the best evidence is only available to those who have already committed themselves to a belief. If you waited to get married until you had decisive evidence for the suitability of the match, you'd never marry. Likewise, political leaders often have to make policy decisions in the absence of decisive evidence.

Without a habit of making resolute commitments when the evidence is only *suggestive*, you'd be too tentative to succeed in life. Such a habit is therefore a virtue, a character trait essential for a good life. And so, if the evidence leans towards the Catholic Church as a credible religious authority, then perhaps trusting it resolutely is a virtue. By implication, it would be virtuous to believe Church teachings even if you cannot see, based on reasons available to you, that the teachings are true.

Some brilliant thinkers have found their way to Catholicism through precisely this line of thinking and it would be a mistake to dismiss it too quickly. Nevertheless, I don't buy it. If I did, the argument would compel me to be a Catholic. And while I think a reasonable person *could* embrace the overall theological substance of Roman Catholicism, I'm not a Catholic.

The Failure of the Catholic View of Faith

The traditional Catholic view of faith gets off the ground based on two initial claims:

1 Were there a God, He would establish a reliable and enduring repository of divine revelation, through which the truths of revelation are dispensed to humanity.
2 The Catholic Church looks like this kind of repository of divine revelation.

One obvious problem here is that, for many, claim 2 just seems wrong. The Catholic Church does *not* look as we would expect God's chosen vessel of revelation to look. Church history is hardly as stainless as the Vatican Council statement would have us believe. The new atheists provide a nice assortment of examples that testify to this point (see, especially, Harris 2004, ch. 3). Although they dwell on the Church's failings at the expense of its achievements (its record of pursuing social justice for the poor should never be downplayed), their concerns cannot be ignored. Even were there some way to reconcile the brutality of the Inquisition and the Crusades with the overall picture of the Church painted by the First Vatican Council, the bloody footprints of history are at least enough to cast doubt on whether the Catholic Church really has the "outstanding holiness" we'd expect of God's chosen repository for divine truth.

And when it comes to believing that a terrestrial institution speaks for God, I'm hesitant to endorse the idea that it's a virtue to make a whole-hearted commitment based on evidence that's mixed. To the extent that the link between the Church and God can be questioned, there's a real risk that trusting the Church as if it were the voice of God on Earth amounts to investing in a fallible human institution the kind of trust that simply cannot be borne by anything merely human. The result may be faithful obedience to commands that, in retrospect, history can only judge with horror.

And this risk does not just apply to trusting the Church. It also applies to investing divine authority in any *book* written by human hands (such as the Bible or Koran). To the extent that the link between the book and God is open to critical challenge, there is, again, the risk of investing in a fallible human creation the kind of trust that nothing human can bear.

Credible human authorities should be trusted but not *without question*. If a trusted human authority says something that seems outrageous, it would at least make sense to investigate the matter. At what point should trust give way when the available evidence counts against a credible source? That depends on the credentials of the authority. If the authority has *divine infallibility*, then the trust should in principle never give way, even to an enormous body of contrary evidence.

And that, of course, is the problem. When we choose to believe that someone (or something) speaks for God, we are choosing to invest them with a degree of authority that, if not identical with God's infallibility, at least approaches it. And if the one in whom we invest such trust is, after all, merely human, the results can be dire.

It's far from obvious that *anything* in this world is the kind of incontrovertible witness to its own divine origins that the First Vatican Council took the Church to be (and that Protestant fundamentalists take the Bible to be). And so, the deep problem with religious faith conceived in this sense is that there's nothing *in* the world that looks enough like a vessel of divine revelation to justify the potentially dire consequences of guessing wrong.

Now this conclusion would be rather devastating for theistic religion if you believed that, were there a God, He would create a reliable and enduring repository of divine revelation – that is, if you believed claim 1 above. But do theists really need to believe this?

Many Christians believe it because they think that human salvation depends on getting our beliefs about God right – and so, any God who desires our salvation would *have* to establish some reliable and enduring repository for divine truth, one that we can recognize as such.

But consider some facts. While numerous religions argue that *they* are the one true receptacle of divine revelation, their arguments rarely convince anyone outside the religious tradition making the argument. What we find convincing on this subject depends largely on upbringing.

To say that salvation depends on getting our beliefs right therefore amounts to saying that whether you're saved will largely depend on your upbringing. But this doesn't seem like a situation a good God would permit. And so, for anyone who believes in a *good* God, there is no small reason to be suspicious of the view that our salvation depends on getting our beliefs right.

A Lutheran Alternative

And this leads me back to Luther's understanding of faith. For Luther, faith is about trusting God, not primarily as a credible authority concerning what to believe, but as a savior. In Luther's view, the Christian message is twofold: first, that there is nothing we can do to overcome the obstacles to our own salvation; second, that we don't have to do anything because God by His grace has done it for us.

The assumption, of course, is that we need saving. And for Luther, what we need saving from is our own sinfulness. For Luther, the essence of sin is alienation from God and from one another. We fail both to love God as we should and to love our neighbors as ourselves. And so we're cut off from the source of all good as well as from our fellows. Since humans find true fulfillment only through communion with God and community with neighbors, we're therefore cut off from authentic happiness.

And experience teaches those of us who try to love as we should that we always fall short. We betray our dearest friends – if not outwardly, then by our inner thoughts. We value fleeting material goods more than the source of all being and life. The more we try to overcome these deficits on our own, the more we confirm our infirmity.

For Luther, faith involves trusting in God's grace to overcome this alienation – which means putting your fate in God's hands, rather than in trying to forge your own fate through your own efforts. Faith in Luther's sense is far more like trusting the pilot of an airplane to get you to your destination than it is like trusting the credibility of a supposed authority. Arriving at your destination does not depend on anything *you* do. It certainly doesn't depend on believing the right kinds of things about the pilot. Your safe arrival depends, instead, on what the *pilot* does.

If you refuse to trust the pilot and so decide to wrest the controls for yourself, even though you don't know how to fly a plane, then chances are you'll crash.[8] For Luther, this insistence on doing it yourself (called works righteousness) is the fundamental impediment to salvation.

It follows, of course, that insistence on being able to get all your beliefs about God right is an impediment to salvation. Getting your beliefs right is every bit as much a matter of your own works, your own efforts, as is more traditional outward activity.

If this view about salvation is correct, the existence of a single reliable repository of divine revelation might actually be an impediment to salvation, rather than a necessary prerequisite for it (a point Luther and his followers may not have adequately appreciated). Such a repository would encourage the practice of trying to save ourselves by devotedly embracing everything this authority declares.

This is not to say that God doesn't reveal Himself, only that He would be unlikely to reveal Himself in *that* way, namely, through an infallible "central authority." But how *would* God – that is, a God that it makes sense to entrust with our very salvation – reveal Himself? If Luther is right about our moral degeneracy, then the only kind of God we could trust to save us would be one who wanted what's best for us despite our unworthiness – in other words, a God who loves unconditionally.

How would such a God of love reveal Himself?

Love and Revelation

Such a God might come to us in a profound person-to-person contact between a finite human and the incomprehensible divine – in other words, through mystical experience. But such experience might prove too overwhelming for finite minds to grasp. We'd get a sense of an encounter with truth but we wouldn't be equipped to put the lessons into a form we could use. And if God is love, He might especially want to teach us about love in ways we can understand.

How might He do it? By writing a book? By establishing a hierarchical institution that issues decrees?

Unlikely. We learn about love not mainly from books or institutional pronouncements but by getting on with the messy business of loving one another. If God's essence is love, it seems we should expect that divine self-disclosure (beyond the ineffable sort that the mystics know) would occur first and foremost in and through loving relationships.

Love has two experiential sides to it: the experience of being loved, and the experience of loving. Mystical experience, being passive, can only offer direct insight into the former (although it might inspire the latter). Since there is nothing God needs from us, our love for God cannot be anything like God's love for us. We come closest to experiencing what it's like to love *as God loves* only when we love our neighbors. Such an experience may acquire the character of divine revelation when it results from surrendering our wills to the loving will that transcends us, so that we are, in effect, *channeling* divine love. When we do so, we feel God's presence in a different but no less profound way than the mystics do. Many deeply religious people report a deep sense of God's love working through them, enabling them to be more unconditionally loving than they could ever have imagined being on their own.

I would argue that it is in experiencing this exalted neighbor-love *from both sides* that a loving God is most perfectly revealed. Does it really make sense to suppose that, if God is love, His chosen vessel of revelation would be an institution or static text? Doesn't it make more sense to suppose that, in those moments when our capacity to love bursts through the usual layers of fear and self-absorption, *we* become the revelation of God?[9]

Since a crucial feature of love is the attention we pay to others, an authoritative book or institution could actually be an *impediment* to love. We'd be in constant danger of paying more attention to the authority than to our neighbors. When gays and lesbians cry out in despair that the uncompromising condemnation of homosexuality is crushing their souls, instead of listening compassionately we may smugly cite Bible verses that condemn their most intimate relationships. When a text or institution becomes for us the very voice of God, it threatens to drown out the voices of the neighbors we should love.

If God *is* a person, there would be more of God in our neighbors than in any book or institution. And so, anything that led us to pay more attention to a book or creed than to our neighbors would be directing us *away* from what is most God-like in the world.

All of this suggests that if God reveals Himself to the world, he wouldn't do so in some book or institution that might, by virtue of its divine authority, drown out the voices of the persons around us; He would, instead, do so through loving encounters with real people. And if we want to extract from these encounters general lessons about God and the good, it seems unlikely that the best strategy would involve referring to a book or pronouncement on high. If we want those lessons to be guided by divine love, wouldn't it make more sense to pursue those lessons in interpersonal conversations characterized by mutual love – that is, conversations in which we strive to let our dialogue be guided by a spirit of unconditional love? Such conversations wouldn't generate certainty. But given how often certainty leads us to *stop* listening, to *stop* caring about others' perspectives, the revelation of a God of love would probably fall short of producing certainty.

Uncertainty would be devastating if our salvation depended on getting our beliefs right. But on a roughly Lutheran view, no such thing is needed. We're free to explore questions of divine truth in empathetic conversations, without fearing that our destinies hinge on getting the right answers. We can have our beliefs without having to create illusory props of infallibility, without needing to adopt, in Dawkins' words, "the presumptuousness whereby religious people *know*, without evidence, that the faith of their birth is the one true faith, all others being aberrations or downright false." If our fate doesn't turn on being right about the ultimate truths, we can cast off that demand for certainty which sees alternative views as a threat.

A God of love, it seems, would stand opposed to the kind of "faith" that alienates us from all those "heretics" who don't believe as we do. And so a God of love – the only kind of God it makes sense to entrust with our salvation – would never make "right belief" a condition *for* salvation. The function of revelation would thus be quite different from what conservative Christians take it to be. Instead of being about showing what we must believe to be saved, it would be a means of building relationships among humans and with God, of helping realize what Martin Luther King called *the beloved community*.

Reason for Trust?

I can already hear the objections. Dawkins may well stand together with James Dobson in protesting this picture of things. "All of this sounds lovely," they might say, "but doesn't it make an astonishing number of *presuppositions*? To trust God as your savior in this nominally 'Lutheran' way assumes that God exists, that God loves us and wants to save us, that God has the means to save us, that we need saving, that we can't save ourselves, and so on. To get to this view of faith as trust, you first need a rich network of religious beliefs – grounding beliefs as you've called them. And by your own admission, these beliefs can't be based on trust in God. So where do these beliefs *come* from? Loving discourse won't do the trick. Atheists love others, but they don't treat what they learn about love as having anything to do with God."

We might restate this objection in terms of the analogy of trusting an airline pilot. When you get on a plane, you trust the pilot to get you to your destination. But this trust doesn't occur in a vacuum. You believe the pilot is qualified to fly the plane and in the right mental and physical condition to fly it. You believe that, in order to get safely to your destination, someone with the expertise to pilot the plane is needed – and that this someone isn't you. And these beliefs don't come from nowhere. *They're rationally justified.* Your beliefs about the pilot's abilities are justified by the intense regulation that the airline industry enjoys. The other relevant beliefs are likewise justified.

And so an act of trust is rational.

But when it comes to trusting God in the way I've proposed, we need a complex framework of grounding beliefs. And if you set aside, as I have done, the authority of religious institutions and texts, it becomes hard to claim that these grounding beliefs are based on the weight of reason and evidence. And so, doesn't my favored version of trust-faith presuppose beliefs that can only derive from the "motivated credulity" that the new atheists despise?

There are several possible replies to this line of objection. One has been developed by Alvin Plantinga (1983, 1993a, 1993b, 2000) in a series of works spanning two decades. In brief, Plantinga's view is that many of our beliefs are not based on other beliefs but are formed in us directly by some kind of cognitive process or faculty (he calls these "basic beliefs"). For example, my belief that there's a pen in front of me isn't something I deduce from other beliefs. Instead, my senses connect me with the world and a cognitive faculty converts sense experiences into an empirical belief: *there is a pen in front of me.*

If the cognitive process generating the belief is functioning properly and is reliable under the current conditions, then my basic belief will be, in Plantinga's terms, "warranted." But how do I know that this cognitive process *is* reliable? We've already encountered this problem in the last chapter. As William Alston notes, there is no noncircular proof for the reliability of my senses. Instead, my empirical beliefs just strike me as correct. They come at me with vivid force. They just seem right.

Plantinga asks us why we shouldn't suppose that our basic religious beliefs are formed in us by a cognitive faculty every bit as reliable as we take the empirical one to be. He even gives this cognitive faculty a name. Following Calvin, he calls it the *sensus divinitatus.* We trust our empirical beliefs because they just seem true to us and we attribute this sense of accuracy to the work of a reliable cognitive faculty. So why not trust religious beliefs that just seem right to us, on the same grounds?

There is much more to Plantinga's line of argument than this. But it isn't my intention to explore Plantinga's theory in detail. There is much of it that I find powerful and convincing but just as much that I find unconvincing. I have numerous technical disagreements, but my strongest objection is this. When I reflect on conversations I've had with those who embrace the beliefs that lie behind their trust in God, it doesn't seem accurate to say that they accept these grounding beliefs because they just seem right to them in something like the way that their empirical beliefs do.

In my own case, I know that my religious beliefs don't feel the same as my belief that there are four beers in the fridge or that I had granola for breakfast. Those beliefs feel like they spring from a reliable faculty. While my religious beliefs are in harmony with the urgings of my faculties, there are crucial elements of my religious beliefs that reach beyond what those faculties generate. It isn't my cognitive faculties that motivate my belief in God. Rather, it's a spirit of hope.

Pragmatic Faith

For many if not most theists, faith in God appears to be a decision to *live in hope* – that is, to live as if a hopeful picture of the world is true. This hopeful picture isn't indifferent to reason and evidence. In fact, central experiential intuitions speak in its favor – inklings of some grander reality that supports and upholds the deepest yearning of the human soul, what Schleiermacher really meant by "the intuition of the Infinite in the finite" and "the feeling of absolute dependence."

Reformed epistemology may play a role in explaining why there is no deep irrationality in trusting these experiential intuitions. But these intuitions do not come to us with all the detail of a distinctive religious picture of the world – one in which, for example, God is a personal spirit who cares about the good. So how do we arrive at such a picture? For most of us, we encounter one sketched out in inherited religious narratives, or a grand theological vision, or a simple sermon – and we are struck by its beauty. It resonates with our deepest hopes.

And we pause and think: It *could* be true. My experience is as consistent with this account of things as it is with any other. And we pause again, and we imagine what it would be like to experience the world through the lens of this story – and we prefer who we are when we see the world in this way. We like better what the world and our experience means. And it *could* be true.

And so we choose to live in hope.

In my case, as with so many others, the hope is that there is a God of love in whom we can trust – a God who preserves what *ought* to endure because its very existence is *good.*

Is this decision to live in hope nothing but wish-thinking? Let's return for a moment to the case of being an airplane passenger. You trust the pilot, and hence can enjoy the flight without paralyzing fear. But you have good reasons to trust the pilot and so your faith is more than just wish-thinking. It's rational.

But suppose you're on a small passenger plane and partway into the flight the pilot collapses with an aneurism. Abruptly, another passenger rises and says, "I'm certified to fly this plane!"

You know nothing about this man. Your only evidence that he's qualified to fly is his word. And so, to trust his flying, you first must trust his word. You must trust *him*, in the absence of any external evidence supporting his trustworthiness.

And just to make matters interesting, let's invoke the prejudices Sam Harris so shamelessly exploits for rhetorical effect throughout *The End of Faith*. Let's suppose the man looks Middle Eastern. There's a copy of an Arab newspaper on his seat. And so, gripped by typical post-9/11 prejudices, the thought immediately enters your head that he might be a terrorist-of-opportunity, seizing on the tragedy to turn the plane into a weapon.

Do you trust him? If you do, you're implicitly endorsing the "grounding beliefs" that imply his trustworthiness: he's qualified to fly the plane and he means to get you safely to your destination. But you are affirming these beliefs without evidence. Given the need for immediate action, there can *be* no evidence beyond his assurances.

Suppose you decide to trust him. Why did you do so? Perhaps because, as far as you can tell, the grounding beliefs for your trust *could* be true. And the alternative to trusting him is . . . what? Suppose the radio is broken. No air traffic controller will talk an inexpert flyer through the process. Suppose the flying conditions are especially tricky. What's the alternative to trust? A few more hours to chat with other passengers before the plane crashes into a mountain?

To trust is an act of hope, a decision to live *as if* the grounding beliefs for such trust are true, in the hope that they are true instead of out of the fear that they are not.

The sense of faith I am proposing here is what Richard Swinburne (1981) calls "pragmatic faith." In describing such faith, Swinburne focuses on the person who believes that "long-term and deep well-being for himself and others . . . are only to be had if there is a God who provides such well-being in this world and in the world to come." This person acts "on the assumption that there is a God – for unless there is, that which is most worthwhile cannot be had" (p. 117).

Historically, the most important philosophical defender of pragmatic faith is William James (1897), who famously developed it in his essay, "The Will to Believe." In that essay, James defends the thesis that "Our passional nature not only lawfully may, but must, decide an option between propositions, whenever it is a genuine option that cannot by its nature be decided on intellectual grounds" (p. 11). It *must* decide because to "leave the question open" carries "the same risk of losing the truth," and is thus itself "a passional decision" (p. 11).

James defends this thesis for what he calls "genuine" options. In a genuine option, we must choose among alternative beliefs, each of which might be true as far as our intellects can discern. Furthermore, putting off a decision amounts for practical purposes to favoring one of the alternatives. And the choice isn't trivial, but has great significance for your life (pp. 3–4).

Suppose you've been married before. You were deeply in love and honestly thought you'd found an ideal mate – but once you were married, hidden incompatibilities surfaced and your marriage collapsed. Now you're in love again. Once again, the person seems an ideal mate. But you know from experience that the evidence is woefully incomplete. The only way to get all relevant evidence is actually to make the commitment. But to do that would be to act *as if* the love of your life is, in fact, an ideal mate. To refuse to decide amounts to deciding against marriage. The time has come to choose. Reason and evidence can take you no further. And the choice you make is hardly trivial.

In cases like this, James argues, your "passional nature" not only *may* decide the matter, but must. You can marry in the hope that you'll enjoy the benefits of a happy marriage. Or you can choose not to marry, fearful that you'll experience another bitter spiral of conflict and dissatisfaction. But you *must* choose, and you cannot choose on the basis of reason and evidence. You must act *as if* one or the other possibility is true.

Human experience – both empirical *and* religious – is open to multiple interpretations. We live in a universe that, in John Hick's words, "is religiously ambiguous, capable both of being seen as a purely natural phenomenon and of being seen as God's creation and experienced as mediating God's presence" (2001, p. 42). And these views hardly exhaust the options (as Hick himself would admit). Human experience does not demand one specific worldview but is compatible with many alternatives.

And yet which worldview we choose matters. It profoundly shapes how we experience the world. Hick argues, in an essay entitled "Seeing-as and Religious Experience," that all our ordinary experience of the world involves an interpretive dimension. He argues that "the true character of the universe does not force itself upon us, and we are left with an important element of freedom and responsibility in our response to it." For Hick, "this uncompelled interpretation of our experience of life is to be identified with *faith* in the most fundamental sense of that word" (1989b, p. 191).

The new atheists typically adopt a worldview that is purely naturalistic. But this worldview isn't compelled by the nature of reality impinging on experience. Their atheism is a matter of *faith*, that is, a way of seeing the world that they have chosen from an array of alternatives about which reason and evidence have nothing decisive to say.

But a different choice than theirs is possible. Religious faith, in the sense I have in mind, involves a choice that is no less rational than theirs – only more hopeful.

The Ethico-Religious Hope Revisited

There are worldviews that can be chosen out of fear. What if there's a supernatural tyrant who smites anyone who doesn't fawn and obey? The fear of this possibility can inspire a passional choice to live as if this worldview were true. The result is what Plutarch calls superstition.

Such superstition is alive and well today and it fuels the fires of atheism just as it did in Plutarch's day. The anger of today's atheists is born in this sea of superstition. Their anger is warranted but it is misdirected by error – specifically, the error of identifying superstitious "faith" with religious faith in any sense of the term. Superstitious belief in a tyrannical God *cannot* inspire *fiducia*. It can inspire fawning obedience but not the self-surrender that Luther advocates, not the act of placing ourselves in God's hands, trusting that He will take care of us.

When God is treated as a tyrant, Lutheran *fiducia* becomes impossible. Trust-faith in the roughly Lutheran sense requires that our choice of worldview be motivated by hope rather than fear. But even that is not enough to characterize it. There are, after all, different things we might hope for. Our hopes might be colored by hatred of our enemies so that what we hope for is their doom – a hope that leads us to embrace a tribal god whose main objective is the humiliating defeat of those we despise.

But such bloodthirsty hope is radically disconnected from religious experience as I've been describing it. The kind of religion I want to defend is precisely that which builds on the foundation laid by that experience. And any religion that builds on that foundation must be true to its content.

And what is that content? It's one that replaces the universe of "pitiless indifference" with a grander vision in which alienation is overcome, enmities reconciled, hostilities dissolved in the sense of a fundamental interconnectedness. The hope for a supernatural ally in our wars against our enemies is common enough but it doesn't have its origins in Schleiermacher's feeling of piety, nor in the numinous visions of the mystics. More likely, it originates in impulses born of evolution, a legacy of the tribalism in which humans came of age. Religious experience, and the hopes that it can generate, are fundamentally at odds with the warrior's faith in a tribal god.

Put simply, the decision to live in hope can be benign or it can be objectionable. What makes it so is the substance of what is hoped for. And when the substance of that hope is that *the universe is fundamentally on the side of goodness*, living in hope may have implications that are better than living without such hope.

The experience of life given by a stripped-down empiricism may lie behind much of what we think of as *sin*. In the face of an indifferent universe, we scramble for security – for enough material possessions to weather the vicissitudes of fate, enough power to control our destinies. In a world of limited resources we jostle for more, careless of how others are hurt. We form cooperative groups to promote survival, but other such groups become rivals and therefore enemies. We vilify and dehumanize them.

Even those close to us can suffer from our anxiety and bitterness in the face of a hostile world. We become self-absorbed in our frantic quest for security. More significantly, we are afraid to love too much, to care too deeply, because in a world of pitiless indifference, to do so is to court grief, to open ourselves to shattering loss.

Religious experience suggests that there may be salvation from this life of fear, this insecure existence in which caring often comes with a crushing price tag. There may be salvation from what we *become* in such a world of "pitiless indifference," as well as salvation from the consequences of existence in such a world. In Christian language, there may be salvation from sin and death. The substance of religious experience tells us that, at its root, the universe is *not* dead matter and energy and blind mechanistic laws. At root, there is something more, something that affirms and lifts up and connects.

Of course, it *may* be just delusional. But there's no compelling reason to think so. And we can choose to live in hope.

In fact, we can hope for the very best imaginable. We can hope that the vista suggested by religious experience and supported by the cosmological argument is nothing less than a fundamental reality that cares about the good and is working to ensure that nothing of genuine value is ever truly lost.

What we have here, of course, is the ethico-religious hope. It is Luther's hope, the only kind that can lead to *fiducia* in his sense – that is, to trusting God as *savior*. If there is any kind of belief-faith that deserves to be called religious, it is this: faith in God, conceived as that being who fulfills our ethico-religious hope. When I speak of religious faith, what I mean is the choice to live in this ambiguous and conceptually malleable universe *as if* our ethico-religious hope were fulfilled.

And what does it look like to live as if this hope has been fulfilled? It involves an act of trusting in a fundamental good at the root of reality, an act of trust which enables us to set aside our frantic quest for security, our fear of death, our bitterness towards competitors for limited resources. It involves the freedom to love without the reticence that comes with the fear of loss. It involves an ability to set aside the fruitless effort to save ourselves by our own works and thereby set aside the concomitant need for certainty, the need to be perfect, and the need to control others' beliefs and behaviors so that they don't compromise our efforts.

This is not the faith that would lead anyone to steal a boy from his loving home, or fly a plane into an occupied building, or convert heretics by torture. Religious faith, conceived as I am suggesting, has its own internal logic that precludes such things.

The Logic of Faith

In the sense I have in mind, religious faith involves living as if our ethico-religious hope were more than just a hope. It involves choosing a world-view, a way of seeing life, which says that the fundamental reality is not blind matter and energy but something that cares about the good and so preserves it. To live as if this is true means that we trust in the object of our hope, which we call God.

If this is what I mean by religious faith, it clearly involves believing beyond the evidence. But that doesn't mean it lacks standards. Dawkins is perplexed when moderate religious voices denounce violent extremists for perverting the faith, since faith, "lacking any objective justification, doesn't have any demonstrable standard to pervert" (2006, p. 306). But if religious moderates mean by "faith" something close to what I am describing, then it *does* have standards, even if they are not the same as those of science.

We've already encountered many of these standards. Religious faith involves embracing a hopeful *interpretation* of the world encountered in experience. As such, it must be true not only to the content of the religious experiences that give it birth but also to the empirical facts. If it rejects the empirical facts, as Young Earth Creationists do, it isn't providing a hopeful interpretation of *this* world at all, but of some fantasy.

Furthermore, because religious faith involves putting one's trust in the transcendent, the transcendent must be construed as trustworthy. Any beliefs about God that render Him capricious, cruel, or vindictive, are thus ruled out by the logic of faith.

The logic of faith also rules out what Dawkins calls "the presumptuousness whereby religious people *know*, without evidence, that the faith of their birth is the one true faith, all others being aberrations or downright false." I have already argued that faith in the Lutheran sense does not require "getting our beliefs right." And so there is no need, on this view of faith, for false certainty. But the logic of faith does more than just erase the need for the presumptuousness Dawkins abhors. It opposes it.

Why? Because faith is an act of *hope*, not recognition of some incontrovertible truth. And more than one religious worldview can satisfy our ethico-religious hope. I am a Christian because the Christian story – a story in which God reaches across the gap between the infinite and the finite, suffers the anguish of finitude, and thereby redeems the world – is a story I find incomparably beautiful. It feeds my ethico-religious hope. But there are other religious stories, in other traditions, which speak powerfully to the hopes of others.

If the basis for my religious belief is a decision to live as if a hoped-for picture of things is true, I cannot condemn others who live in the very same hope, even if their picture differs in its details. I *can* condemn those who live in some bloodthirsty hope fundamentally at odds with the feeling of piety. I can say, "That is not *my* hope and not *my* faith, but something at odds with it." And I can give reasons why the ethico-religious hope is a better thing to hope for than a world of tribal gods at war, in which the violence and divisions of earthly life are reinforced in the transcendent realm. But if I can legitimately live as if a narrative that satisfies my ethico-religious hope is true, then so can you – even if your narrative differs from mine.

And I know from experience that many have been so poisoned against the Christian story that they cannot find in it the beauty and inspiration I find and so will never be moved by it to take the step of trust which is the essential act of faith. Because I want them to share that faith, I would never pressure them to be Christian. By the logic of my faith, I want them to find inspiration where they can.

Finally, *fiducia* involves entrusting ourselves to a God of love – which means inviting a transcendent good to enter our lives and do for us what we cannot do for ourselves. And one of the things we cannot do for ourselves is come to know God through our ordinary cognitive faculties. Empirical investigation and rational inquiry are, in us, finite things. God, if He exists, is not similarly finite. We can't grasp the infinite. Our only hope of knowing it will be if it lays hold of us.

What is needed, in short, is an attitude of expectant readiness to experience the divine. Such expectant readiness may be the first act of trust-faith. If there is a God, the experiential evidence of that fact may come only if we first make this venture of trust.

Such trust involves openness to being moved by a reality that transcends our understanding. It is about being open to encountering a transcendent truth, not about believing whatever we want. Those who adopt a false certainty, who refuse to be budged by reason or evidence, who care not a whit for arguments, exhibit no such openness. To lay yourself fully in God's hands is an act of trust which involves exposing yourself fully to the truth about God, whatever that might be. You are not trusting God so long as you cling tenaciously to your beliefs, refusing to be moved by a truth that transcends them.

Those who believe in this willful way are devoted to their own *image* of God, not to God. And they thus display no real *fiducia*. They are, in the language of Christianity, idolaters.

It should be no surprise that idolatry is rampant, and the new atheists do a fine job of describing this distinctive species of it. But, rather than noticing that it *is* a species of idolatry, one that precludes religious faith as *fiducia*, they identify such idolatry *with* faith. And then they conclude that *faith* is evil.

This is the sort of reasoning I'd expect from religious fundamentalists. But then, maybe that's what the new atheists are.

9

Evil and the Meaning of Life

There's a white elephant in the room. Although I pointed it out in Chapter 2, I haven't looked it in the eye since then. And some may suspect it's started stomping on the furniture.

In his *Letter to a Christian Nation* (2006), Sam Harris notes that, statistically speaking, somewhere in the world right now a little girl is being abducted, raped, and killed. And the same statistics suggest that her parents believe that "an all-powerful and all-loving God is watching over them and their family." Harris asks, "Are they right to believe this? Is it good that they believe this?"

His answer? "No."

According to Harris, this answer contains "the entirety of atheism" and is simply "an admission of the obvious." He encourages his readers to "admit the obvious": that when devout Hurricane Katrina victims drowned in their attics while praying to God for deliverance, they "died talking to an imaginary friend" (pp. 50–2).

With righteous indignation, Harris condemns the "boundless narcissism" of those who survive a disaster only to "believe themselves spared by a loving God, while this same God drowned infants in their cribs" (p. 54).

In a world where evils strike indiscriminately, where villains prosper while children die of cystic fibrosis, anyone who credits an omnipotent God for their earthly fortune, as if God had selectively intervened on their behalf while leaving others to languish, is implying that God plays favorites in a decidedly pernicious way.[1] The god of these faithful is no *God* worth worshipping but just another variant of the *god* of superstition.

But is it even possible to believe in a God worth worshipping in a world where billions survive on less than two dollars a day?

This is just another way to pose the theological problem of evil. The problem is hardly new. Hume (1989) was paraphrasing the ancient Greek philosopher Epicurus when he stated the problem as follows: "Is he willing to prevent evil, but not able? Then is he impotent. Is he able, but not willing? Then is he malevolent. Is he both able and willing? Whence then is evil?" (p. 84).

It's a question no theist should ignore: *Whence then is evil?*

But it's also a question that should be juxtaposed against a related one. We live in a world in which all of us are implicated in what Marilyn McCord Adams (1990, 2006) has called "horrors": crushing evils that seem to strip the lives of those caught up in them of any positive meaning. In such a world, is it possible to view life as worth living *without* believing in a transcendent good that redeems the world?

It may be possible for those of us lucky enough not to have experienced horror or witnessed it firsthand and callous enough that we can ignore its pervasiveness and our own complicity. But what about the rest of us?

What we have here are two interwoven problems. The theological problem of evil is, of course, no problem for atheists; it's simply an argument against God's existence. They call it the "argument from evil." The *problem* is faced by theists who want to reconcile their belief in God with the world's evils.

But one reason why theists want to defend their faith is because of the second problem, sometimes called the *existential* problem of evil. This problem isn't about how to reconcile God's existence with the world's evils but how to find positive meaning in life despite them. And for many, the only viable solution comes from the promise of a transcendent good that fulfills our ethico-religious hope – in other words, from *God*.

The Evidential Argument from Evil

The argument from evil is a challenge to the existence of God traditionally conceived as omnipotent, omniscient, and perfectly good. But I have defined God less precisely – as a transcendent being who fulfills our ethico-religious hope.

To fulfill that hope, God would have to be good, and He would have to be greater than any evil (in the sense that, given God's existence, evils would cease to have ultimate significance). But this isn't the same as being all-powerful. So why can't we just sidestep the problem of evil altogether by admitting that God isn't omnipotent?

Unfortunately, the problem won't evaporate so easily. Even if we accept that God is not all-powerful, we may still ask: Why does evil look so significant if it isn't? If reality is fundamentally on the side of goodness, why don't we all have a clear sense of God's redemptive work, an awareness that evils are fleeting while the good eternal?

Let me consider this problem in concrete terms. Not long ago, the distracted negligence of a home daycare provider combined with plain bad luck to take the life of my friend's 18-month-old son, a gentle boy fiercely loved by his parents. In the face of this tragedy, my friend and his wife have been sustained by a religious faith which promises that everything good and beautiful about their child has been embraced by the deepest reality in the universe. Their little boy's potential was not lost on that terrible day, but has been *actualized* in the bosom of God.

On Dawkins' view, there's no such God to embrace this child's soul. For Dawkins, the boy is gone – and while memories survive, these too will eventually disappear with the deaths of those who now remember him. The material universe doesn't care about us or our loves. It grinds on, eventually destroying everything whose existence we treasure.

But if my friends are right and Dawkins wrong about the nature of the universe, why did the wheels of chance and human negligence snuff out their son's precious life at all? The way that events unfold in the empirically observable world more closely fits Dawkins' picture of things than theirs.

And shouldn't we base our worldview on the available evidence? The evils in the world, atheists might argue, comprise a telling body of evidence, in the face of which our ethico-religious hope amounts to nothing but irrational "wish-thinking." This deeper problem of evil persists even if we concede that God isn't omnipotent. In its simplest terms, the problem is that a broadly theistic picture of the world seems unlikely, given the empirical evidence.

This deeper problem is strongly reminiscent of the so-called *evidential argument from evil*, which has become the dominant version of the argument in philosophical circles since William Rowe (1979) first sketched it out. Even though this "evidential argument" explicitly targets the existence of a traditional God, complete with omnipotent powers, looking at it may offer insight into the deeper problem of evil.

The basic thrust of the evidential argument is this: An all-powerful and perfectly good God would not allow an evil to exist *unless there were a morally sufficient reason* to allow it. Evil that doesn't meet this condition is gratuitous.

But if we look at the evils in the world, many *seem* gratuitous (Rowe's example is the painful death of a fawn burned in a forest fire). And so, the world *looks* like one in which there does not exist an all-powerful and perfectly good God. The evils we see may not *prove* there is no God, but they make atheism the view that best fits the evidence.[2]

How can theists respond to this argument? The traditional way is to offer a "theodicy" – that is, an *explanation of why* a good and all-powerful God would permit the world's evils.

Theodicies

Among theodicies, two basic approaches are especially important. The first focuses on "moral evils" – that is, wicked choices and their evil consequences – and argues that a good God must allow them out of respect for human freedom.

In the words of Richard Swinburne (1998), "It is intrinsically good (good for us) that we shall have much responsibility, and make significant choices between many good and bad alternatives" (p. 159). In creating humans, God has created beings of great intrinsic value. But He has also created beings whose dignity hinges on being *responsible agents*, with the freedom to make choices with real consequences for good or ill – what Swinburne calls *efficacious* freedom (p. 11).

Out of respect for that freedom, God must not merely give us space to form evil intentions but to carry them out. Were an all-powerful God to do His best to eliminate the evil consequences of our choices, no one could ever affect the world for ill. And there would be nothing left for me to accomplish were I to take a stand against wickedness. The same good ends would have been realized had I done nothing.

And so, out of respect for efficacious freedom, God must do *less* than His best to prevent evil. Perhaps God's morally optimal strategy for opposing wickedness would be to quietly encourage and support human beings in *their* efforts to resist wickedness, through the urgings of conscience and the inspiration of prophetic voices.

To step in with a show of divine omnipotence would convey a dramatic message that our efficacious freedom is restricted by an all-seeing God; and this would arguably impact such freedom far beyond the frequency of these interventions. It might discourage many from choosing to take a courageous stand against wickedness. To step in *covertly* – through "chance" events, for example – might not have the same effect. But if it became routine – if rapists invariably tripped and fell whenever they were about to attack – efficacious freedom would evaporate. To preserve efficacious freedom, covert intervention would need to be sufficiently infrequent that we'd still feel we have as much freedom to do ill as we have to do good.

While divine interference beyond quiet encouragement would mean less moral evil in the world, it would also diminish efficacious freedom. Deciding the optimal balance between these things is no easy matter and critics routinely challenge "free will" theodicies on precisely this point. Wouldn't just a little more intervention, a bit more show of divine muscle, produce a better balance?

Stated in such general terms, this question might seem easy to rebuff. After all, to decide whether God could have achieved a better balance between protecting efficacious freedom and limiting moral evil, we'd need to know what an optimal balance looks like, and *whether* the scope of moral evil in the world is consistent with such a balance. But that requires a God's-eye view of things. Hence, no mere human can honestly say that it appears as if the scope of moral evil exceeds what an optimal divine policy would allow.

But if we consider the skeptic's question in more concrete terms, it has more force. Consider: was preserving Hitler's efficacious freedom really *worth* the enormous suffering and death that resulted from his choices? The answer seems obviously "no." Given the enormity of the horror resulting from Hitler's choices, intervening covertly to restrict Hitler's freedom would surely have produced the better balance, wouldn't it?

But this way of framing things may betray a confused understanding of what Swinburne and others actually mean to say. As I have argued elsewhere (Reitan 2000), when theists argue that God allows horrific evil to be done out of respect for free will, we shouldn't take them to mean that Hitler's freedom is so valuable that preserving it is worth the costs in untold affliction. Rather, we should take them to mean that God has an *obligation* to respect freedom, one that morally binds Him even when the exercise of that freedom has horrific consequences. The nature of God's relationship to the world, as its creator and sustainer, may impose upon Him unique duties that tie his hands.

For what it's worth, my own view is that, insofar as everything in the world depends absolutely on the creative and sustaining work of the creator, the world's integrity as a separate reality, something in its own right apart from God, may depend on a radical abdication on God's part. The act of creation may be inseparable from an act of radical divine self-restriction. Self-imposed limits on what God can legitimately do in relation to the world may constitute the very condition for the world's existence *as a reality separate from God*. And this may be *especially* true for the independent existence of free beings. If so, then when moral horrors are perpetrated, God may be constrained so radically that all He can do is look on and weep.

Obviously, these ideas, to be convincing, require much fuller development than what I can offer here. But they're suggestive enough to show that, for all we can tell, God may have reasons why He not only may but *must* permit the wicked to carry out their vicious plans.

But not all evils result from wicked choices. Some of the worst suffering is brought on by disease, famine, and natural disaster. While these "natural evils" are often exacerbated by human choices (people *chose* to neglect the New Orleans levies), it isn't reasonable to trace all the harms from natural evils back to human negligence. So how do we reconcile *these* evils with God's goodness?

One ancient solution is to blame them on the wicked choices of supernatural creatures. To preserve the efficacious freedom of angels, God must allow them the same opportunity we have to act for good or ill. Angels must have the freedom to fall.

But there are obvious problems here. We have ample evidence that *humans* who make bad choices exist, and we can trace much evil directly to them. But there is no real evidence for the existence of fallen angels. We can fully explain natural evils by appeal to predictable physical laws. Furthermore, the hypothesis that demons are to blame for AIDS and earthquakes is, for most people today, a dead hypothesis.

Finally, free will theodicies leave unexplained the fundamental problem at the heart of the evidential argument from evil: why does all this evil – whether it comes from the free choices of villains or demons – *look* so significant? Why isn't God present in the midst of suffering, wiping away the tears even if He can't prevent the tragic losses that inspire them? While some profess feeling such a comforting presence, so many do not.

For all of these reasons, many thinkers look to a different theodicy to make sense of the world's evils. The most important alternative may be what theologian John Hick (2001) has called the "soul-making theodicy."

The basic thrust of this theodicy is that the world has a different purpose than to be a pleasure palace where we can enjoy ourselves without fear of hardship and suffering. Its purpose, instead, is to provide a context in which each of us can develop into the best kind of moral being we can be, suitable for intimate communion with God. And the best kind of moral being is one who has participated actively in her own development, through her own free choices. In Hick's words, "virtues that have been formed within the agent as a hard-won deposit of right decisions in situations of challenge and temptation are intrinsically more valuable than ready-made virtues created within her without any effort on her own part" (p. 43).

What this means is that God would create us as imperfect creatures with the capacity to freely participate in our own self-development; but it also means He would put us in a world *suitable* for such development.

What would such a world look like? First, Hick thinks our self-development may require that God put Himself at an "epistemic" distance from us – distant from our lived experience and hence from what we can readily know – since the immediate presence of our infinite creator would swamp us, compromising our capacity to evolve as independent selves. And so we'd need to live in a world that runs by its own rules, rather than by God's constant agency, and "from within which God is not overwhelmingly evident" (p. 42). God's presence will have to be an ambiguous thing, felt fleetingly and intermittently at best, so that we can be "on our own" enough to develop into fully formed independent selves.

Furthermore, "The development of human personality – moral, spiritual, and intellectual – is a product of challenge and response" (p. 46). And so we need to live in a world that challenges us, one "within which we have to learn to live on penalty of pain or death" (p. 46). Hick thinks that it is "by grappling with real problems" in a world *not* designed to cater to our needs that we "develop in intelligence and in such qualities as courage and determination" (p. 47). And it is when we struggle together with other human beings in such a world that we "develop the higher values of mutual love and care, self-sacrifice for others, and commitment to a common good" (p. 47).

But such a world will have tragedies – and these will have to strike indiscriminately. A world in which disaster only strikes the wicked or foolish wouldn't serve our self-development. In such a world "wrong deeds would obviously bring disaster upon the agent while good deeds would bring health and prosperity." And under these conditions "truly moral action, action done because it is right, would be impossible" (p. 50). Furthermore, in such a world compassion for the needy would evaporate in the sweeping judgment that they all deserved what they got.

This theodicy, while important, faces significant challenges. We'd never praise a grade school teacher who created a "room of death" in which her students' survival depended on solving grade-appropriate math problems, reading to grade level, and helping each other selflessly along the way. Even if such a room did contribute to the intellectual and moral growth of some students (while traumatizing others, killing some, and driving not a few towards greater selfishness), we wouldn't say it was worth the cost.

And yet, we *do* think teachers should challenge their students in ways that can cause bitter disappointment. Consider how traumatic a failing grade can be. The problem with the "room of death" is that it inflicts costs beyond the teacher's power to repair. The teacher cannot make it up to little Sally's corpse. When we consider whether the evils in this world are the sort that God, wanting to facilitate "soul-making," would allow, we also need to consider the resources at God's disposal for *transforming* what would otherwise be intolerable loss into something good. While the world's evils seem insurmountably terrible from our human perspective, this may only be because we lack an appreciation of the broader context God has created for their redemption.

Because of human wickedness, the evils of this world may exceed what is strictly necessary for *soul-making* (surely the Holocaust didn't need to happen). Out of respect for efficacious freedom, God may be forced to permit these horrors. But the resources at His disposal for redeeming natural evils *might also redeem these excessive moral ones.* God's goodness may not demand that He prevent all evils; but it may well demand that He *redeem* them all, so that evil will never be the final word in any human life – an insight which leads Hick as well as others (such as Marilyn Adams 2002 and 2006, and Thomas Talbott 2001) to insist that a doctrine of universal salvation is essential to any successful theodicy.[3]

It is the role of *redemption* in God's relation to the world that strikes me as the most important element of Hick's soul-making theodicy. Other elements are less than convincing, at least in the precise forms that Hick lays them out. Most notably, his theodicy is far too anthropocentric, largely ignoring the living world outside of humanity and the suffering that is an elemental part of the process of evolution.

But in stressing the possibility of redemption, Hick has raised an important consideration when reflecting on the argument from evil. If my parents, in my childhood, permitted me to endure suffering that they knew, in the grand scheme of my life, would prove to be transient and trivial, that would require a far less powerful justifying reason than would be called for were they to permit me to suffer a lifelong and debilitating affliction. Often, advocates of the argument from evil present the evils of this world as if they are afflictions of the latter sort: devastating and life-crushing. They argue that a good God could have no good reason to allow such evils.

But while the evils of this world may be devastating and life-crushing on the assumption that there is no God who is acting to redeem them, these very same evils have a very different character if it turns out that we live in a universe in which our ethico-religious hope is fulfilled. If we assume that materialists like Dawkins are right, that the whole of reality is encompassed by the world of matter and energy that science can explore, then the evils that many endure in this life are monumental. If what happens to us on this mortal coil, over the course of a few decades of material existence, comprises the *entirety of our existence*, then many lives are swamped by evil.

But if a redeeming God exists, this picture of things is false. The evils of the world are then situated in a grander context, and they cease to be as dominant a feature of life as they would be in a materialist's universe.

It may well be that many of the atheists who pose the argument from evil are envisioning the evils of the world as they look from an atheist perspective. In other words, they are begging the question: they are *assuming* that God does not exist, attaching to the evils of the world the significance they would have, *given* that assumption, and then demanding a reason why God would permit evils which have such overwhelming significance. But if a redeeming God exists, they do not have such overwhelming significance after all. When we reflect on the adequacy of theodicies such as those of Swinburne and Hick, we need to keep this in mind. We should *not* ask whether these theodicies give an adequate account of why God would permit evils that actually strip lives of meaning. Rather, we should ask whether they give an adequate account of why God would permit evils that He can and does redeem.

Do they? There is obviously more to be said on both sides of that question. After all, the persistent question remains: if the evils of the world really aren't that significant in the grand scheme of things, why do they *seem* so significant? Many purported revelations of God do promise redemption. But even for those raised with those promises, the immediacy and vividness of life's tragedies often drown out mere assurances of a redeeming God at work.

When we ask why God would permit us to experience evil as so significant, we are asking about what might be called a "second-order" evil.

The first-order evils – the tragic losses, debilitating illnesses, and deliber-ate violations – are attended by this second order evil: God is not vividly present in the midst of them, assuring us of redemption.

But for both kinds of evil, we need to avoid question-begging. If there *is* a redeeming God, then second-order evils are redeemed, too. It is one thing to ask why God would permit one to languish for one's entire existence under the delusion that evil has overwhelming significance. It is something else to ask why God would permit this for the relatively transient mortal phase of a vaster existence. For any and all of these evils, the question of why God would permit them requires us to suppose that there are vistas of reality that transcend our understanding – vistas that may not just put *evil* into perspective but also the fact that it can seem so overwhelming.

And these same vistas do something else, too. They point the way to an altogether different strategy for responding to the argument from evil, one which I turn to now.

A Limited Perspective

This alternative strategy begins by asking a question: If God had a justify-ing reason for permitting the world's evils, should we *expect* to be able to see it from our limited perspective? If not, then we cannot move from "I don't see any justifying reason God would have for permitting this evil" to "There appears to be no such reason." Stephen Wykstra clarifies this point with an example:

> Searching for a table, you look through a doorway. The room is very large – say, the size of a Concorde hangar – and it is filled with bulldozers, dead elephants, Toyotas, and other vision-obstructing objects. Surveying this clutter from the doorway, and seeing no table, should you say: "It does not appear that there is a table in this room"? (Wykstra 1990, p. 151)

Obviously, the answer is no. Were there a table, you wouldn't expect to be able to see one. And so, failing to see one provides no good reason to think there is no table.

Likewise, if God had a reason for allowing evil, we shouldn't expect to be able to discern it. Insofar as God is the transcendent creator of the universe, just about everything God understands lies outside our compre-hension. If, within His vast ocean of understanding, God discerns a justi-fying reason for allowing an evil to exist, the probability that this reason would also fall within our puddle of understanding is very low. And so we shouldn't expect to see a justifying reason for evil, even if God has one.

Given this reality, it's actually rather remarkable that we're able to develop theodicies that give us some sense of why God *might* allow many of the evils in the world. Of course they don't explain every evil to our satisfaction. But then, evolutionary theory has not yet explained every complex biological system to our satisfaction. And Dawkins has rightly insisted that mysteries which have yet to be explained in Darwinian terms are no reason to reject Darwin's theory.

Theodicies are fundamentally metaphorical. In our experience we find cases in which *we'd* permit a preventable evil (because it may teach our son responsibility, or give the student the chance to make the right deci-sion for the right reason, or provide our daughter with a chance to build character by facing the challenge herself). And we make metaphorical gestures. They don't quite track, because we are *not* God and our situation *isn't* God's. But that they give us some sense of why a benevolent God might permit the evils of the world, given how unlikely it is that God's reasons would be accessible to us, may tell us just how much (or little) evidential weight evil has against belief in God.

And what happens when God is conceived, not with the precise list of characteristics found in traditional theism, but as the fulfillment of our ethico-religious hope? Evil's evidential force is clearly weaker when leveled against God conceived in those less precise terms.

And what about when we incorporate the cosmological argument into our body of evidence? That argument tells us it is reasonable to believe in a transcendent and essentially mysterious reality. What implications might such a deeper reality have for the significance of the evils we encounter? If it's reasonable to believe that there are orders of reality beyond our com-prehension, this is akin to saying it is reasonable to believe there are places in the Concorde hangar where tables and mice and cows could be hiding, which are entirely beyond our capacity to uncover no matter how diligently we search.

Dawkins claims that the empirical world looks just as we'd expect it to look "if there is, at bottom, no design, no purpose, no evil, no good, noth-ing but pitiless indifference." But the cluttered Concorde hangar looks just as we'd expect it to look if there were no table – and, especially if there are entire regions of the hangar that cannot be investigated even in principle, this fact carries little evidentiary weight.

And it isn't just the cosmological argument that supports the reality of such inaccessible regions. So does the testimony of the mystics. So do the less vivid but more widespread religious feelings, the sense of something vast and inexplicable beneath the surface of the world, something *good* holding us in its embrace. If we haven't experienced these things, they'll weigh less heavily in our assessment of the evidence – but that doesn't mean we can ignore them.

The evidential argument from evil rests on the judgment that *our* inability to see a morally sufficient reason for God to allow the evils in the world is evidence that there is no such reason (and hence no God). But this "evidence" is weakened by theodicies that, for all their limitations, give some sense of why a transcendent God might permit evils that at first appear gratuitous. It is weakened by the reasonableness of believing that there are orders of reality that defy human understanding. It is weakened further by reports of experiential encounters with such an ineffable reality. And this weakened evidence then needs to be weighed against the evidence, however modest, that there *is* a transcendent good – evidence offered by experiential reports, with varying degrees of vividness, of encounters with such a good.

It may turn out, for those who haven't had personal religious experiences, that a weighing of the evidence still pushes the scale away from the existence of a perfectly good and all-powerful God. But I'm by no means convinced of this – and I'm even less convinced that it pushes the scales away from the existence of a God less precisely conceived – one who fulfills our ethico-religious hope.

But even if it did, that is hardly the end of the story. Whatever the weight of the evidence, we're surely *not* talking here about a case against God's existence so formidable that we have no reason to hope.

Horrors

If our lives depended on finding a mouse in the cluttered Concorde hangar, it would make perfect sense to step through the doorway *in the hope* that one is there – that is, to act *as if* one is there to be found. And if, in our search, we encounter the occasional encouraging sign – something that looks like it might be a mouse dropping; what look like gnaw marks on a table (!!) that we find behind a bulldozer – it would be entirely reasonable to keep on living in that hope.

If our lives depended on finding a mouse, it *wouldn't* be reasonable to conclude that there is no mouse, and to act accordingly, just because, standing in the doorway and looking over the clutter, we couldn't see one peeking out from under one of the dead elephants.

And for many human beings, there is a sense in which their lives *do* depend on the existence of God. Their lives are so grim that, without a transcendent good to redeem them, it would appear to be better had they never lived at all. Human beings live in a state of radical vulnerability to what Marilyn McCord Adams calls horrors: evils that seem to "engulf the positive value of a participant's life" (1990, p. 211).

A mother, running late for a morning meeting, rushes out the door with both her children. The older son is to be dropped off at preschool, the baby girl at a nearby daycare. When the preschool lets out, the daycare's minivan will bring the son to the daycare, where he will wait with his baby sister until their mother gets off work.

The mother gets to work, leaving the car in a sunny lot. It's a hot day. She makes it to her meeting and has a productive day. At five o'clock she gets in her car and drives to the daycare. Her son runs to her. She picks him up and kisses his head, then looks around for her baby girl. Not seeing her, she asks one of the daycare workers.

"I'm sorry, ma'am. You didn't drop her off this morning."

The reply, tentative and apologetic, doesn't have the tone of something that should tear a life apart. But it does. The mother's hands go numb. Her son falls from her grasp. It feels as if all the darkness in the world is pressing outward from inside her. *No. Impossible.* But she has no memory of unstrapping that precious little girl, of carrying her into the daycare. No memory, in the rush of the morning, the urgency to get to her meeting on time.

Driving to the daycare after work, looking forward to seeing her children, she never looked at what was in the back seat. And now her knees give out and the sobs escape even before she makes it to the car, even before she sees what's there.

Someone is soothing the son, who stands at the daycare door. The mother is beating at the car windows with her fists. In her imagination the baby girl is screaming for mommy, for comfort, as the car grows hotter and hotter, while all the while the mother is in her stupid meeting, talking about stupid contracts, feeling relieved that she'd made it to work on time.

And the son, distressed beyond understanding by his mother's behavior, breaks free of the daycare worker and runs towards her – into the path of an oncoming car.

This story is loosely based on real events. And there are life stories bleaker than this. Horror is real. According to the 2007 Global Monitoring Report put out by the World Bank, there are at present more than one billion people on earth living in "extreme" poverty (that is, on less than $1 per day).[4] Such poverty is not only dire in itself but renders the poor terribly vulnerable to exploitation, disease, and natural disasters. I could fill a book with harrowing stories of human lives crushed by a combination of poverty, brutal abuse, and the grim indifference of nature.

But that isn't needed, I think, in order to convince most readers that there are horrors in the world so devastating that those who undergo them feel as if their entire lives are stripped of positive value, as if they'd be better off dead – while those who are implicated in them, once they come to appreciate the full measure of their complicity, are torn apart by self-loathing.[5]

If there is a God, His reasons for permitting such evils are hidden from us. And, as Marilyn Adams has pointed out, even if traditional theodicies give some general sense of why God might create a world in which evils exist, these theodicies bring no comfort to the mother as she turns away from her infant's corpse just in time to see her son crushed under the wheels of a screeching car. It won't give meaning to her life. It won't eliminate the horror.

Her existence has, in a few heartbeats, become worse than a void. It's become a space of affliction compared to which the void would be preferable.

This woman needs *salvation*.

Who can give it to her? Us?

Morality demands that we care about horror's victims – a demand that the most privileged among us have consistently failed to live up to. Those of us in the developed world who are honest with ourselves know that our affluence is possible only because of a global economic system that disenfranchises great swaths of humanity. But to preserve the pleasures of our lives from contamination, we ignore or minimize this reality. And so we don't do enough to alter even those economic realities over which we have some control.

Salvation won't come from human beings, religious or secular. While the Council for Secular Humanism *has* established a charitable organization (Secular Humanist Aid and Relief Efforts, or S.H.A.R.E.), more of the council's resources go to fighting religion than to lifting people out of poverty. Human beings everywhere find it easier to tear down than to build up, so they operate under the delusion that paradise will blossom on its own once the sources of evil are identified and wiped out. The West focuses on wiping out Muslim extremists, who focus on wiping out Israel and the western contagion. Religious zealots focus on destroying heresy while the atheist zealots focus on destroying religion. And all the while, the hungry masses continue to starve.

Salvation will not come from humanity; and there is no better hope from the forces of nature. Nature solves problems of overpopulation and resource stresses by the mechanistic infliction of famine and pestilence – horrors on top of horrors.

Can horror victims *save themselves*? According to Dawkins, "The truly adult view . . . is that our life is as meaningful, as full and wonderful as we choose to make it. And we can make it very wonderful indeed" (2006, p. 360). Is he right? Can the mother who's just seen her children die find meaning by *choosing* not to let their deaths and her own complicity bring her down? Do the starving masses only have themselves to blame if their lives aren't "very wonderful indeed"? Would Dawkins really have us believe that the most shattered souls on the planet could escape the pit of horror if only they got themselves an attitude adjustment or pulled themselves up by the bootstraps?

Dawkins is speaking from a place of extraordinary privilege. His statement is not just appallingly naive, but appalling. The victims of horror are broken by the wheels of an indifferent universe, by human cruelties, and by their own imperfections. Horror does not just afflict those with the personal resources necessary to bounce back.

So who will save them from lives that have been shattered so fully that they seem not worth living? *How* can they be saved?

The Defeat of Horror

Adams points out that the very horror that "threatens to rob a person's life of positive meaning" also "cries out not only to be engulfed, but to be made meaningful through positive and decisive defeat" (1990, p. 211).

To *engulf* evil is to drown it out with a weightier quantity of good. To *defeat* it involves fitting it into a larger whole which gives it positive meaning. Discordant notes, by themselves, may be nothing but unpleasant. Surround them with pretty melodies and the overall experience may be pleasant but the notes remain an ugly interruption. But a great composer can build a melodic line with increasing levels of discord, reaching a climax in which those very same discordant notes give rise to a cathartic resolution – and the notes are turned into an integral part of something beautiful. *That* is defeat. *That* is what horrors demand.

And when it comes to the most horrific evils, Adams argues that merely terrestrial goods have no hope of defeating them. Only a transcendent good – only something like God – can do that.

To say that God defeats horrors is to say that God responds by *making* them an integral part of something valuable – which, I should note, is nothing like claiming that horrors were never really bad at all. It is one thing to say that God is so resourceful He can turn a monumental evil – say the Holocaust – into an element of a greater whole that gives positive meaning to the experiences of its victims. It is something else to say that the Holocaust is part of the "best of all possible worlds," and that the Nazis were therefore agents of the good. The latter is appalling. The former – which says that God can take the worst that we can throw at Him and find a way to turn it to the good – is not.

In *Christ and Horrors* (2006), Adams interprets Christian theology in terms of horror and God's effort to defeat it. She explores both why God might create a world in which we are radically susceptible to horrors and how He might act to defeat such horrors. And defeat them He must, if He is to show love to their victims.

We can imagine that God is motivated by His loving nature to create something other than Himself (a finite reality, like our material world) and then to love it *for what it is*. Such love would express itself, in part, by respecting that finite reality enough to let it be what it is: something that does its own thing according to rules suitable to it. But a loving God would also want *relational union* with this reality. And so He would design it to evolve according to its own rules towards forms that can enter into relationship with God: conscious agents like ourselves.

But as soon as conscious life is part of a finite reality, there emerges the capacity to experience finitude. That which is susceptible to damage and disintegration is now able to *experience* this from the inside, as suffering and death. And when conscious agents capable of forming loving relationships exist in a finite universe, they will make attachments to other finite things. And so they will know loss and grief. When a finite reality is allowed to be itself – to run according to its own rules – these experiences may hit some of us with shattering force. We are "radically vulnerable to horrors" (Adams 2006, p. 39).

To *protect* creatures from horror would mean not respecting the finite world as it is enough to let it be what it is. God would not be allowing it to be truly *other*, a reality distinct from Himself that can relate to Him in a genuinely "I–Thou" relationship. But to allow horror to be the final word in the lives of conscious subjects would also be contrary to love. If *that* were required of God, it might prove immoral for God even to create a world containing finite conscious beings.

God could (and presumably would) engulf horrors with the overwhelming goodness of the beatific vision. But horrors demand more. They cry out for defeat. How is God to defeat them? Not surprisingly, Adams proposes a Christian answer: God defeats the horrors we endure by *becoming human and enduring them along with us*. Horrors thereby become a pathway to solidarity with God. "If God takes God's stand with the cursed," Adams notes, "the cursed are not cut off from God after all" (p. 41).

Here, Adams is pursuing an idea that Simone Weil, in her own way, pursued more than half a century ago. For Weil, the greatest horror of all is God's absence in the midst of suffering. According to Weil, the divine act of creation is by necessity an act of withdrawal, in which God "renounces being everything" (1952a, p. 79). To create something *other* than Himself, an infinite God would need to forge a space of finitude in which God is absent, because "were we exposed to the direct radiance of his love, without the protection of space, of time, and of matter, we should be evaporated like water in the sun; there would not be enough 'I' in us to make it possible to surrender the 'I' for love's sake" (pp. 78–9).

And so our existence as individual selves apart from God *requires* God's absence; but that absence also makes it possible for earthly suffering to rise to the level of *affliction* – by which she means immersion in anguish so complete that one feels utterly abandoned, even by God (Weil 1951, pp. 120–1). If God is the fulfillment of our ethico-religious hope, affliction is the feeling that this hope has been dashed.

Weil hears just such affliction in Christ's cry from the cross: "My God, my God, why hast thou forsaken me?" But that cry is not the end of the story. As Weil sees it, the most perfect love has such a purity of intent that it seeks nothing for itself, not even the loved one's presence. And so it persists, undiminished, even in the loved one's total absence. Such love is nothing less than the perfect love of God. And so, when such love *for*

God is expressed in the very place where God is *not*, God comes to be paradoxically present in that place of absence. Love bridges the gap of infinite distance.[6]

Weil saw in Christ's crucifixion the fulfillment of this impossible possibility, the creation of the pathway for God to extend grace to the very midnight of the soul. God became human and experienced with us the raw sense of God's absence and thereby came to be present with us in the place of outer darkness, the very space where God seems to have forsaken us. In fact, God has become more fully with us in that place of abandonment *than anywhere else*. For in that place, He is not the ineffable Infinite. When we descend to the deepest place of personal horror, God is there with a human face. Horror is defeated by becoming the very means of connecting us most intimately to God.

For both Adams and Weil, Christ's Atonement is conceived in these terms – as a way for God to be uniquely present with humanity in the very place where God is experienced as utterly absent. I am a Christian in part because I do not personally see another way for God to *defeat* horror (although I see many ways He might engulf it). But my imagination is far too limited for me to move from "This is the only way *I* can see for God to defeat horror," to "There is no other way for God to defeat horror." Other religions may have their own resources for explaining horror's defeat.

I share this account, then, not to convert readers to Christianity but to offer an example of what the defeat of horror would look like. And this example is not merely hypothetical. For many years I volunteered as a facilitator for experiential nonviolence workshops in prisons. Often, in these workshops, participants would share their life stories – more often than not stories of horror, in which the distinction between perpetrator and victim was lost in a sea of outrage and despair. But some of these prisoners who'd endured such horrors were now living with a sense of hope, joy, and compassion that I would hardly have credited had I not witnessed it.

For many, the transformation came when they were in the pit of desolation, looking upward, seeing nothing but darkness. Stripped of hope, lost to the pitiless indifference of a world that had heaped upon them misery and bitterness, they had the sudden sense of someone *with* them in the pit, crying out, "My God, my God, why hast thou forsaken me?" And recalling childhood stories of crucifixion and resurrection, their despair was transfigured. Suddenly they felt that everything they could hope for was real, and was there beside them, even in the darkest places.

Sources of Meaning

For most horror victims, the sense that their lives have positive meaning may depend on the conviction that a transcendent good is at work redeeming evil. Is the evidential case against the existence of such a good really so convincing that it warrants saying to these horror victims, "Give up hope"? Should we call them irrational when they cling to that hope or when those among the privileged live in that hope for the sake of the afflicted?

What does moral decency imply about the legitimacy of insisting, as the new atheists do, that any view of life which embraces the ethico-religious hope should be expunged from the world?

In an essay entitled "The Dignity of Human Life," the Kierkegaard scholar David Swenson reflects on the common view of happiness, in which a happy life is one abundant in diverse goods, not just material property but friends, meaningful work, exposure to great art, bodily health, adventures that get the blood pumping, and the like (Swenson 1981, p. 23).

Swenson does not deny that these things are good. They have value and should not be trivialized. But the empirical world of pitiless indifference does not richly bless everyone with these things. Quite the contrary. If these things were the measure of a meaningful life, most lives would be impoverished.

And so, Swenson argues, there's something fundamentally wrong with any view of life which holds that the possession of such diverse goods is what gives *meaning* to life. In Swenson's words,

> all such views of life inevitably imply a privileged status for the happy individual . . . To choose them as the end and aim of life constitutes an injury to the mass of men who are not so privileged. This one thought alone is of so arresting a quality as to give the deepest concern for every man who has the least trace of human sympathy and human feeling. (Swenson 1981, p. 25)

Swenson insists that, for "the fundamental source of inspiration in my life, I need something that is not exclusive and differential, but inclusive and universal." His compassion will permit nothing but "a spring from which all men may refresh themselves," that is, a source of meaning available to all, no matter what fate the blind indifference of nature and human cruelty have in store (p. 25).

For Swenson, this wellspring comes from a view of life according to which *caring about the good*, rather than *possessing a diversity of goods*, is the source of meaning. Put another way, it comes from being moral. But under what conditions will caring about the good confer genuine meaning, even for those horror victims who have seen the things they care most about stripped away? It will bring meaning on the condition that "duty is the eternal in man, or that by which he lays hold of the eternal; and only through the eternal can a man become a conqueror of the life of time" (p. 27).

If the *eternal* cares about the good, then those of us who likewise care, even when we are in the grip of horrors, will be aligned with the eternal, with the fundamental truth behind the shifting vagaries of time. In fact, the most wrenching horror strikes when we witness the pitiless destruction not merely of something we care deeply about, but something we care deeply about *because we recognize its existence to be genuinely good*. When we value what we *should* value, when we love deeply what calls out for such love – when we are truly moral – we are also most vulnerable to horror.

Experiencing horror in its fullness is thus a sign of being connected to the good *in the right way*. But will such a connection to the good give a sense of meaning to life if it is seen as a futile gesture in the face of a universe that, at bottom, doesn't care?

I think, on the contrary, that John Bishop (1998) is right to say that in a universe taken to be pitilessly indifferent to the good, though we might still see it as our duty to live lovingly, it is hard for ordinary human beings to resist the conclusion that "suffering, finitude and death . . . make a mockery of commitment to such a life, robbing it of its meaningfulness and point" (p. 183). For ordinary human beings with ordinary human failings, to see a life guided by morality and compassion as meaningful, rather than as a cold and alienating duty, requires that we see it as our purest connection to the eternal.[7]

To choose this view of life, to live as if it were true, is simply to live as if our ethico-religious hope has been fulfilled. It's to live *as if there is a God* – which may ultimately be the only way to show solidarity with those whose lives have been shattered by horror.

And there's something that those who live in this way tend to discover: it doesn't feel as if they're living a lie. It feels, instead, as if they've finally stumbled into the truth behind the surface appearances of things. They experience what Schleiermacher was talking about when he spoke of *the intuition of the Infinite in the finite*, and *the feeling of absolute dependence*.

They read the mystics with the sense that here, in its fullness, is what they experience only dimly.

This experience isn't *proof* that our ethico-religious hope is not in vain. The great German philosopher Hermann Lotze, after rigorously examining various theodicies, concludes that there is no "speculative proof for the correctness of the religious feeling upon which rests our faith in a good and holy God, and in the destination of the world to the attainment of a blessed end" (1886, p. 127). From an intellectual standpoint, evil cannot help but be a problem for theism – an enigma that admits of no easy solution.

Theists ought to wrestle with this mystery, not hide from it. But such wrestling is entirely compatible with living in the hope that a transcendent good is working to redeem the world. And sincerely living in this hope opens windows of experience that, while not unraveling the mystery of evil, do balance the scales of evidence. More significantly, we should take to heart Lotze's warning (p. 128) against solving the mysteries of life by simply "sacrificing all that is most essential and supreme in life" to a cold intellect as pitilessly indifferent to the good as is the universe in which Dawkins believes.

The extremity of human need reaches upward towards a transcendent hope. The afflicted cry for a savior, and others, moved by compassion, reach upward with them. And some of us who do so discover that a superficial account of life's meaning begins to fall away and something more profound takes its place.

Somewhere, even as I write this, a girl is being raped and murdered. Her parents believe in a transcendent God of love who will redeem even the most shocking horrors.

Are they right to believe this? Is it good that they believe this?

In the darkness of affliction, Harris's answer rings hollow.

10

The Root of All Evil?

Throughout this book, I have been defending the legitimacy of theistic religion, not in *any* conceivable sense, but conceived in a particular way. I have argued that for devoted theists, "God" names a transcendent being that fulfills our ethico-religious hope.

Of course, many so-called theists, both historically and today, are not *devoted* to God but live in fawning servility towards a deity they take to be an almighty tyrant – what Plutarch would call the god of superstition. It has never been my intent to defend the legitimacy of *such* theistic "religion."

As noted in Chapter 1, defending theistic religion isn't quite the same as defending belief in God. For Schleiermacher, the essence of religion is a certain kind of consciousness – a "feeling" of piety that arises in us both when we gaze outward at the wonders of the universe (the intuition of the Infinite in the finite) and when we look inward to the mystery of our own existence (the feeling of absolute dependence). Belief in God, by contrast, is part of theology – by which Schleiermacher means the effort to explain the *meaning* of pious feelings. Theistic *religion*, in the sense I have been defending, takes the distinctive religious consciousness – which sometimes rises to the level of a vivid mystical experience – and interprets it to mean that our ethico-religious hope has been fulfilled.

I have used the cosmological argument to make the case that belief in a transcendent realm, in which our ethico-religious hope *might* be fulfilled, is reasonable. Mystical experience feels like an encounter with such a realm and its optimistic character offers reason for hope – a hope, or so I have argued, that neither science nor the problem of evil can dash. But nothing in our experience establishes that this hope is, in truth, fulfilled. To believe in its fulfillment is consistent with the world of experience, but reason and evidence do not demand that we so believe.

The final step comes from faith, understood as the decision to live in hope – that is, to live as if what we hope for is true. In the case of the ethico-religious hope, what this means is that we put our trust in God. We choose to live as if the evils of the world and the pitiless indifference of nature are *not* the final word in life because there is a transcendent being that cares about the good enough to save it. Experiential religion gestures towards a hazy possibility and faith fleshes it out in the most hopeful conceivable terms.

With respect to the kind of theistic religion I'm defending, I don't believe that faith can be displaced by a preponderance of reasons. But that doesn't mean it's irrational. To deny human beings this faith is to condemn many to a worldview according to which the horrors that shatter so many lives will never be redeemed. When religious experience gestures towards a transcendent and redemptive good, it's not irrational to live as if that good is real – that is, to set aside cynicism and despair, and to love what is good wholeheartedly, without the timidity or paralyzing anxiety that so often accompanies the fear of loss.

It's now time to directly consider whether religion in this sense "poisons everything," whether it's "the root of all evil," whether faith as I've described it "is surely the devil's masterpiece." It's time to consider whether religion in this sense – what I presumptuously want to call *true* religion – really is one of the forces bringing human civilization ever closer to the abyss.

While nobody can deny that "religion" in some other senses has historically contributed to violence, it seems intuitively implausible to blame religion in *every* sense – especially the sense I have been staking out. My aim has been to show that it's entirely possible to have a deep religious faith in God that is both consistent with reason and morally benign.

In fact, I would go further and say, with Schleiermacher, that any "religion" that propagates cruelty and violence is fundamentally disconnected from the religious consciousness and from the mystical developments of that consciousness in which the ethico-religious hope seems more than just a dream. In an important sense, any "religion" that begets violence or encourages brutality is not really religion at all.

But if this is right, we need to consider why the history of religion is so tainted. The new atheists might argue that this bloody history shows that even the benign religion I have been developing cannot sustain itself, that there is something about religion even in this sense that primes the faithful for corruption. If we want to see the end of religious violence and persecution, we must exterminate religion even in my seemingly benign sense because even in this form it carries the seeds of horror.

My general answer to this view is that the problem doesn't lie with religion at all. The problem lies with *humanity*, with tendencies endemic to human beings who are by disposition tribal, who want easy answers, who hunger for security and cheap validation. If "true" religion is hard to maintain, it's because it is humans who are maintaining it. To condemn religion for that reason would be no wiser than condemning science because most people who attempt to do science do it badly or denouncing the Sibelius Violin Concerto because only the rarest of violinists can play it well. It would be no wiser than condemning technological innovation because human beings routinely direct such innovation to the manufacture of weapons of mass destruction.

Like these other things, religion has something of worth to contribute when it *isn't* corrupted. Our task should be to encourage and celebrate religious virtuosity and to resist its corruption, not stamp religion from the world.

But let us explore these ideas more carefully by considering some of the more significant accusations that the new atheists heap on religion's doorstep.

The Need for Certainty

Sam Harris acknowledges much of what I have said about the nature of religion. He sees the importance of religious experience for understanding the origins of religion, even though he tries to squeeze all such experience into his own Buddhist brand of nature mysticism. He also sees the importance of *hope* in motivating religious faith. "The allure of most religious doctrines," he claims, "is nothing more sublime or inscrutable than this: *things will turn out well in the end.* Faith is offered as a means by which the truth of this proposition can be savored in the present and secured in the future" (2004, p. 70).

Harris seems to see this hope as purely directed towards the future (things *will* turn out well) rather than being about the nature of the universe – that when we care about the good by promoting it in the limited ways we can, we are in alignment with the deepest reality. More significantly, he thinks religion cannot make do with hope alone. The essential act of religious faith, for him, is "to presume knowledge where one has only pious hope" (p. 225). He thinks it is "indisputable" that the "literal correspondence" of religious doctrines with reality "is of sole importance to the faithful" (p. 70). It isn't enough for the faithful to live in the hope of such a correspondence. What religion demands, on Harris's view, is that the correspondence between what is hoped for and what is real be written in stone, a matter beyond dispute. And this insistence on certainty is, for Harris, a wellspring of unreason and brutality.

Undeniably, religious communities throughout history have attempted to preserve the *illusion* of certainty by remorselessly persecuting every "heretic" whose differing beliefs might threaten that illusion. And I share Harris's horror at these practices. But when most religious people I know insist that their beliefs are a matter of faith, they are acknowledging with those very words that *they do not know*, that what they believe is *not* beyond dispute. It is because of this very fact – that their beliefs are a matter of faith, not knowledge – that religious moderates endorse pluralism and interfaith dialogue rather than holy war and the Inquisitor's rack.

The problem is not with faith as such but with the tendency to treat faith *as if* it were knowledge – a tendency that springs from an all-too-human hunger for certainty. Why do we have that hunger? The answer seems clear enough. We need to *know* in order to *know what to do*. Uncertainty about whether or not there are rabid wolves in the forest can be deadly. If we know there are none, we can spare ourselves the precious resources we might otherwise have wasted guarding against them. If we know they are there, we can act to protect ourselves. Uncertainty either way is risky.

But when it comes to the ultimate character of the universe, our experience is too conceptually malleable to afford certainty. As Hick (1989b) says, "the true character of the universe does not force itself upon us, and we are left with an important element of freedom and responsibility in our response to it" (p. 191).

Dawkins, apparently, cannot stand such uncertainty – and so he insists that the empirical world is all there is and that anyone who disagrees with him is a fool. Stenger cannot endure uncertainty and so insists (with words that a friend thought had to be a joke) that "science has advanced sufficiently to be able to make a *definitive statement* on the existence or non-existence of a God having the attributes that are traditionally associated with the Judeo-Christian-Islamic God" (2007, p. 11).

The craving for certainty, especially when it comes to matters where certainty is impossible, can be dangerous. In a different world, under different conditions, the false certainty that fuels Fred Phelps's rabid homophobia might have culminated in a violent campaign of extermination rather than the hateful picketing his church now pursues. And in a different world, under different conditions, the false certainty that fuels the rabid atheism of Dawkins and Hitchens and Harris might have inspired a crusade against religion far more bloody than the crusade of words they now pursue.

False certainty often leads to the kind of aggressive self-righteousness that drenches every page of Hitchens' book. It leads to battle lines being drawn against those with a different view. It leads to taking joyous delight in stomping all over what others find sacred – either physically, such as when the Taliban smashed Buddhist relics in Afghanistan, or verbally, such as when Dawkins (2006, p. 31) calls the God of the Old Testament "arguably the most unpleasant character in all fiction" (and then launches into his hyperbolic characterization of this "capriciously malevolent bully").

Consider this last example. It isn't enough for Dawkins to say what I want to say about the Old Testament picture of God, namely this: if we take the Old Testament to be offering a literal and inerrant picture of God, ignoring how the authors' cultural assumptions might be in play or how the image of God evolves through the text, we are left with a picture closer to the god of superstition than to any God worthy of devotion.

Dawkins cannot content himself with something along these lines. He has to ridicule, grinding the reverent feelings of other human beings underfoot with obvious glee. He never considers the possibility that, in the Old Testament, the sectarian image of a tribal god was slowly transformed by religious encounters with a transcendent good and that this evolving image of God testifies to the power of the divine to transfigure the superstitions that arise from other sources (such as from our psychological tendency to read agency into the merciless forces of nature). He never considers this view because he is full to the brim with a false certainty that leads him to treat ancient texts with nothing but scorn, oblivious to the possibility that the sacred might lurk amidst the errors.

The lure of false certainty is entirely predictable, an ordinary human failing that infects atheists as readily as it does the religious – and, ironically, it seems especially pervasive when it comes to matters about which certainty cannot be had. The reason is clear enough. The ultimate nature of reality is not just a matter about which certainty is impossible. It is also of utmost significance for human life. How can we guard against the hunger for certainty when it comes to such critically important issues?

In fact, I have already given my answer. The need for certainty springs from the conviction that we must know the truth in order to know what to do. In other words, it springs from the view that in some sense, *our salvation depends on getting our beliefs right.* Like the fundamentalists, the new atheists are gripped by this same conviction. This is especially clear in Harris's case. For him, unless we get our beliefs right – unless, that is, we convert the world to atheism – we are doomed.

If we want to escape this morbid need for certainty, a roughly Lutheran understanding of faith offers the avenue: when it comes to the ultimate nature of reality, we can let go of the need to get it right by trusting that our ultimate salvation comes from a transcendent benevolence rather than from anything *we* do or think. Only then can we release ourselves from the need for certainty.

In short, faith in the sense I've been defending here is *not*, as Harris seems to think, a special pathway to false certainty. Rather, it is its antidote. Perhaps the reason why the new atheists are so prone towards false certainty is because they cannot avail themselves of this antidote.

Indifference to the Goods of This World

Another recurring accusation against religion is that, by offering a "better world" beyond this one, religion leads to a cavalier attitude towards the fragile goods of this life. It makes it easier to throw away life as if it were trivial. Dawkins claims that "religious faith is an especially potent silencer of rational calculation" because it shuts off the self-interested motives that usually inhibit violent conflict (not to mention suicide bombing). It achieves this through "the easy and beguiling promise that death is not the end and that a martyr's heaven is especially glorious." And for Dawkins, the "take-home message" is that "we should blame religion itself, not religious *extremism*" for the willingness of religious fanatics to treat human life cavalierly (2006, p. 306).

The new atheists seem to think that if only they could convince everyone that every good is impermanent – if only we came to understand that death is truly the *end*, that *nothing* of value survives its hungry maw – then we'd treasure and protect life with all the care that its fragility demands. Promise a transcendent reality that preserves the good beyond the finitude of the empirical world and we'll all start throwing earthly goods about like so much trash.

All of this might follow *if* religion teaches that we shouldn't care about the apparent goods of this life because they really have no value. If religion teaches that the transcendent realm is the only realm in which real goods reside, and that everything on this mortal coil is valueless, then indifference to human life may well result.

But even if some religious traditions teach this, such teachings are hardly essential to religion. The form of religion I have been defending embraces the hope that the fundamental reality cares about the good. Such a hope implies that this fundamental reality will act to preserve what has objective value from the ravages of time and the blind indifference of nature. After all, when we care for something in any real sense, we show that care by nurturing and protecting it.

But to say that the good is preserved despite the seeming indifference of nature is not to say that terrestrial goods aren't really good after all. Nor is it to say that our actions cannot do any harm (if you break my son's arm, you've done real harm even though, with proper care, he'll eventually be good as new). Instead, it is to say that, whatever harm is done by us and by natural forces, there is a transcendent good that will redeem it.

Most significantly, if the fundamental reality cares about the good, then we become most in tune with reality when we care about the good, too. And, as I just mentioned, when we care for something, we show that by nurturing and protecting it. We are finite physical creatures living in a material world. Whatever the nature of the transcendent reality, and however it nurtures and protects the good, *we* can only nurture and protect it in its terrestrial aspect. In Simone Weil's words, "The fact that a human being possesses an eternal destiny imposes only one obligation: respect. The obligation is only performed if the respect is effectively expressed in a real, not a fictitious way; and this can only be done through the medium of Man's earthly needs" (1952b, p. 6).

There is only one way in this mortal life to show our care for one another – and that is by meeting the needs we have in this life. In negative terms, this means *not* ignoring or despising the mortal lives which, for all of their impermanence, still embody real value.

And so, if we want to align ourselves with the ultimate reality, we must feed the hungry, heal the sick, protect the weak, liberate the oppressed, nurture our children, share our time with those we love, and refrain from inflicting needless injury on anyone. *This* is essential to what it means to live in the ethico-religious hope. To live with a cavalier disregard for life is to take the seemingly pitiless indifference of nature as our role model, to act as if life and joy and love really are as meaningless as, on Dawkins' view, the universe says they are.

In short, if there are forces at work inspiring a careless disregard for the value of human life, they do not have their origin in the ethico-religious hope or in any religion built around that hope.

And there is one more issue that deserves consideration. Is it really true that we would care about life and its goods all the more if we came to believe that the seeming impermanence of it all were the ultimate truth? Pierre Teilhard de Chardin warns that belief in such impermanence may have a very different effect:

> Multiply to your heart's content the extent and duration of progress. Promise the earth a hundred million more years of continued growth. If, at the end of that period, it is evident that the whole of consciousness must revert to zero, *without its secret essence being garnered anywhere at all*, then, I insist, we shall lay down our arms – and mankind will be on strike. The prospect of a *total death* (and that is a word to which we should devote much thought if we are to gauge its destructive effect on our souls) will, I warn you, when it has become part of our consciousness, immediately dry up in us the springs from which our efforts are drawn. (Teilhard de Chardin 1969, pp. 43–4)

To care for others, to nurture them and promote their welfare, takes effort. It is an effort of love. We may well ask, with Teilhard de Chardin, whether when we exert that effort any of us are *really* operating in the belief that it will all come to naught in the end. Perhaps, on the contrary, every such effort of love amounts to living in the hope – however implicitly – that what we are nurturing will not die.

If so, then stamping out that hope may have implications far more dire than what the new atheists are willing to admit.

A Cause of Violence

In *god is not Great*, Christopher Hitchens offers a litany of contemporary examples of how, in his view, religion foments violence. "In Belfast," he tells us, "I have seen whole streets burned out by sectarian warfare between different sects of Christianity, and interviewed people whose relatives and friends have been kidnapped and killed or tortured by rival religious death squads, often for no other reason than membership of another confession" (2007, p. 18).

Concerning the ethnic conflicts between Croats, Serbs, and Muslims that rocked the former Yugoslavia, Hitchens has this to say:

> It would have been far more accurate if the press and television had reported that "today the Orthodox Christian forces resumed their bombardment of Sarajevo," or "yesterday the Catholic militia succeeded in collapsing the Stari Most." But confessional terminology was reserved only for "Muslims," even as their murderers went to all the trouble of distinguishing themselves by wearing large Orthodox crosses over their bandoliers, or by taping portraits of the Virgin Mary to their rifle butts. Thus, once again, *religion poisons everything*, including our own faculties of discernment. (Hitchens 2007, p. 22)

Dawkins and Harris offer examples of their own and the supposed take-home message is always the same: religion is a cause of violent strife, especially across "confessions." Where intractable conflicts rage on for years, where group hatreds perpetuate intergenerational bloodbaths, at the root of it all we find . . . religion.

In his book, *The Dawkins Delusion?* (McGrath and McGrath 2007), Alister McGrath offers his own response to this accusation. The first point he makes is that not all religions are the same. McGrath points to his own faith as an example of religion that stands opposed to violence. "I write," he says, "as a Christian who holds that the face, will and character of God are fully disclosed in Jesus of Nazareth. And as Dawkins knows, Jesus of Nazareth did no violence to anyone." He goes on to point out that the Christian ethic calls us to "turn the other cheek" in the face of violence and rage – a call that is not just "about the elimination of the roots of violence"; it is "about its *transfiguration*" (2007, p. 76).

McGrath goes on to point out that religion, for all its bloody history, is not alone in generating violence: "The history of the twentieth century has given us a frightening awareness of how political extremism can equally cause violence. In Latin America millions of people seem to have 'disappeared' as a result of ruthless campaigns of violence by right-wing politicians and their militias. In Cambodia, Pol Pot eliminated millions in the name of socialism" (p. 77). He then discusses how, in the former Soviet Union, violence "was undertaken in pursuit of an atheist agenda – the elimination of religion" (p. 78). He concludes that "human beings are capable of both violence and moral excellence – and that both of these may be provoked by worldviews, whether religious or otherwise" (p. 79).

I agree with most of what McGrath says here but I wonder if he might not have conceded too much to Dawkins and the rest. It is true that in some sense of the word, "religion" has been and continues to be a cause of violence. But there may be something important to learn from the fact that so much inter-group violence is perpetrated in the name of non-religious worldviews or ideologies, and that so much of this violence looks very similar to the paradigm cases of religious violence trotted out by the new atheists. It may be that all of these instances of inter-group violence, religious and nonreligious, can be explained in terms of the same basic human motivations.

If so, it seems a stretch to blame religion *as such* for the violence in Belfast and Bosnia – about as much of a stretch as it would be to blame economic theories for the Cold War. When one racial group brutally oppresses another, we blame racism, not race. When people of different nations go to war out of misplaced pride, we blame nationalism, not nationality. When rival ethnic groups practice "ethnic cleansing," we blame ethnocentrism, not ethnicity.

Likewise, I would suggest that what we should blame for all the violence that has been done in the name of God is not *religion* but what might be dubbed *religionism*. Behind each of these "isms" lies a common human tendency: the drive to divide humanity into in-groups and out-groups, to define oneself in terms of group membership, and to define one's group against rivals.

In a brilliant essay entitled "The Idea of Collective Violence," John Ladd (1991) explores the phenomenon of "collective violence," which he defines as "violence that is practiced by one group on another and that pertains to individuals, as agents or as victims, only by virtue of their (perceived) association with a particular group" (p. 19). Perpetrators of collective violence act as agents of a group and their targets are chosen, not for any individual characteristics they possess but by virtue of their perceived membership in the targeted group. Obviously, the usual examples of religious violence are a *species* of collective violence in this sense.

As Ladd sees it, perpetrators of collective violence rationalize their acts according to a distinctive ideological framework which he sketches out in terms of five key "premises" or "doctrines":

1   The Doctrine of Bifurcation, according to which the world is divided into two groups – a "Chosen Group" and an "Other Group" – that are "irretrievably separated and divided";

2   The Doctrine of Moral Disqualification, according to which members of the Other Group are perceived as "moral outcasts" who "lack the minimum attributes necessary for being members of the moral community, or even for being human";

3   The Doctrine of the Double Standard, which establishes two distinct moralities, one for interactions with those who belong to the Chosen Group and hence to the moral community (a standard that demands respect and concern), and a different one for interactions with Others who fall outside the moral community and may thus be treated in ways that would never be permitted in relation to the Chosen;

4   The Doctrine of Group Mission, "which assigns a plenary mission, often divinely commanded, to the members of the Chosen Group to protect the Chosen Group and its values from perceived threats to it by the Other Group";

5   The Doctrine of Zero-Sum Struggle, according to which the two groups are "locked in a conflict for which compromise or reconciliation are absolutely inconceivable," and which is such that the flourishing of one group can only be achieved by the defeat or destruction of the other. (pp. 40–1)[1]

In developing his theory, it is quite obvious that Ladd's template is Nazism. But he also sees racism as falling squarely within it. And at its worst moments, the Cold War was fueled by those in the grip of this sort of ideology, with capitalism and communism serving as the basis for division.

What Ladd has done, I think, is pinpoint the basic ideological structure that underlies the most intractable and brutal cases of inter-group violence. Belief in God, as such, has nothing to do with it. A certain vision of what gives meaning to life has nothing to do with it. Clearly, the ethico-religious hope has nothing to do with it.

At root, this kind of violence is motivated by a pattern of thinking that probably has its origins in the tribalism in which humanity evolved. Members of one's own tribe or clan were to be trusted and treated with respect. Other tribes were rivals and, more often than not, enemies.

We've left the tribalism behind. We've found ways to live together in great cosmopolitan cities in which, in principle, our common humanity is enough to justify mutual regard. But the legacy of tribalism remains and can be used with sinister art by ambitious leaders to consolidate power in the name of defeating a common enemy.

And, beyond mere instinct, there is a powerful psychological allure to such in-group/out-group ideology. In his classic *Anti-Semite and Jew*,

Jean-Paul Sartre (1948) beautifully characterizes this allure. While he looks explicitly at anti-Semitism, his analysis applies just as readily to racism or classism or what I am dubbing "religionism."

The first attraction of the anti-Semitic worldview is that it gives worth to the individual simply by virtue of being a member of the Chosen Group, without the need to *do* anything at all. Sartre describes the mindset as follows:

> By treating the Jew as an inferior and pernicious being, I affirm at the same time that I belong to the elite. This elite, in contrast to those of modern times which are based on merit or labor, closely resembles an aristocracy of birth. There is nothing I have to do to merit superiority, and neither can I lose it. It is given once and for all. (Sartre 1948, p. 27)

You can rest assured of your own value, regardless of whether you amount to anything in life, regardless of how petty your concerns or how morally suspect your character. You have value because you are white rather than black, American rather than Mexican, Sunni rather than Shi'ite.

Secondly, the anti-Semitic worldview assures its adherent that all will be well with the world if only the Other Group is put down. Achieving a good life, a harmonious society, does not require creative efforts to *build* anything. All that's needed is to *destroy*. "Underneath the bitterness of the anti-Semite is concealed the optimistic belief that harmony will be re-established of itself, once Evil is eliminated" (p. 43). Evil, of course, is identified with the Jew.

"The more one is absorbed in fighting Evil," Sartre continues, "the less one is tempted to place the Good in question. . . . He is in the breach, fighting, and each of his outbursts of rage is a pretext to avoid the anguished search for the Good" (pp. 44–5). There is no need to do the hard work of building a good life; such a life will simply blossom on its own amidst the ashes that remain once the Jews (or blacks or Israelis or Protestants) have been destroyed.

Finally, anti-Semitism provides an outlet for our ugliest impulses while preserving the illusion of a clean conscience. The anti-Semite metes out sadistic brutality upon the Jew as a means of ushering in the Good for the Chosen Group and thus sees himself as a "sanctified evildoer," as a "criminal pure of heart." He "accords esteem . . . to all forms of violence. Drunk with evil, he feels in himself the lightness of heart and peace of mind which a good conscience and the satisfaction of a duty well done bring" (p. 50).

Sartre's analysis springs from his own existential philosophy, and so he weds anti-Semitism to the struggle to avoid taking responsibility for creating meaning in one's life. But even apart from this philosophical perspective, his analysis has enormous power. It offers a coherent picture of the psychological motivation that lies behind ideologies of collective violence as described by Ladd.

Together, the ideology and its motivation offer a comprehensive framework for understanding what is going on not just in anti-Semitism and racism and ethnic hatreds, but also long-standing religious animosities. The explanatory power of this picture is one of its great attractions. Religious violence is not something special, with some uniquely "religious" motivation not discoverable in other forms of collective violence. On the contrary, it is but the same ideologies adapted to use religion – instead of race or nationality or political ideology – as the tool for division.

When ideologies of collective violence co-opt religion, what we have is religionism, an evil every bit as pernicious as racism. And the seeds of a unique brand of such religionism – one that divides the world between the enlightened atheists and the benighted "faith-heads" (to borrow Dawkins' disparaging phrase, the "kike" or "chink" or "faggot" of his preferred bigotry) – are found in the angry ravings of the new atheists.

The culprit behind religious violence isn't religion as such, but religionism. And its essential feature – the ideology of collective violence that divides up the world between the children of light and the children of darkness – is so hard for humans to resist that the new atheists, so appalled by religionism's influence, almost immediately fall prey to it themselves. When I reflect too long on the new atheists, I am in dire danger of falling prey to it myself.

The Hope of the World?

I want to end this book by considering a possibility that never enters the minds of religion's cultured despisers. It is the possibility that religion – in something like Schleiermacher's sense, something like the sense I have been developing here – may actually be our best hope against the bifurcating ideologies and other dangerous forces that pose such a real threat to human beings all over the world.

But first, I need to acknowledge what will be evident to anyone who looks carefully at real-world religion. The kind of religion I have been defending is, in the real world, inevitably entangled with other things that also go by the name "religion."

The view of religion I've been defending is mainly religion in a *personal* form: it is about individual feelings, the private hopes they inspire, and the beliefs that spring from a personal decision to embrace the most optimistic interpretation of lived experience. While it can express itself in community with others, and while such social expression is natural and inevitable for social animals, religion in this sense remains essentially personal. By contrast, sociologists of religion tend to follow Emile Durkheim in viewing religion as an essentially social phenomenon, one that inculcates allegiance to metaphysical beliefs as a means of social control.[2]

Durkheim isn't making this up. He is describing a real phenomenon in human culture. And there is no doubt that religion in my sense is entangled with religion in Durkheim's sense. Religious institutions that engage in extensive social control *also* offer theologies that resonate with personal religion feelings and worldviews that promise the fulfillment of moral hopes. Social structures that work to inspire obedience to social norms (often through the promise of supernatural punishment and reward) *also* provide a venue in which persons inspired by religious feelings can share and cultivate those feelings in community with others.

And religion in my sense is also clearly entangled with religionism and superstition. One might even view these other entanglements as arising when the drive for social control takes a more sinister turn. One way to control groups of people is to pander to the insipid desires that Sartre sees lurking behind every anti-Semite. It may be in the interests of the elite to secure their privileged status by feeding these base impulses. In a Marxist vein, Sartre notices that the "owning classes" can use anti-Semitism to "substitute for a dangerous hate against their regime a beneficial hate against a particular people." Anti-Semitism "channels revolutionary drives toward the destruction of certain men, not of institutions. An anti-Semitic mob will consider it has done enough when it has massacred some Jews and burned a few synagogues" (p. 44). Likewise, religionism can be invoked to channel the dissatisfaction of the disenfranchised.

The transcendent visions of religious experience defy easy domestication by institutional forces. It is far easier to control people through fear. And so there may be an incentive for institutions seeking social control to displace the God of religion with the god of superstition, the god who can inspire servile obedience.

Such displacement may not be too difficult. The God of religion is mysterious, hard to capture in the imagination. But if Dawkins and Dennett are correct, the god of superstition may be a pervasive product of human evolution. We are primed by millennia of evolution to see agency in nature.[3] And we are at the mercy of nature. But nature, at least as it appears to an empirical eye, is hardly a nurturing caretaker. This combination yields, quite readily, belief in a dangerous supernatural tyrant who must be appeased on pain of death.

Dawkins and Dennett are quite right to think that belief in the god of superstition can be explained as a product of human evolution. If so, then this tyrannical deity will be readily available as an image to be used by establishment forces. And one of the most important uses may be to *control* communities formed around authentic religious experience.

It is an interesting fact of history that the founders of new religions and religious movements have tended to be social critics whose visions were a threat to the establishment. In the Christian tradition, Jesus is the obvious example (although Martin Luther also comes to mind).[4] These visionaries do not absorb their beliefs and values from religion as a social institution in Durkheim's sense. But their religious visions do attract followers. Countercultural communities arise that pose a threat to the establishment.

Religion in Durkheim's sense may arise as much from the attempt to subvert these countercultural religious communities as in an attempt to regulate the general population. And infecting the image of God with the god of superstition may well be a useful means of subversion, at least if it is done incrementally. The joyous message that God has redeemed the evils of the world is changed, in careful stages, to the message that God will save *you* from the evils of the world *if* you comply with His wishes. And this message is then changed to the message that God will cast you into the fires of hell if you do *not* comply. The oriental despot has neatly displaced the God of love.

Of course, all of this is speculation, quite a bit sketchier than Dennett's speculations in *Breaking the Spell*. But my purpose is to set the stage for considering a possibility – namely, that what I am presumptively calling true religion is nothing short of the hope of the world.

To reflect on this possibility, let us consider again the religious vision of Simone Weil. As I mentioned in Chapter 7, Weil never joined the Catholic Church, even though her religious vision was explicitly Christian and her deepest personal friendship was with a Catholic priest, the Reverend Father Perrin. Her reasons for remaining outside the Church are powerfully expressed in her correspondence with Father Perrin. In a particularly telling passage in her final letter to him, she chastised him (something she did with great hesitation) for using the word "false" when he meant "nonorthodox" – even though he quickly corrected himself (1951, p. 96). This mistake was one she took to violate the spirit of Christ who, as "Truth," could not endorse a "confusion of terms" so clearly incompatible "with perfect intellectual honesty" (p. 96). She saw in this mistake a more far-reaching flaw in Father Perrin's character. "I believe," she said, "this imperfection comes from attaching yourself to the Church as to an earthly country. As a matter of fact, as well as being your bond with the heavenly country, it is a terrestrial country for you. You live there in an atmosphere of human warmth. That makes a little attachment almost inevitable" (p. 96).

But such attachment struck Weil as unacceptable. "The children of God," she insisted

> should not have any other country here below but the universe itself, with the totality of all the reasoning creatures it ever has contained, contains, or ever will contain. That is the native city to which we owe our love . . . Every existing thing is equally upheld in its existence by God's creative love. The friends of God should love him to the point of merging their love into his with regard to all things here below. (Weil 1951, p. 97)

This profound religious vision (so at odds with the pugnacious sectarianism that the new atheists equate with religiosity) was the very thing that motivated Weil's refusal to join the Church. She judged herself to be susceptible to the very same imperfection she saw in Father Perrin. She could not join the Church without attaching herself to it as one would to a terrestrial country, with the kind of allegiance that leads to thinking in terms of *us* and *them*. In an earlier letter, she confessed being too easily influenced by anything collective, so that "if at this moment I had before me a group of twenty young Germans singing Nazi songs in chorus, a part of my soul would instantly become Nazi" (p. 53).

What worried her about joining the Church was the in-group/out-group perspective that membership in *any* distinctive community seems to engender even in the noblest souls. And such a division was fundamentally at odds with the substance of her religious experience. It was her religiosity – her intimate personal connection with the divine – that motivated her refusal to join anything that jeopardized the *universal* benevolence, the connection to *all* humanity, which she took to be the essential expression of that religiosity.

Few of us have this kind of fierce and uncompromising will to resist belonging to a human community. Most of those who share Weil's religious vision will gravitate to other people, form associations, and find support for their commitment to a life of love within a community of similarly inspired persons. And despite the risks of such association, risks that Weil was painfully conscious of, there are also benefits. It is when we work together in community that we can do the most good, even if it is also in such associations that we are most susceptible to corruption. And in actual practice, it is impossible to show love to "all the reasoning creatures" that the world has ever contained. But we can *rehearse* such universal benevolence in the microcosm of a human community, and then take the skills learned from such rehearsal out into our wider associations.

And if we cannot resist joining a human community, it may be better to join one united around a religious vision that warns against in-group/out-group dichotomies, than to join one that lacks this intrinsic check on tribal thinking and bifurcating ideology. The possibility I want to consider is that when the more sinister forces of social control wrap their fingers around true religion, when they seek to subvert it and tame it and use it, they have enclosed a power that possesses by its very nature the capacity to resist and to transform these forces.

What these forces hold is something rooted in a good that transcends the world. It is a patient power that works by shining light, by revealing truth, by nurturing a spirit of compassion, by inspiring a vision in which in-group/out-group dichotomies mean nothing. In much the way that the Zoroastrian God, Ahura Mazda, set a trap for Angra Mainyu by creating a world that the Devil could not resist, the transcendent good has drawn to itself the forces of control and domination, of tribalism, of fear and superstition. They close around it like greedy fingers seeking to trap and tame a powerful prize. But unlike other things they might seize, religion in its essence says *no* to them.

While that *no* can be silenced for a time, it always rises up again. When ideologies of collective violence entangle religion to create *religionism*, there remains at the core something whose essence is at odds with every ideology of division. Race cannot say *no* to such ideology. Ethnicity cannot say *no*, nor can nationality. Only religion can.

Sweep religion from the world, as the new atheists dream, and the forces motivating collective violence will close around other things – things like racial difference, national identity, economic ideology. But these other things lack religion's power to resist the clutching fingers from within. And so, the dark powers that the new atheists falsely identify with religion will finally be free of religion's moderating influence. Finally, the quiet light that has been keeping us from the abyss all these ages will be gone. The real root of evil, the poison of the world, will turn nation against nation, tribe against tribe, race against race – and since there is nothing in *national* identity, or *tribal* identity, or *racial* identity that inherently says *no* to dichotomies and to violence, it will be the end of us all.

I must admit that Sam Harris's hyperbolic rhetoric of doom is getting to me. Of course this picture is an overstatement. But so is Harris's. And his picture strikes me as being a good pinch further from the truth than mine.

Notes

Introduction

1 The "scant six pages" are found on pp. 240–6 of *Breaking the Spell* (Dennett 2006).

2 I have attacked the Christian doctrine of hell repeatedly (Reitan 2001, 2002a, 2002b, 2003, 2007b; Kronen and Reitan 2004) as well as the traditional Christian condemnation of homosexuality (see Reitan 2007a; Kronen and Reitan 1999).

3 Dawkins' BBC documentary, *The Root of All Evil?*, was given its title not by Dawkins but by the wise decision-makers at the BBC. In *The God Delusion*, Dawkins' only comment on the title is that it was too sweeping. Surely religion isn't the root of *all* evil (p. 1).

4 One reason why Schleiermacher's approach to Christian theology lost its foothold on popular religious consciousness is because a number of theologians, most notably Karl Barth, worried that Schleiermacher's theology flirted with pantheism, that his emphasis on religious consciousness turned the believer's attention inward rather than toward God, and that his ideas made one's salvation depend not on God's work but on our achieving the right kinds of conscious states. There was also significant suspicion of Schleiermacher resulting from Schleiermacher's own willingness to radically reinterpret central Christian doctrines (most significantly, the doctrine of the Incarnation). I think that most of these worries are actually misplaced; and while I disagree with Schleiermacher on a number of concrete issues – including the feasibility and coherence of a strong doctrine of Incarnation – I do not believe that his overall approach to theology should be dismissed on account of specific conclusions with which one might disagree. But defending these points falls well outside the scope of what I am doing in this book.

5 McGrath says: "I do not accept this idea of faith, and I have yet to meet a theologian who takes it seriously. It cannot be defended from any official declaration of faith from any Christian denomination" (2005, p. 85).

6   Dawkins sketches out his theories about these impulses in Chapter 5 of *The God Delusion*. Dennett proposes his evolutionary account of religion's origins in Chapters 4 and 5 of *Breaking the Spell*, and then develops his view of its memetic and cultural development in Chapters 6–8.

7   He doesn't use these precise words, but it is such a pervasive theme in *The God Delusion* that I doubt anyone would challenge that this is what Dawkins thinks.

Chapter 1: On Religion and Equivocation

1   In fact, this isn't Russell's only image of religion, although it dominates his later thinking. His understanding of religion was more sympathetic earlier on. While he never accepted *theism*, in a 1912 essay, "The Essence of Religion," he expresses strong affinity for what he takes religion to be *about* in general. He even describes the "essence of religion," in a way evoking Schleiermacher, as "the subordination of the finite part of our life to the infinite part" (1961a[1912], p. 575).

2   John Hick (1989a) explicitly endorses this idea (pp. 3–5).

3   Pickering (1975), p. 36.

4   Pickering (1975), p. 21.

5   Zaehner (1997) takes Marxism to be a religion in substantially these terms.

6   Dawkins explicitly says he means to show that great scientists "who sound religious usually turn out not to be when you examine their beliefs more deeply" (p. 14).

7   A similar statement, if less eloquent, appears in Einstein (2007), p. 5.

8   Schleiermacher repeats this idea in various ways through the *Speeches*. His most complete statement of it reads as follows: "The contemplation of the pious is the immediate consciousness of the universal existence of all finite things, in and through the Infinite, and all temporal things in and through the Eternal" (p. 36).

9   In the *Speeches*, Schleiermacher notes that reflection on pious feelings can lead to interpretations in terms of "principles and ideas," and "if you call them religious . . . you are not in error. But do not forget that this is scientific treatment of religion, knowledge about it, and not religion itself" (pp. 46–7). A bit over a century later, William James (1914) expresses a similar sentiment. He claims "that feeling is the deeper source of religion, and that philosophical and theological formulas are secondary products" (p. 431).

10 Part of the difficulty here is that the terms Dawkins uses to characterize God are themselves ambiguous. Under some understandings of these terms, I will admit to believing in a God as described – but not if "interventionist" and "miracle-wreaking" imply violations of natural laws (as Dawkins clearly

intends); not if "thought-reading" is taken to mean anything like what the psychics among the X-Men enjoy; not if "sin-punishing" is taken to refer to the classical doctrine of hell or to worldly hardships imposed in response to specific sins; not if "prayer-answering" is taken to refer to the idea that we can secure good fortune by bowing our heads and fervently asking for what we want.

11 With respect to the Bible, I think he's just wrong about this, because the content of the Bible does not lend itself to a fundamentalist reading. The spirit of the whole clashes too often with isolated passages.

12 What he strives to rescue is Buddhist mysticism, which he claims has nothing even remotely like it in the canons of Christianity, Judaism, or Islam. Apparently, he's never read Schleiermacher, arguably the most important Christian theologian of the last three centuries, whose theology is grounded in precisely the sort of phenomenological study of inner conscious states that Harris takes to be Buddhism's hallmark.

Chapter 2: "The God Hypothesis" and the Concept of God

1 In a sense, I agree. Assuming the God Hypothesis is true, I think we can reasonably expect an observable universe to exist. On the assumption that the God Hypothesis is false, I don't think we could have any reason to expect a universe to exist. My reasons are developed in Chapter 6.

2 Kant offers a concise development of this line of argument in the *Critique of Practical Reason* (1993, pp. 130–8). His full development of these ideas is found in *Religion within the Limits of Reason Alone* (1960). John Hare (1996) offers one of the best recent examinations and developments of Kant's argument.

3 Schleiermacher does not for a moment believe that the source of our feeling of absolute dependence is indifferent or malign. In his mature theology, love and wisdom turn out to be God's most central and important attributes (1928, pp. 726–37).

Chapter 3: Divine Tyranny and the Goodness of God

1 See http://datelinehollywood.com/archives/2005/09/05/robertson-blames-hurricane-on-choice-of-ellen-deneres-to-host-emmys/ (Accessed 2 November 2007).

2 See http://mediamatters.org/items/200509130004 for complete quote and video footage. (Accessed 2 November 2007).

3 For a full transcript of the exchange, see http://www.actupny.org/YELL/falwell.html (Accessed 2 November 2007).

4 The passage is quoted in Lutes (n. d.), p. 6. The statement originally appeared in the April 2004 issue of the *Focus on the Family Newsletter*.

5 Stated during a May 23, 2004 television simulcast to hundreds of churches entitled "The Battle for Marriage." Quoted in Lutes, p. 6.

6 Dobson's unwillingness to listen compassionately to alternative perspectives and experiences (especially those that highlight the harmfulness of his teachings) is characteristic, it seems to me, of those whose view of God is a confused mix of the loving God of religion and the tyrannical god of superstition. On some level they're conscious of the contradictory picture but they fear what acknowledging that contradiction would entail. And so they shut their ears (or their doors) to anything that might force them to acknowledge it, including the anguished cries of those hurt by their ideology.

Chapter 4: Science, Transcendence, and Meaning

1 See also Gould (1997) in which he first introduced the term "Nonoverlapping Magisteria."

2 Some may think there is more to be said here. Dawkins (2006) mentions the interesting activity, pursued at the secular humanist summer camp, Camp Quest, of trying to disprove the existence of an "invisible, intangible, inaudible unicorn" (p. 53). Isn't belief in such a unicorn superstitious, even though we cannot gather empirical evidence against its existence, even in principle? My view is that such a belief isn't superstitious but *nonsensical*. A unicorn is defined in terms of certain empirical properties – size and shape and the like. A unicorn wouldn't be a unicorn if it lacked a distinctive horse-like *shape* – and having a shape requires discernible boundaries, that is, *visible* or *tangible* boundaries. The Camp Quest exercise asks us to imagine such an empirical entity, and yet *also* imagine that it lacks all empirical properties. But to lack all empirical properties is to fail to be an empirical entity at all. That God lacks all empirical properties is not nonsensical, since God is not an empirical entity but a transcendent one. It isn't nonsense to say that a transcendent being – a being who falls outside the empirical world – exists even though it lacks empirical properties. But it is incoherent to say this of some object or creature whose very conception is empirical.

3 As reported by BBC News on November 23, 2004, http://news.bbc.co.uk/2/hi/americas/4034787.stm. Accessed June 25, 2007.

4 See the full report at http://www.usatoday.com/news/offbeat/2006-08-18-chocolate-mary_x.htm. Accessed June 25, 2007. A photo of the chocolate dripping, alongside the Virgin Mary prayer card, is included with the online article.

5 http://blogs.usatoday.com/ondeadline/2006/08/chocolate_virgi.html. Accessed June 25, 2007.

Chapter 5: Philosophy and God's Existence, Part I

1 My explication of the first "Way" here is an elaboration of what Aquinas (1952) sketches out in pt I, q. 2, art. 3 of the *Summa Theologica*. Likewise, my summaries of the remaining "Ways" are drawn from the same article from the *Summa*.

2 Actually, the fourth way seems to me entirely unpersuasive, verging on silly. But a colleague and friend of mine who is a much better Aquinas scholar than I am assures me that the apparent silliness of the argument arises only because I am interpreting it through my thoroughly contemporary paradigms and assumptions, rather than in the light of Aquinas's own metaphysical system. Since I trust my colleague and know Aquinas to be a profound thinker, I think it's more intellectually responsible to say I don't understand the argument than to say that it's hogwash. Dawkins, however, prefers the approach typical of my less intellectually responsible students: if you don't understand what someone is saying, assume they're being incoherent and call them idiots.

3 Robin Collins (2003) offers a forceful statement of this argument.

4 See Miller (1999), Chapter 5, for an accessible critique of Behe by a biologist who is also a theist.

5 Robin Collins (2005) has challenged this "multiverse" objection to the fine-tuning argument but it remains one of the more popular responses to it.

6 See Aquinas (1952) pt I, q. 3, art. 7.

Chapter 6: Philosophy and God's Existence, Part II

1 See Clarke (1998), pp. 8–18, especially pp. 10–12. Clarke used the terms "self-existent" and "independent" interchangeably but "self-existent" seems the more helpful term.

2 William Rowe (1970) develops this reply to Edwards in greater philosophical detail.

3 If existence did add to our idea of a thing, then we could never discover that there existed something corresponding to a concept whose existence was for us a matter of doubt. Suppose I were wondering whether there are any living albino humpback whales. Since I don't know whether there are any, "existence" isn't part of my idea. But then suppose I encounter such a whale. Since it exists, it would turn out *not* to correspond with my idea (since my idea doesn't include existence). By treating existence as a real predicate, I'm forced to an absurd conclusion.

4 Dawkins' citation for the passage from Malcolm (which he quotes on p. 83 of *The God Delusion*) refers his readers to the entry on the ontological argument from the Internet Encyclopedia of Philosophy.

5 I think this version of PSR may amount to a different formulation of the same basic idea that Alexander Pruss (2004) expresses in his "restricted" PSR: "If *p* is a true proposition and possibly *p* has an explanation, then *p* actually has an explanation" (p. 167). Pruss proposes his version of PSR as a concession to those who worry that some things – specifically chance events and free choices – *cannot* be explained.

6 I am indebted to Gordon Barnes for pointing out this line of objection.

Chapter 7: Religious Consciousness

1 Two excellent and comprehensive biographies of Weil's life are those of Simone Petrement (1976) and David McLellan (1990). For a briefer and more controversial treatment, see the provocative recent biography by Francine du Plessix Gray (2001).

2 How we interpret an experience may, however, have important implications. Zaehner notes that for the monistic mystic, the experience of identity with God is the highest possible spiritual attainment. Spiritual growth has, from this perspective, an *endpoint*. But loving union with God will have no such endpoint. God is infinite, and so there will always be more for the finite creature to discover. And so, even if James is right that the two forms of mysticism are different interpretations of the same basic experience, the difference in interpretation may influence the *possibilities for future experience*. If the theist is right, the monist may cease to pursue spiritual growth where such growth remains possible.

Chapter 8: The Substance of Things Hoped For

1 In the twentieth century, in *Why I Believe* (1969), Pierre Teilhard de Chardin developed an argument similar to Lotze's, but in more individualistic and experiential terms. Like Lotze, he takes the data of science seriously in developing his religious worldview.

2 See Kertzer (1998) for a detailed discussion of the Edgardo Mortara case.

3 John Hick (1987, pp. 3–4) offers a concise treatment of the distinction between these senses of "faith."

4 Aelred Graham (in G. D. Smith 1962, pp. 710–16) offers a helpful summary of these ideas.

5 These visible signs of a divine commission can be variously characterized. Graham (in Smith 1962), following the language of the Nicene Creed, identifies "the distinctive qualities of unity, holiness, catholicity and apostolicity" as the chief signs of the Church's "divine origin" (p. 703).

6 This definition appears in Aquinas (1952) *Summa Theologica* II–II, q. 2, art. 9. In his entry on faith in *The Catholic Encyclopedia* (highly respected as a resource on all things Catholic), Hugh Pope quotes Aquinas's definition but indicates it is from the *Summa* II–II q. 4, art. 2 (see Pope 1909, p. 756). This error is reiterated throughout the web and even in several scholarly books. Apparently, *The Catholic Encyclopedia* enjoys considerable credibility, at least with respect to Aquinas, leading numerous writers to have faith in its citations – even when they're wrong.

7 On this point, see especially the section from the *Summa* that *The Catholic Encyclopedia* erroneously cites as the source of Aquinas's famous definition, namely *Summa* II–II, q. 4, art. 2.

8 I do not, however, think that those who "crash" trying to save themselves are eternally damned. An omnibenevolent God would, it seems, make such crashes into learning opportunities. And given an indefinite opportunity to learn, even the most recalcitrant will eventually hand the controls over to God. See Reitan 2003 and 2007b for developments of these ideas.

9 It would also make some sense to suppose that such a God would reveal Himself by coming to us as a human person, as in the Christian teaching of the incarnation. The doctrine of biblical inerrancy strikes me as polluting this essentially Christian understanding of God's strategy for divine revelation.

Chapter 9: Evil and the Meaning of Life

1 It isn't similarly problematic to express gratitude to God for one's existence, for the goods of the world, and for the promised redemption of the world's evils. Also, we might believe that God's capacity to intervene in the world is limited, perhaps by the broader moral purposes for which God created the world. On this picture of things, to view life's blessings as the transcendent good breaking through the veil of time and space *when and where it can* – and hence to thank God for those blessings – doesn't entail belief in a God who plays favorites.

2 An older version of the argument, called the *logical argument from evil*, maintained the stronger conclusion that the world's evils *prove* there is no God. Critics (especially Plantinga 1974) rightly noted that God could have justifying reasons for permitting evil and so evil in the world doesn't disprove God. Hence, the "logical" argument has given way to the more modest evidential one.

3 On Hick's view, soul-making may well continue *after* death, in some post-mortem state potentially involving anguished struggle. Such struggle would continue until the soul-making project succeeded, since failure would entail evil that is ultimately unredeemed, and thereby unjustified – something a perfectly good God would not permit. See Hick (2001), p. 52.

4   See Table 2, on p. 13 of the report overview, available online at
    http://siteresources.worldbank.org/INTGLOMONREP2007/Resources/3413191-
    1179404785559/Overview-GMR07_webPDF-corrected-may-14-2007-2.pdf.
5   Often, the perpetrators of horror are themselves victims, who protect them-
    selves from the anguish of a life stripped of apparent meaning by siding with
    a universe of pitiless indifference in order to avoid the horror of having their
    values crushed by it.
6   See especially Weil (1951), pp. 123–7, and Weil (1952a), pp. 139–44. What I
    am offering here is an interpretation of Weil's provocative and often paradoxically
    stated ideas. For another interpretation, similar in many respects to mine, see
    Diogenes Allen (1990), pp. 201–3.
7   John Hare (1996) develops a similar point in *The Moral Gap*.

Chapter 10: The Root of All Evil?

1   Ladd does not name this fifth premise as he does the first four. I do so here
    to preserve parallel structure.
2   See Pickering (1975) for a collection of Durkheim's most important sociolog-
    ical reflections on religion.
3   See Dawkins (2006), pp. 182–3, for a concise statement of this idea. Dennett
    (2006) develops these ideas more fully, especially in Chapter 5 of *Breaking the
    Spell*.
4   In his admirable recent book, *The Politics of Jesus*, Obery M. Hendricks, Jr. (2006)
    traces out the revolutionary character of Jesus' ministry and then explores the
    subsequent efforts of the dominant classes to domesticate that message for the
    sake of social control.

References

Adams, M. M. (1990) "Horrendous Evils and the Goodness of God," in *The Problem of Evil*, eds. Adams and Adams, pp. 209–21.

Adams, M. M. (2002) "Neglected Values, Shrunken Agents, Happy Endings: A Reply to Rogers." *Faith and Philosophy* 19: 487–505.

Adams, M. M. (2006) *Christ and Horrors: The Coherence of Christology*. Cambridge University Press: Cambridge.

Adams, R. M. (1979) "Divine Command Metaethics Modified Again." *Journal of Religious Ethics* 7: 66–71.

Adams, M. M. and Adams, R. M. (1990) *The Problem of Evil*. Oxford University Press: Oxford.

Allen, D. (1990) "Natural Evil and the Love of God," in *The Problem of Evil*, eds. Adams and Adams, pp. 189–208.

Alston, W. P. (1983) "Christian Experience and Christian Belief," in *Faith and Rationality: Reason and Belief in God*, eds. Plantinga and Wolterstorff, pp. 103–34.

Alston, W. P. (1991) *Perceiving God: A Study in the Epistemology of Religious Experience*. Cornell University Press: Ithaca, NY.

Alston, W. P. (2004) "Religious Experience Justifies Religious Belief," in M. L. Peterson and R. J. Vanarragon (eds.) *Contemporary Debates in Philosophy of Religion*. Blackwell Publishing: Oxford, pp. 135–45.

Anselm (1998) "Proslogion," in *Anselm of Canterbury: The Major Works*, eds. B. Davies and G. R. Evans, trans. M. J. Charlesworth. Oxford University Press: Oxford. (First published in 1078.)

Aquinas, T. (1952) *Summa Theologica*, trans. The Fathers of the English Dominican Province (revised by D. J. Sullivan). Encyclopedia Britannica: Chicago. (Originally published in 1273.)

Behe, M. J. (1996) *Darwin's Black Box: The Biochemical Challenge to Evolution*. The Free Press: New York.

Bishop, J. (1998) "Can There be Alternative Concepts of God?" *Noûs* 32: 174–88.

Boyce, M. (1979) *Zoroastrians: Their Religious Beliefs and Practices*. Routledge & Kegan Paul: London.

Christian, C. W. (1979) *Friedrich Schleiermacher*. Word Books: Waco, TX.

Clarke, S. (1998) *A Demonstration of the Being and Attributes of God and Other Writings*, ed. E. Vailati. Cambridge University Press: Cambridge. (Originally published in 1705.)

Collins, R. (2003) "God, Design, and Fine-tuning," in *God Matters: Readings in the Philosophy of Religion*, eds. R. Martin and C. Bernard. Longman: New York.

Collins, R. (2005) "The Many-worlds Hypothesis as an Explanation of Cosmic Fine-tuning: An Alternative to Design?" *Faith & Philosophy* 22: 654–66.

Copleston, F. C. and Russell, B. (1964) "The Existence of God: A Debate between Bertrand Russell and Father F. C. Copleston," in *The Existence of God*, ed. J. Hick. Macmillan: New York.

Dawkins, R. (1995) *River Out of Eden: A Darwinian View of Life*. Basic Books: New York.

Dawkins, R. (2006) *The God Delusion*. Houghton Mifflin: Boston.

Dennett, D. C. (2006) *Breaking the Spell: Religion as a Natural Phenomenon*. Penguin Books: New York.

Dennett, D. C. (2007) "The God Delusion" (March letter to the editor in response to January 11, 2007 review by H. Allen Orr). *The New York Review of Books* 54(3). Available from http://www.nybooks.com/articles/19928 (Accessed 6 April 2007).

Dobson, J. (2001) *Bringing Up Boys: Practical Advice and Encouragement for Those Shaping the Next Generation of Men*. Tyndale House: Carol Stream, IL.

Du Plessix Gray, F. (2001) *Simone Weil*. Viking: New York.

Edwards, P. (1959) "The Cosmological Argument," *The Rationalist Annual*. Pemberton: London, pp. 63–77.

Egner, R. E. and Denonn, L. E. (eds.) (1961) *The Basic Writings of Bertrand Russell*. Simon & Schuster: New York.

Einstein, A. (2007) *The World as I See It*. The Book Tree: San Diego.

Flew, A., Hare, R. M., and Mitchell, B. (2005) "Theology and Falsification," in *Ten Essential Texts in the Philosophy of Religion: Classic and Contemporary Issues*, ed. S. Cahn. Oxford University Press: New York, pp. 462–72.

Frank, P. (1947) *Einstein: His Life and Times*. A. A. Knopf: New York.

Gould, S. J. (1989) *Wonderful Life: The Burgess Shale and the Nature of History*. W. W. Norton: New York.

Gould, S. J. (1992) "Impeaching a Self-appointed Judge." *Scientific American* 267: 118–21.

Gould, S. J. (1997) "Nonoverlapping Magisteria." *Natural History* 106: 16–22.

Gould, S. J. (1999) *Rocks of Ages: Science and Religion in the Fullness of Life*. Ballantine: New York.

Griffiths, P. J. (1999) *Religious Reading: The Place of Reading in the Practice of Religion.* Oxford University Press: New York.

Hare, J. E. (1996) *The Moral Gap: Kantian Ethics, Human Limits, and God's Assistance.* Clarendon Press: Oxford.

Harris, S. (2004) *The End of Faith: Religion, Terror, and the Future of Unreason.* W. W. Norton: New York.

Harris, S. (2006) *Letter to a Christian Nation.* Alfred A. Knopf: New York.

Hendricks, O. M. (2006) *The Politics of Jesus: Rediscovering the True Revolutionary Nature of Jesus' Teachings and How They Have Been Corrupted.* Doubleday: New York.

Hick, J. (1987) *Faith and Knowledge: A Modern Introduction to the Problem of Religious Knowledge.* Macmillan: London.

Hick, J. (1989a) *An Interpretation of Religion: Human Responses to the Transcendent.* Yale University Press: New Haven, CT.

Hick, J. (1989b) "Seeing-as and Religious Experience" in *Faith*, ed. T. Penelhum. Macmillan: New York, pp. 183–92.

Hick, J. (2001) "An Irenaean Theodicy," in *Encountering Evil: Live Options in Theodicy*, ed. S. T. Davis. Westminster John Knox Press: Louisville, KY, pp. 38–51.

Hitchens, C. (2007) *god is not Great: How Religion Poisons Everything.* Twelve: New York.

Hume, D. (1989) *Dialogues Concerning Natural Religion.* Prometheus Books: Buffalo, NY. (First published in 1779.)

James, W. (1897) *The Will to Believe and Other Essays in Popular Philosophy.* Longmans, Green: New York.

James, W. (1914) *The Varieties of Religious Experience: A Study in Human Experience.* Longmans, Green: London.

Kant, I. (1958) *The Critique of Pure Reason*, trans. N. Kemp-Smith. The Modern Library: New York.

Kant, I. (1960) *Religion within the Limits of Reason Alone*, trans. T. M. Greene and H. H. Hudson. Harper & Row: New York.

Kant, I. (1993) *Critique of Practical Reason*, trans. L. W. Beck. Prentice Hall: Upper Saddle River, NJ.

Kertzer, D. I. (1998) *The Kidnapping of Edgardo Mortara.* Vintage: New York.

King, M. L. (1986) "Pilgrimage to Nonviolence," in *A Testament of Hope: The Essential Writings and Speeches of Martin Luther King, Jr.*, ed. J. M. Washington. HarperCollins: San Francisco.

Kretzmann, N. (1999) *The Metaphysics of Creation: Aquinas's Natural Theology in Summa Contra Gentiles II.* Clarendon Press: Oxford.

Kronen, J. and Reitan, E. (1999) "Homosexuality, Misogyny, and God's Plan." *Faith and Philosophy* 16: 213–32.

Kronen, J. and Reitan, E. (2004) "Talbott's Universalism, Divine Justice, and the Atonement." *Religious Studies* 40: 249–68.

Ladd, J. (1991) "The Idea of Collective Violence," in *Justice, Law, and Violence*, eds. J. B. Brady and N. Garver. Temple University Press: Philadelphia.

Leibniz, G. (1965a) *Monadology and Other Philosophical Essays*, trans. P. Schrecker and A. M. Schrecker. Bobbs-Merrill Educational Publishing: Indianapolis.

Leibniz, G. (1965b) "On the Ultimate Origination of the Universe," in *Monadology and Other Philosophical Essays*, pp. 84–94. (Written in 1697.)

Leibniz, G. (1965c) "Monadology," in *Monadology and Other Philosophical Essays* (1965), pp. 148–63. (Written in 1714.)

Leibniz, G. (1973) "Discourse on Metaphysics," in *Leibniz: Discourse on Metaphysics/Correspondence with Arnauld/Monadology*, trans. G. R. Montgomery. Open Court Publishing: La Salle, IL.

Lotze, H. (1886) *Outlines of the Philosophy of Religion: Dictated Portions of the Lectures of Hermann Lotze*, trans. G. T. Ladd. Ginn: Boston.

Lutes, J. (n. d.) *A False Focus on My Family*. Soulforce Booklet: Lynchburg, VA.

Mackie, J. L. (1982) *The Miracle of Theism: Arguments For and Against the Existence of God*. Clarendon Press: Oxford.

Malcolm, N. (1960) "Anselm's Ontological Arguments." *The Philosophical Review* 69: 41–62.

Martin, M. (1990) *Atheism: A Philosophical Justification*. Temple University Press: Philadelphia.

Martin, M. (1991) *The Case Against Christianity*. Temple University Press: Philadelphia.

McGrath, A. (2005) *Dawkins' God: Genes, Memes, and the Meaning of Life*. Blackwell Publishers: Oxford.

McGrath, A. and McGrath, J. A. (2007) *The Dawkins Delusion? Atheist Fundamentalism and the Denial of the Divine*. InterVarsity Press: Downers Grove, IL.

McLellan, D. (1990) *Utopian Pessimist: The Life and Thought of Simone Weil*. Poseidon Press: New York.

Melanchthon, P. (1965) *Melanchthon on Christian Doctrine: Loci communes 1555*, trans. and ed. C. L. Manschreck. Oxford University Press: Oxford.

Menssen, S. and Sullivan, T. D. (2007) *The Agnostic Inquirer: Revelation from a Philosophical Standpoint*. Eerdmans: Grand Rapids, MI.

Miller, K. R. (1999) *Finding Darwin's God: A Scientist's Search for Common Ground Between God and Evolution*. HarperCollins: New York.

Mills, D. (2006) *Atheist Universe: The Thinking Person's Answer to Christian Fundamentalism*. Ulysses Press: Berkeley, CA.

Morris, R. (1990) *The Edges of Science*. Prentice Hall: New York.

Persinger, M. A. (1987) *Neuropsychological Bases of God Beliefs*. Praeger Publishers: New York.

Petrement, S. (1976) *Simone Weil: A Life*, trans. from the French by R. Rosenthal. Pantheon Books: New York.

Pickering, W. S. F. (1975) *Durkheim on Religion: A Selection of Readings with Bibliographies*. Readings trans. J. Redding and W. S. F. Pickering. Routledge & Kegan Paul: London.

Plantinga, A. (1974) *God, Freedom, and Evil*. Eerdmans: Grand Rapids, MI.

Plantinga, A. (1983) "Reason and Belief in God," in *Faith and Rationality: Reason and Belief in God*, eds. A. Plantinga and N. Wolterstorff, pp. 16–93.

Plantinga, A. (1993a) *Warrant and Proper Function*. Oxford University Press: New York.

Plantinga, A. (1993b) *Warrant: The Current Debate*. Oxford University Press: New York.

Plantinga, A. (2000) *Warranted Christian Belief*. Oxford University Press: New York.

Plantinga, A. (2007) "The Dawkins Confusion: Naturalism ad absurdum." *Books & Culture: A Christian Review* 13(2). Available from http://www.christianitytoday.com/bc/2007/002/1.21.html (Accessed 4 April 2007).

Plantinga, A. and Wolterstorff, N. (eds.) (1983) *Faith and Rationality: Reason and Belief in God*. University of Notre Dame Press: Notre Dame, IN.

Plutarch (1993) "Superstition," in *Plutarch: Selected Essays and Dialogues*, trans. and ed. D. Russell. Oxford University Press: Oxford, pp. 1–12.

Pope, H. (1909) "Faith," in *The Catholic Encyclopedia: An International Work of Reference on the Constitution, Doctrine, Discipline, and History of the Catholic Church*, Vol. 5: 752–9. Robert Appleton: New York.

Pruss, A. (2004) "A Restricted Principle of Sufficient Reason and the Cosmological Argument." *Religious Studies* 40: 165–79.

Putnam, H. (1981) *Reason, Truth, and History*. Cambridge University Press: Cambridge.

Reitan, E. (2000) "Does the Argument from Evil Assume a Consequentialist Morality?" *Faith and Philosophy* 17: 304–19.

Reitan, E. (2001) "Universalism and Autonomy: Towards a Comparative Defense of Universalism." *Faith and Philosophy* 18: 222–40.

Reitan, E. (2002a) "Eternal Damnation and Blessed Ignorance: Is the Damnation of Some Incompatible with the Salvation of Any?" *Religious Studies* 38: 429–50.

Reitan, E. (2002b) "Sympathy for the Damned: Schleiermacher's Critique of the Doctrine of Limited Salvation." *Southwest Philosophy Review* 18: 201–11.

Reitan, E. (2003) "Human Freedom and the Impossibility of Eternal Damnation," in *Universal Salvation? The Current Debate*, eds. R. Parry and C. Partridge. Paternoster Press: Carlisle.

Reitan, E. (2007a) "Love the Sinner, Hate the Sin? The Case of Homosexuality." *Free Inquiry* 27: 42–3.

Reitan, E. (2007b) "A Guarantee of Universal Salvation?" *Faith and Philosophy* 24: 413–32.

Rowe, W. (1970) "Two Criticisms of the Cosmological Argument." *The Monist* 54: 441–59.

Rowe, W. (1979) "The Problem of Evil and Some Varieties of Atheism." *American Philosophical Quarterly* 16: 33–41.

Rowe, W. (2007) *Philosophy of Religion: An Introduction.* 4th edn. Thomson Wadsworth: Belmont, CA.

Russell, B. (1961a) "The Essence of Religion," in *The Basic Writings of Bertrand Russell*, eds. R. E. Egner and L. E. Denonn, pp. 565–76. (Originally published in 1912 in *The Hibbert Journal*, vol. 2.)

Russell, B. (1961b) "Why I am Not a Christian," in *The Basic Writings of Bertrand Russell*, eds. R. E. Egner and L. E. Denonn, pp. 585–97. (Originally a lecture delivered in 1927.)

Russell, B. (1997) "Is There a God?" in *The Collected Papers of Bertrand Russell*, eds. J. C. Slater and P. Kollner, vol. 11. Routledge: London, pp. 542–48. (Written in 1952.)

Sagan, C. (2006) *The Varieties of Scientific Experience: A Personal View of the Search For God*, ed. A. Druyan. Penguin Press: New York.

Sartre, J.-P. (1948) *Anti-Semite and Jew.* Schocken Books: New York.

Schleiermacher, F. (1928) *The Christian Faith*, eds. H. R. Mackintosh and J. S. Stewart. T&T Clark: Edinburgh. Translation (multiple translators) of the 2nd German edition of 1830. (Original title: *Glaubenslehre.*)

Schleiermacher, F. (1958) *On Religion: Speeches to its Cultured Despisers*, trans. J. Oman. Harper & Row: New York.

Schleiermacher F. (1987) *Servant of the Word: Selected Sermons of Friedrich Schleiermacher*, trans. D. DeVries. Fortress Press: Philadelphia.

Scriven, M. (1966) *Primary Philosophy.* McGraw-Hill: New York.

Smith, G. D. (ed.) (1962) *The Teachings of the Catholic Church: A Summary of Catholic Doctrine.* Vol. II. Macmillan: New York.

Smith, G. H. (1979) *Atheism: The Case Against God.* Prometheus Books: Buffalo, NY.

Stace, W. T. (1960) *Mysticism and Philosophy.* J. B. Lippincott Company: Philadelphia.

Stenger, V. J. (2007) *God: The Failed Hypothesis.* Prometheus Books: Amherst, NY.

Swenson, D. F. (1981) "The Dignity of Human Life," in *The Meaning of Life*, ed. E. D. Klemke. Oxford University Press: Oxford, pp. 20–30.

Swinburne, R. (1981) *Faith and Reason.* Clarendon Press: Oxford.

Swinburne, R. (1998) *Providence and the Problem of Evil.* Clarendon Press: Oxford.

Talbott, T. (2001) "Freedom, Damnation, and the Power to Sin with Impunity." *Religious Studies* 37: 417–34.

Tanner, N. P. (ed.) (1990) *Decrees of the Ecumenical Councils, Volume II.* Sheed & Ward: London.

Teilhard de Chardin, P. (1969) *How I Believe*. Harper & Row: New York.

Van Biema, D. (2006) "God vs. Science." *Time Magazine* (5 November): 49–55.

Weil, S. (1951) *Waiting for God*, trans. E. Craufurd. G. P. Putnam's Sons: New York. (Originally published in 1950.)

Weil, S. (1952a) *Gravity and Grace*, trans. A. F. Wills. G. P. Putnam's Sons: New York. (Originally published in 1947.)

Weil, S. (1952b) *The Need for Roots*, trans. A. F. Wills. Routledge & Kegan Paul: London. (Originally published in 1949.)

Wise, K. (2000) "Geology," in *In Six Days: Why Fifty Scientists Chose to Believe in Creation*, ed. J. F. Ashton. Master Books: Green Forest, AR, pp. 351–5.

Wittgenstein, L. (1953) *Philosophical Investigations*, trans. G. E. M. Anscombe. Macmillan: New York.

Wittgenstein, L. (1961) *Tractatus Logico-Philosophicus*, trans. D. F. Pears and B. F. McGuinness. Routledge & Kegan Paul: London.

Wolpert, L. (2007) *Six Impossible Things Before Breakfast: The Evolutionary Origins of Belief*. W. W. Norton: New York.

Wykstra, S. J. (1990) "The Humean Obstacle to Evidential Arguments from Suffering: On Avoiding the Evils of 'Appearance,'" in *The Problem of Evil*, eds. Adams and Adams, pp. 138–60.

Zaehner, R. C. (1957) *Mysticism Sacred and Profane: An Inquiry into Some Varieties of Praeternatural Experience*. Clarendon Press: Oxford.

Zaehner, R. C. (1961) *The Dawn and Twilight of Zoroastrianism*. Phoenix Press: New York.

Zaehner, R. C. (1997) "Dialectical Materialism," in *Encyclopedia of the World's Religions*. Barnes & Noble Books: New York. (Originally published in 1959 as *The Hutchinson Encyclopedia of Living Faiths*.)

Index